Digital Humanities and Material Religion

Introductions to
Digital Humanities – Religion

Edited by
Claire Clivaz, Charles M. Ess, Gregory Price Grieve,
Kristian Petersen and Sally Promey

Volume 6

Digital Humanities and Material Religion

An Introduction

Edited by
Emily Suzanne Clark and Rachel McBride Lindsey

DE GRUYTER

ISBN 978-3-11-060465-8
e-ISBN (PDF) 978-3-11-060875-5
e-ISBN (EPUB) 978-3-11-060817-5

Library of Congress Control Number: 2021952069

Bibliographic information published by the Deutsche Nationalbibliothek
The Deutsche Nationalbibliothek lists this publication in the Deutsche Nationalbibliografie;
detailed bibliographic data are available on the Internet at http://dnb.dnb.de.

© 2022 Walter de Gruyter GmbH, Berlin/Boston
Cover image: Social network visualization. With friendly permission of Martin Grandjean.
Printing and binding: CPI books GmbH, Leck

www.degruyter.com

Table of Contents

Part 3 Intersections of the Digital and Material: Tools, Questions, and Processes

Acknowledgements

This book is itself in some sense an exercise in digital materiality. Its editors and contributors live across continents and have navigated various remote conferencing and collaborative workspace platforms to conceptualize, write, gather, and create the book you are either reading on a screen or holding in your hands. The editors have many people to thank for bringing the book to completion. First, the contributing authors have demonstrated tremendous patience as the project faced unpredictable challenges extending from various quarters, professional, institutional, personal, and medical—to say nothing of the global pandemic that has seized so much of everyone's time and energy as the book has come into final stages of editing and production. We thank you for your scholarship and collegiality. We are also indebted to the *Introductions to Digital Humanities—Religion* series editors Claire Clivaz, Charles M. Ess, Gregory Price Grieve, Kristian Petersen, and Sally Promey for the opportunity to develop this volume. We also thank the editorial team at DeGruyter for shepherding this project through. Katrin Mittmann has been especially generous with her time and expertise, even as we corresponded across many time zones and life seasons. And this book would not exist without Ulla Schmidt's expert attention to the too-often invisible labor of manuscript production. *Danke.* Saint Louis University graduate research assistants William Potter and Kelly Bratkowski provided invaluable assistance at various points in the editorial and production process. Your futures are very bright indeed. Finally, we thank our families, friends, students, and other interlocutors whose ears we have bent and whose insights have sharpened our own thinking. This is a waypoint in a long conversation and we are excited to see where it goes.

https://doi.org/10.1515/9783110608755-001

Emily Suzanne Clark and Rachel McBride Lindsey

Chapter 1
Digital Materiality: Possibilities of Interpretive Frameworks in the Academic Study of Religion

What do the digital humanities have to do with material religion? At first these modes of interest and analysis seem wildly at odds. Clicks and bricks. The one concerned with turns to big data and the erasure of former bounds of time and space; the other with turns to granular particularity and haptic proximity. While there are very good reasons for surmising that digital humanities and material religion make for strange bedfellows, this volume demonstrates that the gulf between them may be more of a useful fiction than an interpretive necessity. Indeed, rather than a case of opposites attracting, the chapters in this volume demonstrate how both digital humanities and material culture studies are turns of a common wheel—that is, the academic study of religion—and both have something to teach all of us about disciplinary formations, priorities, and the future of the field.

But perhaps we are getting ahead of ourselves. As the first to focus on the intersection of material religion and digital humanities, this book was daunted with challenges from conceptualization through editing. While both editors have researched and published work on material religion since the beginnings of our careers, we are both more recent scholars of digital humanities. In fact, we both came to this intersection of material religion and digital humanities largely through our teaching. The undergraduate classroom is a generative space for interdisciplinary work. This was certainly the case for both of us. While this volume does not directly engage with pedagogy (another volume in this De Gruyter series will focus specifically on teaching), it seems right to begin our volume with the classroom, as it was there that we both began to consider the challenges and possibilities that develop at the meeting of digital humanities and material religion.

https://doi.org/10.1515/9783110608755-002

1.1 Locating Material Religion and Digital Humanities

"Thwack thwackthwack thwack." Syncopated sounds filled the classroom on the lowest floor of Spring Hall, a brand new, state of the art residence hall on the campus of Saint Louis University, where students in "Arch City Religion: Religious Life and Practice in St. Louis" were giving presentations of research they had conducted in Forest Park over the course of the spring semester. Forest Park is a municipal park, dating to the years after the American Civil War and larger in acreage than Central Park in New York City. The grounds were home to the Louisiana Purchase Exposition in 1904, a belated centennial celebration of the 1803 charter, and a stone's throw from the 1904 Olympics, after St. Louis stole the show from Chicago to host the first Olympiad to be held in the United States. Once home to an amusement park and baseball fields, today Forest Park boasts a zoo, museums, ponds, tennis courts, trails, playgrounds, golf course, and outdoor municipal theater among other attractions. It is public space that straddles the boundary between St. Louis City and St. Louis County, a borderlands fraught with histories of racism, xenophobia, and economic injustice that shape the region through the present.[1] It is not typically recognized as a "religious" place. But students in Arch City Religion were rethinking the relationship between urban space and the categories, ideas, practices, and experiences of religion. The thwacking was part of this process.[2]

Of the several student groups in the class, one group set out to investigate the statues of Forest Park. From *The Apotheosis of St. Louis* in front of the Saint Louis Art Museum, to a statue of St. Francis gifted to the city by the widow of a cantankerous car salesman, to monuments to Confederate soldiers and German immigrants, to a small Ganesha shrine tucked into foliage at the zoo, to name just a few examples both official and otherwise, the statues of Forest Park have linked the material history of a city to constructions of the sacred— built worlds of profound meaning in ordinary spaces. But these students did not simply *see* this material history. They wanted to hear it—or at least an echo of it.

---

1 For an overview of the racial politics of place in St. Louis, see Walter Johnson, *The Broken Heart of America: St. Louis and the Violent History of the United States* (New York: Basic Books, 2020).

2 This pedagogical activity was inspired by the American Religious Sounds Project, a richly generative digital humanities initiative directed by Amy De Rogatis and Isaac Weiner. See, *American Religious Sounds Project*, https://religioussounds.osu.edu/ (accessed October 22, 2021).

So they traipsed through Forest Park, one student holding an audio recorder, the other thwacking statues with sticks.

In keeping with previous Western hierarchies of the senses, "digital worlds" have prioritized sight and sound over other sensations. Despite Willy Wonka's imaginative technologies—transporting chocolate bars and naughty boys through electromagnetic waves—at the outset of the third decade of the twenty-first century we still lack the ability to transport haptic objects through time and space at the speed with which we can sound and image.[3] Digital proxies of material worlds are always translations: plots on a map, glimpses and echoes of embodied life, interpretive datasets of lived experiences. Digital technologies have indeed introduced new ways of encountering and analyzing the material worlds of religion. And, in turn, digital materiality, a term this volume introduces for scrutiny, has teased us into recognizing yet another site of mediating bodies. But such digital translations are fields ripe for misinterpretation—the perennial hazard of any exercise in translation. What does it mean to identify an object of study that has been re-rendered from physical to digital form? What, in that moment, is the object of study? More to the point, even as digital technologies have introduced new ways of encountering and analyzing the material worlds of religion, while often celebrated as liberatory, digitization can freight anew the longstanding baggage of institutional imperialism. These students were not wrong. They wanted to find a way to register the materiality of objects, specific objects with specific histories in specific places encountered at specific times, using aural technologies that could be uploaded to digital platforms that untethered those sounds to time or place. But in the course of thwacking statues, they broke open the ways we, as students of the study of religion, are trained to think about material cultures and digital worlds.

Out further west, undergraduate students at Gonzaga University scanned images on the third floor of the university's library. These images came from the archives of the Jesuits West Province that were held in the library's special collections. In those archival boxes and file folders were a variety of documents and artifacts that captured the late-nineteenth and early twentieth-century Jesuit missions to Native communities in the Pacific Northwest. Slowly and meticulously, these students scanned photographs of Catholic sacramental life as practiced by Columbia Plateau peoples and Jesuit priests, hand-written translations of Catholic prayers rendered in Kalispel Salish, and glass lantern slides depicting Catholic cosmology and theology.

The images, already once removed from the religious practice, took one more step further away from their original, material context. This brought an interest-

---

3 Roald Dahl, *Charlie and the Chocolate Factory* (Alfred A. Knopf: New York, 1964).

ing combination of consequences. By making these materials digital—or rather, by creating digital translations of these artifacts—the images became accessible to students and researchers across the country and to the wider Inland Northwest community, including descendants of those in the photographs. As one pair of students enhanced the clarity of a scan, they realized that to clean up a blemish in the image, they would have to lighten the skin of a Native man's face. While it would make the image sharper, they decided it was not the right thing to do. (Their professor agreed.)

Before and during their scanning, the students worked through a variety of the archival materials, including a priest's traveling vestments, books of sacramental records, a branding iron for the mission's livestock, business ledgers, and even sacred relics. Though the students had felt, smelled, and listened to the sacramental objects from the mission field in the archive, their scanned images of events like the Corpus Christi processions of the 1920s lacked that material resonance. In other cases, the digital facsimiles seemed to better capture the vibrancy of the originals. One group scanned image slides from a mission's glass lantern show. Glass lantern or magic lantern shows became popular in the nineteenth century as a way to travel to faraway places or tell lively stories via projected images. An antecedent to the Kodak Carousel, magic lantern shows used lenses, a light source, and the stained-glass plates to project images onto a screen. The glass lantern slides in this archival collection were primarily didactic and used to tell biblical stories or teach theological lessons. The slides were small, and without their traveling projector equipment, they had to be raised to the light to reveal their images. They were interesting but not altogether exciting for the students who directly handled them. However, these same slides were made more vivid in the scanning and digital presentation, especially one of a devil surrounded by red and orange flames. The digital scan of a glass lantern slide depicting the Annunciation, when the angel Gabriel revealed to Mary that she would be the mother of Christ, better revealed the texture and color of their garments and the facial expressions of the cherubim flanking their conversation. The digitization process seemed to flatten some materials, but for others, it offered a richer way of seeing them. Making digital, material religion is a process of give and take.

In both classrooms, students and professors of religion were confronting the as-yet-undefined concept of "digital materiality," a category this book aims to limn in anticipation of future scholarship and pedagogy. Rather than gloss over the numerous acts of translation that freight material objects in intimate proximity to daily life into digital objects of academic analysis and interpretation, the analytic concept of digital materiality thrusts these acts of translation into sustained scrutiny. The digital, however defined, can of course invoke, reflect, echo, and anticipate haptic worlds of embodied experience. It can—the singular here seems decidedly too shallow—also be a generative world of connection, mediating people and communities separated by voluntary or involuntary distances, geospatial, temporal, and otherwise. In a field long accustomed to naming what is so often imperceptible to all-too-human limitations of perception—deities, spirits, ghosts, ancestors, collective effervescences of human experience—the invisible ubiquity of the digital brings us to another threshold. To be sure, the meeting of these two interpretive fields, the digital and the material, is never fully achieved. One of the great sleights of hand of modern technology is the promise to replicate and reproduce lived experiences in digital form—a promise that may have been implicit in recent decades suddenly became center stage during the global coronavirus pandemic that seized global life as this volume came to completion. It is an old sell, dating at least as far back as the daguerreotype in the middle of the nineteenth century, and that, itself, drew upon previous promises of the magic lantern and panorama paintings to transport beholders beyond their sense horizons, as one early advocate of the educational promises of the camera enthused.[4]

All this to say, the interpretive field of the digital material inevitably draws us into renewed scrutiny of embodiment and affect—to ask what it is to position digital practices and pedagogies at the center of a field that has struggled to recognize and to take seriously the embodied experiences giving shape and form to definitions of the sacred. This volume began by asking a seemingly simple question that yielded no easy answer: How has material religion become digital? Along the way, we realized that this is not even the right question to ask. It presumes a one-way process of material religion becoming digital rather than considering the challenges and possibilities born from their intersection. In the course of attempting to answer that original question, better, grittier, stickier questions emerged: is the direction of causality and consequence singular or multidirectional? That is, can we conceive of a "material digitality" as readily as a "digital materiality"? Is "digital materiality" a new order of inquiry or an old one in updated technological garb? Over the last two decades, the academic study of religion has experienced "turns" in both material studies and digital scholarship. While these turns may at first glance seem unrelated, or at most coincidental, both approaches to the study of religion interrogate processes of mediation and together point to critical disciplinary advances in the twenty-

---

4 Jenna Supp-Montgomerie's work on the telegraph presents yet another site in which to explore antecedents of digital materiality. See, Supp-Montgomerie, *When the Medium Was the Mission: The Atlantic Telegraph and the Religious Origins of Network Culture* (New York: New York University Press, 2021).

first century. This book considers these processes from a variety of perspectives and sub-disciplines within the field of religion in order to theorize the implications of these two turns in scholarship, offer case studies in methodology, and reflect on various tools and processes that mediate between the material and the digital.

To better understand the intersection of these two turns in scholarship, and the ramifications of their intersection, it is first helpful to consider the terms: digital humanities and material religion. Definitions vary for these terms and disagreements among scholars are not uncommon. As such, it is not surprising that bringing these two concepts together is not simple or straightforward but instead opens a new and exciting scholarly vein of questions.

1.2 Naming the Field: Religion, Digital Humanities, and Material Culture

Perhaps the most existential question in the academic study of religion is one of boundaries—what *is* religion? What *counts* as religion within the scope of study? One need only to look briefly at the range of scholarship over the last century to notice major shifts and competing claims, from institutional studies and analyses of creed to studies of practice, lived experience, and public life.[5] Numerous books offer historical overviews of definitions of religion, analyses of various definitions, and/or attempts to define the term anew. Not all religion scholars agree on a definition, but something about the pursuit of that term and understanding it pulls the field together. When considering what united her and her fellow Yale Religion Department colleagues, Kathryn Lofton argued that it "is the effort to define religion" that brings together the field.[6] Whether one studies a region, a tradition, a methodology, a theme, a language, all focus on making better sense of this "thing" called religion, what it does, and how it works.

---

5 A full list of such studies extending from various "critical turns" over the last fifty years is seemingly inexhaustible. Accounts of these turns can be found in monographs by this chapter's authors. See also, Emily Suzanne Clark, *A Luminous Brotherhood: Afro-Creole Spiritualism in Nineteenth-Century New Orleans* (Chapel Hill: University of North Carolina Press, 2016) and Rachel McBride Lindsey, *A Communion of Shadows: Religion and Photography in Nineteenth-Century America* (Chapel Hill: University of North Carolina Press, 2017). Additionally, see Ashon Crawley, *Blackpentecostal Breath: The Aesthetics of Possibility* (New York: Fordham University Press, 20016), for an exemplary study that holds these critical paradigms to account.
6 Kathryn Lofton, "Religious history as religious studies," *Religion* 42.3 (2012): 385.

For Lofton, the ontology of the field is in the scholarly practice of naming the object of study, not in a specimen that is discovered, pinned, and dissected. As the disciplinary claims of previous generations confront criticisms of the artificiality of those boundaries, the precision of the object of study becomes more difficult to name, let alone analyze and interpret. The emerging framework of "digital religion" is no exception. What *is* digital religion? Do we use the same tools of inquiry, developed in previous generations from very different contexts of communication and assembly, to name and understand it? Does it—whatever *it* is—confirm, modify, or unsettle the discipline? Is it a species of embodied, lived religion, or is it a threat to those conventional modes of experience? Can it be both at once?

Scholars of religion are well aware of the difficulties of defining complex terms. These questions are not new, and indeed one goal of the series in which this volume is published is to demonstrate the complexity and urgency of attending to religion and digital humanities. But such questions are nevertheless essential to pose at the outset of this volume as we seek to consider one of the many borderlands in the study of religion today—one where material studies confronts digital humanities, or, more accurately, where embodied life confronts digital cultures. Is this indeed an epistemic borderlands or a rupture of other dimensions?

Defining digital humanities, likewise, is not an easy task. The term as we know it and use it is a few decades old but with a longer history. (As of late 2021, there is no entry for "digital humanities" in the Oxford English Dictionary.[7]) And it is a history full of debate. Within the history of that term, academics have identified digital humanities as the thing that will save the humanities, as merely a passing fad, and as a methodology not separate from but now embedded in the humanities (and that's all just within the pages of *The Chronicle of Higher Education*). Before the introduction of the term "digital humanities," the "field" went by terms including humanities computing, eHumanities, humanist informatics, literary computing, and more.[8] Some continue to use those terms somewhat interchangeably, while others see a distinction between digital humanities in its current mode and its predecessor humanities computing (simply using comput-

---

7 OED Online. September 2021. Oxford University Press. http://www.oed.com.ezp.slu.edu (accessed September 21, 2021).

8 Melissa Terras, Julianne Nyhan, and Edward Vanhoutte, "Introduction," in *Defining Digital Humanities: A Reader*, Melissa Terras, Julianne Nyhan, and Edward Vanhoutte, eds. (Farnham, Surrey: Ashgate, 2013); and Edward Vanhoutte, "The Gates of Hell: History and Definition of Digital | Humanities | Computing," in *Defining Digital Humanities*.

ers to do humanities research).[9] The advent of the internet, advanced digital visualizations, distant reading of texts, multimedia archives, optical character recognition (OCR), and more have all changed the humanities in some way.

In 2004, Susan Schreibman, Ray Siemens, and John Unsworth, explained the term through an articulation of its "goals": "using information technology to illuminate the human record, and bringing an understanding of the human record to bear on the development and use of information technology."[10] Others emphasize methods. Matthew Kirschenbaum called digital humanities "a common methodological outlook."[11] In their 2012 volume *Digital_Humanities*, Anne Burdick, Johanna Drucker, Peter Lunenfeld, Todd Presner, and Jeffrey Schnapp advocated for a digital humanities that "asks what it means to be a human being in the networked information age and participle in fluid communicates of practice, asking and answering research questions that cannot be reduced to a single genre, medium, discipline, or institution." In short, it is a field that supports "a global, trans-historical, and transmedia approach to knowledge and meaning-making."[12] Rafael Alvarado defined digital humanities as "a social category, not an ontological one."[13] Using the concepts of genealogies and networks, Alvarado saw the term as one that centered community, namely a group of people trying to figure out digital humanities as they went.

This tour of definitions is not meant to be exhaustive but rather to gesture to the variety within the field and how the combination of "digital" and "humanities" opens new directions for scholars. It is "a nexus of fields within which scholars use computing technologies to investigate the kinds of questions that are traditional to the humanities."[14] In our own experiences as instructors, researchers, and project directors, we have found collaboration across fields of ex-

---

9 John Unsworth, 'What is Humanities Computing, and What is it Not?', in *Jahrbuch für Computerphilologie*, G. Braungart, K. Eibl and F. Jannidis eds. (Paderborn: Mentis Verlag, 2002), 71–84.
10 Susan Schreibman, Ray Siemens, and John Unsworth, "The Digital Humanities and Humanities Computing: An Introduction," in *A Companion to Digital Humanities*, Susan Schreibman, Ray Siemens, and John Unsworth, eds. (Malden, MA: Blackwell Publishing, 2004), xxiii.
11 Matthew Kirschenbaum, "What is Digital Humanities and What's It Doing in English Departments?" in *Debates in the Digital Humanities*, Matthew K. Gold, ed. (Minneapolis: University of Minnesota Press, 2012), 4.
12 Anne Burdick, Johanna Drucker, Peter Lunenfeld, Todd Presner, and Jeffrey Schnapp, *Digital_Humanities* (Cambridge: The MIT Press, 2012), vii.
13 Rafael C. Alvarado, "The Digital Humanities Situation," in *Debates in the Digital Humanities*, 50.
14 Kathleen Fitzpatrick, "Reporting from the Digital Humanities 2010 Conference," *ProfHacker*, 10 July 2010, https://www.chronicle.com/blogs/profhacker/reporting-from-the-digital-humanities-2010-conference/25473

pertise, including highly specialized coders and developers, to be a hallmark of digital humanities practice. Digital forms "point to a new way of working with representation and mediation," and so the digital humanities also prompts us to "approach culture in a radically new way."[15] A primary way to understand the field of digital humanities, then, is to start with those who identify with the field of digital humanities; know about big projects, platforms, and databases made and used by other digital humanists; read the literature in the journals or books; attend DH conferences; and otherwise associate their scholarly practices with DH. But perhaps more than that, not so different than the field of religion, it is a field brought together by the pursuit of similar questions about technology and human experience and a desire for collaboration within a scholarly community. Indeed, what better reflects the humanities than a definition that eschews tradition and opts for one with nuance, flexibility, and complexity?

Rather than become tied to a straightforward definition of digital humanities, this volume attempts to open the category up even further. In its early years and still today, digital humanities has been dominated by scholars whose home discipline is English or Literature. The field often emphasizes using technological tools to manipulate, re-examine, re-organize, or "hack" a text (a source-base as familiar to as it is contested within the study of religion). As the tour through definitions revealed, many digital humanities scholars think of the field as one about tools. This volume considers digital humanities as the use of technological tools to do humanities research connected with the study of religion as well as humanist analyses of technology. In this way, we think about digital humanities as both a methodology and a theory. Digital tools, digital media, and digital techniques draw our attention to the methods of digital humanities scholars. Unexamined assumptions about technology, culture, and religion remind us that theory matters too. Technology is forever altering the world for our religious subjects and for our modes of inquiry. Therefore, we consider digital humanities to include both the deployment of particular tools or methods to engage material religion as well as theoretical analyses of technology's intersection with material religion.

---

15 David M. Berry, "Introduction: Understanding the Digital Humanities," *Understanding Digital Humanities*, David M. Berry, ed. (New York: Palgrave MacMillan, 2012), 2.

1.3 Material Religion

The meeting of material culture and digital humanities is more than academic exercise. It is born, in the essays in this volume, of efforts to account for the multimodal realities of modern life, in which human behaviors, experiences, and aspirations are worked out in physical and digital contexts, neither of which is hermetically sealed from the other. To take but one example from the chapters that follow, in James Edmonds's ethnography of Habib Syech bin Abdul Qadir Assegaf, the grittiness of Indonesian cities and digital recordings of his performances of *salawat* are each of central importance to understanding this culture of devotion. To separate what is "materiality" from what is "digital" is to create artificial boundaries that preclude fuller understanding of this devotional and cultural experience. In Edmonds's telling, efforts to regulate access to digital recordings of Habib Syech's blessings complicate narratives of accessibility even as they confirm the deep entanglement of digital and material worlds.

When describing the material turn in religious studies, Sonia Hazard has argued that this field is defined by "the claim of material things and phenomena—objects, practices, spaces, bodies, sensations, affects, and so on—to a place at the center of scholarly inquiry."[16] Centering the material might seem a scholarly move away from the digital. "Isn't the digital by necessity virtual?" one might ask. Perhaps. But what is most generative here is the centering of the processes of mediation and translation that scholars of religion have long made in their interpretive leaps from objects, bodies, places, and texts into such categories as belief, tradition, world, and human. In this way, the "digital material" not only claims a new category of analysis but also throws light on the deeper interpretive processes and energies at work in the study of religion. The material and the digital are perhaps better visualized as the upside down of each other on a common thread rather than opposite ends of a spectrum. Still, a brief overview of the material culture turn in the study of religion is instructive preface to the chapters that follow.

Jules David Prown, an art historian who pressed the study of ordinary objects, explained material culture through a focus on the production and reception of those objects. He argued that "human-made objects reflect, consciously or unconsciously, directly or indirectly, the beliefs of the individuals who commissioned, fabricated, purchased, or used them, and, by extension, the beliefs

---

16 Sonia Hazard, "The Material Turn in the Study of Religion," *Religion and Society: Advances in Research* 4 (2013): 58.

of the larger society to which these individuals belonged."[17] To be sure, object study is certainly an important component of material religion, but the study of material religion is more than an examination of religious stuff. The study of material religion recognizes a broader significance to the material. When explaining the significance of materialities, scholar of religion and art Sally Promey argued that the "material is all around us." Explaining further, Promey writes, "We are literally material beings in a material environment, populated with material objects, situated amidst the material stuff of nature, bound in intimate and more distant relations with other persons through shared material habits and habitats."[18] Material religion prompts a recognition that religion is always framed by materiality, through objects, embodied practice, built and natural environments, and more. That is, material religion is never only an expression of belief, but also that which generates human experience and, in turn, gives rise to the cultivation of meaningful associations.

It is almost formulaic to begin a conversation on material religion with an acknowledgment of the field's historical focus on belief and ideas, but rather than being just a historiographical cliché, such an acknowledgment emphasizes the significance of the material turn in the field. The historical centering of belief in the study of religion went hand-in-hand with the original focus on Protestant Christianity in the field of religious studies. The history of the study of religion is overwhelmingly Christian and Euro-centric. With Protestantism's claim of "sola fide," by faith alone, the practice and material sides of religion became associated with "corrupt" Catholicism and so-called "primitive" non-Christian religions. However, the field of religious studies has, at least in theory, expanded beyond this original Protestant focus and exponentially benefited from that development. This does not mean that material religion replaces material for belief. Rather, as religion scholar David Morgan explains, "forms of materiality—sensations, things, and performance—are a matrix in which belief happens as touching and seeing, hearing and tasting, feeling and emotion, as will and action, as imagination and intuition."[19]

---

17 Jules David Prown, "The Truth of Material Culture: History or Fiction?" in *American Artifacts: Essays in Material Culture*, eds. Jules David Prown and Kenneth Haltman (East Lansing: Michigan State University Press, 2000), 11. For a critique of the primacy of "belief" in analyses of material culture, see Lindsey, *A Communion of Shadows*, 12–14.
18 Sally M. Promey, "Religion, Sensation, and Materiality: An Introduction," in *Sensational Religion*, ed. Sally Promey (New Haven: Yale University Press, 2014), 4.
19 David Morgan, "Introduction: The matter of belief," in *Religion and Material Culture: The Matter of Belief*, ed. David Morgan (New York: Routledge, 2010), 8.

With this move away from centering belief, studies in material religion began to grow in popularity in the 1990s with pivotal works like Sally Promey's *Spiritual Spectacles: Vision and Image in Mid-Nineteenth-Century Shakerism* (1993), Colleen McDannell's *Material Christianity: Religion and Popular Culture in America* (1995), David Morgan's *The Sacred Gaze: Religious Visual Culture in Theory and Practice* 2005), and more. Contemporary to these works was another shift in religious studies that further emphasized the material side of religion called "lived religion." Folklorist Leonard Primiano articulated a theory of "vernacular religion" in the early 1990s that has been eclipsed in scholarship by "lived religion" over the next several decades.[20] Theorized by scholars like Robert A. Orsi in *The Madonna of 115th Street: Faith and Community in Italian Harlem, 1880 – 1950* (1985; 2002 second edition), Marla Frederick's *Between Sundays: Black Women and Everyday Struggles of Faith* (2003), Marie Griffith's *Born Again Bodies: Flesh and Spirit in American Christianity* (2005), and David Hall's edited 1997 volume *Lived Religion in America: Toward a History of Practice*, "lived religion" emphasized analyses of practice and, by extension, material worlds of practice, in the study of religion. Initially theorized primarily by specialists in the study of American religion, the footprint of lived religion has extended far beyond this subfield.

Demonstrating the wider significance of the material turn in religious studies is the creation of the *Material Religion: The Journal of Objects, Art and Belief* in 2005. Avoiding a simple focus on just material culture itself, the journal pursues "how religion happens materially." According to *Material Religion*'s founding editors, Birgit Meyer, David Morgan, Crispin Paine, and S. Brent Plate, the "materialized study of religion begins with the assumption that things, their use, their valuation, and their appeal are not something added to a religion, but rather inextricable from it."[21] In other words, the material is not just a flashy addition to the substance of religion but rather a foundational element of traditions and communities. The journal editorial board reflects the expansive nature of material religious studies and the wide appeal of the approach. Editorial board members past and present have their expertise in Islamic Studies, African Religions, Chinese Religions, American Religion, and more. Perhaps one of the jour-

---

20 Leonard Primiano, "Vernacular Religion and the Search for Method in Religious Folklife," *Western Folklore* 54 (Jan. 1995): 37– 56. Vernacular religion, perhaps given Primiano's training as a folklorist, was initially more intentionally attentive to artifacts in time and place than early studies of lived religion.

21 Birgit Meyer, David Morgan, Crispin Paine, and S. Brent Plate, "The Origin and Mission of *Material Religion*," *Religion* 40.3 (2010): 209. Tellingly, the Protestant shadow of "belief" remains a primary category of analysis even in this flagship journal.

nal's most influential issues was the "Key Terms in Material Religion" install-
ment in 2011, which included a wide array of terms including sacred, touch,
sensation, ritual, thing, medium, and even belief. References to the digital
were fleeting in the issue, but those few connections to digital production and
engagement signaled rich possibilities.

The material turn in the study of religion happened alongside the digital
turn and the growth of the field of digital humanities. These developments, we
contend, ought not be seen as separate. After all, religious studies and digital
humanities are both inherently interdisciplinary fields whose conversations are
enriched from intellectual and scholarly cross-pollination.

1.4 Digital Humanities and Religion

The digital's intersection with religion did not begin with digital humanities.
In the late 1990s, "online religion" caught the attention of researchers and popular media.[22] A 1996 *Time* magazine article, "Finding God on the Web," suggest-
ed a growing trend among the American faithful. At a time when search engines
found fewer than half a million hits for "God" (today Google finds nearly 2 bil-
lion), the cover story drips with anticipation about the digital revolution:

> Like schools, like businesses, like governments, like nearly everyone, it seems religious
> groups are rushing online, setting up church home pages, broadcasting dogma, and estab-
> lishing theological news groups, bulletin boards, and chat rooms. Almost overnight, the
> electronic community of the Internet has come to resemble a high-speed spiritual bazaar
> where thousands of the faithful—and equal numbers of the faithless—meet and debate
> and swap ideas about many things many of us had long since stopped discussing in public,
> like our faith and religious beliefs. It is an astonishing act of technological and intellectual
> mainstreaming that is changing the character of the Internet and could even change our
> ideas about God.[23]

As Americans had done previously with photography, radio, and television, the
internet and its promises of digital community became an indispensable part of
American religion. Five years after the *Time* report, the *Pew Internet & American
Life Project* "found that about 28 million Americans, or 25% of the Internet pop-

---

22 Scholars researching the affinity between religion and media have theorized about religion
and the internet/online communities since the early 2000s, especially how new digital media is
shaping religious practice. For example, see Heidi Campbell, ed., *Digital Religion: Understanding
Religious Practice in New Media Worlds* (London: Routledge, 2012).
23 Ramo, Joshua Cooper and Greg Burke, "Finding God on the Web," *Time*. December 16, 1996.

ulation, visit religious cyberspace, with more than 3 million seeking spiritual material on any given day." The Pew report revealed that more Americans searched for "spiritual material online" than "traded stocks or bonds or mutual funds online, or [did] online banking, or participated in online auctions, or used Internet-based dating services, or placed phone calls online." More than 90 % of these "Religion Surfers," in the study's nomenclature, were Christian. Jewish, Buddhist, and "no affiliation" were each under 2%; Muslims were 0.6%; and 3% were "other religion."[24] The study did not account for race, class, or gender.

Scholars, too, attempted to make sense of what the new frontier of cyberspace meant for the study of religion. In her 2004 book, *Give Me That Online Religion*, Brenda Brasher claimed the "cyberworld" as a "an arena of public life where relations of authority and power are played out" and sought to demonstrate the new identities, hierarchies, and social inequalities that it produced among religious groups and persons.[25] Brasher recognized the seachange afoot in modern religion, even if her scholarly approach to those changes were anchored in a previous episteme of analysis. She was hardly alone in this tumult. It was not until 2018 that the American Academy of Religion adopted Guidelines for Evaluating Digital Scholarship, just one institutional marker of the dramatic changes taking place not only in modern religion but in the ways scholars are trained and practice scholarship in the digital world.[26] Indeed, despite the seeming affinity between religious studies and digital humanities, scholars of religion have been slower than other fields to join that conversation—this despite, as we will see, the centrality of theology and religious life in the history of digital humanities.[27]

We suggest that there have been at least three main digital humanities modes in the study of religion to date: "concordance" (efforts to locate and upload as many sources as possible); "annotation" (including social media, crowdsourcing initiatives, and metadata tagging, as well as scholarly output in more conventional

---

24 Elena Larsen, "Are Internet users singing out for that online religion?" Pew Internet & American Life Project, Pew Research Center, last modified 23 December 2001, https://www.pe wresearch.org/internet/2001/12/23/introduction-14/
25 Brasher, *Give Me That Online Religion* (New Brunswick, NJ: Rutgers University Press), 2004.
26 Theodore Vial, Timothy Beal, Christopher Cantwell, Kristian Peterson, Jeri E. Weiringa, "Guidelines for Evaluating Digital Scholarship," *American Academy of Religion*, https://www. aarweb.org/AARMBR/AARMBR/About-AAR-/Board-of-Directors-/Board-Resolutions-/Guide lines-for-Evaluating-Digital-Scholarship.aspx, accessed December 22, 2020.
27 Christopher D. Cantwell and Hussein Rashid, "Religion, Media, and the Digital Turn: A Report for the Public Sphere Program," whitepaper, December 2015; accessed 21 July 2019, https:// s3.amazonaws.com/ssrc-cdn1/crmuploads/new_publication_3/religion-media-and-the-digital-turn.pdf

forms); and "data mining and visualization" (maps, galleries, sounds, etc.). There are outliers to these categories, of course, and the boundaries across these modes are often porous as individual projects frequently draw from more than one. Current work may constitute an emergent fourth model that pushes beyond employing digital tools to answer questions grounded in pre-digital disciplinary epistemologies; that, in short, teach us to think differently about religion.

Given the slowness of religious studies and theology to join other humanities disciplines in the employment and scrutiny of "the digital," it is easy to forget that the study of religion was at the beginning of the digital turn. In 1951, Italian Jesuit Roberto Busa and Paul Tasman, an employee with IBM, together created a machine-generated concordance of the entire works of Thomas Aquinas. Busa had proposed a mechanical concordance during his doctoral studies, but it took some time for the technology to catch up with his imagination. Busa and Tasman began with over 1,000 cards on which Busa recorded Aquinas's writing and created a computer-generated concordance. Computational work in the humanities, then, developed from a Jesuit and a computer executive crafting alternative uses for science technology. The 1980s saw the creation of a CD-ROM version of the *Index Thomisticus*, and internet users have been able to consult this project since 2005.[28] Though Busa's computational-driven research was based on a text analysis insight (he theorized that the preposition "in" was key to understanding Aquinas's understanding of God's holy presence), Busa first had to transform one material form to another—a codex into a punch card for the machine technology to read—before he could work with the digital text. His concordance is largely regarded not only as the first attempt to use nascent computing technologies for linguistic analysis in the service of theological study, but as "the beginning of humanities computing" in general. It is perhaps telling that the pursuit of a fuller account of Thomistic "faith and reason" was prolegomenon to digital humanities.[29]

Following Busa's model, many of the most transformative digital projects in the study of religion in the last decade have seized upon the ability of digital media to compile, preserve, and disseminate texts, objects, and moments that had once been limited by factors of accessibility to local archives or the happen-

---

28 To consult with the *Index Thomisticus* today, see http://www.corpusthomisticum.org/it/index.age

29 Roberto Busa, "The Annals of Humanities Computing: The Index Thomisticus," *Computers and the Humanities* 14 (1980): 83–90; Thomas Nelson Winter, "Roberto Busa, S.J., and the Invention of the Machine-Generated Concordance," *The Classical Bulletin* 75.1 (1999): 3–20; and Anne Burdick, Johanna Drucker, Peter Lunenfeld, Todd Presner, and Jeffrey Schnapp, *Digital_Humanities* (Cambridge: The MIT Press, 2012), 123.

stance of one's environs. Indeed this "concordance" model constitutes much of the energies and efforts in digital religion today.

Still, even though Busa's Thomistic concordance animated the beginnings of what we now call digital humanities and religious users were lighting up Alta-Vista and dominating chat groups in the early years of popular internet usage, as late as 2015 Tim Hutchings observed that "religion is at best a marginal theme in digital humanities conferences and debates."[30] In recent years the Association of Digital Humanities Organizations—the largest DH scholarly community—has hosted panels on religion and theology and the American Academy of Religion now facilitates a number of DH-themed panels and papers at its annual meetings. Slow as the field may be to seeing itself in the history of digital humanities, as the digital vernacular of GIS, XML encoding, datasets, and computational analyses have shifted our disciplinary episteme, it seems appropriate now to scrutinize digital tools and platforms as mediated fields of translation.

The next move in digital humanities and religion, then, we propose, is to turn the field's focus to the material. Early studies at the intersection of digital humanities and religion used digital tools to analyze religious writings and explorations of religion on the internet, and these projects revealed the vast possibilities of digital religion. This volume creates a space for questions that feel both new and old about material religion and technology. Religious people have long engaged with the technology of their day—using new tools and technologies to see the world in different ways, connecting with religious communities at large distances, moving the boundary of the unknowable a little bit further, and marveling at the ways they can engage the divine. Scholars too are forever developing new methodologies prompted by current research tools. The technology and tools used by religious people and scholars of today are different from the past, but regardless of our temporal focus, whether it's the ancient world or today, religion is not disconnected from the larger world. Does digital technology prompt new questions or does it remix questions the field has asked before? The chapters presented in this volume answer the question with the scholar's favorite reply: "well, both."

---

30 Tim Hutchings, "Digital Humanities and the Study of Religion," in *Between Humanities and the Digital*, eds. Patrik Svensson and David Theo Goldberg (Cambridge: MIT Press, 2015), 283.

1.5 Volume Overview

The chapters in *Digital Humanities and Material Religion: An Introduction* are organized in three sections. The first section, "Emerging Frameworks of Digital Materiality," expands on the complicated processes we've begun to articulate here. In "Promiscuous Affiliation: Evangelical Women, Biblical Mediation, and Digital Infrastructures of Conversion," Suzanne van Geuns and Pamela Klassen introduce readers to the world of Christian bloggers and how their products are confessional and intimate as well as material and capitalist. These Christian bloggers share their testimonies, biblical exegesis, and aesthetics with readers and send those readers into "internet conversion funnels": links to products sold by retailers, and the blogger, as an affiliate marketer, gets a small payment if a purchase is made. Biblical womanhood thus includes entrepreneurial spirit as these women's "confessional production snugly intertwines Biblical references with commercialization efforts." The clicks and charisma matter and then mediate, materialize, and monetize salvation.

In "Digital Scriptures, Material Religion and the Digital Humanities: An Interdisciplinary Framework for Curating Digitized Sacred Texts Online," Arjun Sabharwal builds on an interdisciplinary framework combining digital curation, material religion, and the digital humanities in approaching the digital preservation and representation of sacred texts. In this context, digital curation aims to provide stable and meaningful access and use for purposes of worship, education, and faith curation. Material religion—and within that, digital religion—serves as a context for some of the material presented herein, but the primary focus in the chapter is on technologies used in religious practices. Digital humanities, in turn, focuses on the use of digital technologies and techniques to represent text and data in humanistic inquiry and interpretive practices central to religious communication. As a digital initiatives librarian, an academic appointment within his university library, Sabharwal offers critical insight to questions surrounding the curation of material and digital artifacts: How does digital curation fit into the broader context of material religion? How do approaches such as digital preservation, remediation, social curation, text encoding, and data visualization comprise digital curation strategies? How do curatorial strategies fit into the culture of religious communities?

The second section of this text is titled, "How the Material Becomes Digital: Methods in Digital Material Religion." In "Visiting Religious Spaces in the Digital Realm: The MAVCOR Digital Spaces Project in Historical Context," Emily C. Floyd and Meg Bernstein smartly compare past and present. These authors bring our attention to the ongoing MAVCOR Digital Spaces Project, which produces high-resolution images of religious spaces, using both drone, giga-pixel, and 360º photography, and consider this project in light of its historical antecedent. Proxy pilgrimage in medieval Europe allowed an analog version of virtual religious experience through illustrated guides that created mental pilgrimage journeys. The comparison is particularly useful for identifying what the digital experience of religious space emphasizes: "the visual over the tactile, aural, or olfactory; solitude rather than community; pixels rather than practice."

In "Balinese Religio-cultural Imaginaries and Rituals of Digital Materiality," Urmila Mohan applies an anthropological and historical framework to explore how Balinese Hinduism in Indonesia may be studied through digital images (photos and videos) and the use of messaging and social media applications such as WhatsApp and Instagram. The study of Balinese culture and religion is a process of unpacking religio-cultural imaginaries long created and mediated by various agents from the time of Dutch colonialism. Against this historic backdrop, how, and to what end, does the production and circulation of digital imagery influence Balinese religious identity and values? How does it shape the social and cultural impetus to act and perceive a certain way in order to be suitably Balinese? This chapter will explore these questions in a transmedia manner, proposing the study of rituals *around* media and rituals *for* media. In one example, divination and healing via smart phone video chats highlights digital materiality's role in continuing religious practices. In another instance, heritagization through pre-wedding digital photos and videos, illustrates how digital materiality facilitates Balinese self-fashioning and cultural re-presentation. Across these and other examples, digital materiality becomes the intersection of the material and digital, through the movement between analog and virtual, real and imaginary, and the tangible and intangible that shapes and sustains Balinese identity.

The final section, "Intersections of the Digital and Material: Tools, Questions, and Processes," continues the focus on methodology. In "Material, Maternal, Embodied, and Digital: Objects and Practices in Natural Parenting," Florence Pasche Guignard investigates the ideas and practices of natural parenting, asking a number of critical questions and unearthing fascinating intersections and ironies along the way. In particular, the intersection of natural parenting with technology is a curious one due to the contrast between ideas and practices that are embodied and material and the mediated use of online platforms and digital tools to share ideas and create community. While there is much in digital humanities scholarship on the innovative tools scholars can use in their research, Pasche Guignard brings our attention to new questions and new sites of analysis that come from paying attention to the digital side of being human.

In "(Re)Enchanting the Digital: Technological Manifestations of Baraka," James Edmonds considers the popular Islamic performer Habib Syech bin

Abdul Qadir Assegaf through analysis of his disavowal of "centralized technological presentation of his performances or himself." Noticing that Habib Syech promotes his appearances on social media and other digital platforms, but does so in a way that subverts their authority as communicative networks, Edmonds focuses attention on the disruptions between the performer's intent and the digital behaviors of the thousands of people who gather in rice fields, stadiums, and other large venues across Asia and the Middle East almost daily over the last twenty years. Edmonds argues that Habib Syech's disavowal of technology and participants' use of technology does not hinder his popularity, but rather allows for a different manifestation of technological existence. In the chapter in this volume, Edmonds juxtaposes recordings of Habib Syech's performances—which, despite his wishes, have been uploaded to YouTube and Facebook and recorded to CD—to "the culture of sharing that often enables global communication." Such recordings offer what Edmonds calls a "(re)enchantment of the material" by creating conditions for "technological manifestations of *baraka*" through creative reconfigurations of performance.

In "Beyond Recognition? Orphan Objects, Decolonization, and Religious Histories of the Spanish Americas," Barbara E. Mundy and Dana Leibsohn consider the importance of decolonialization in digital/material religion and the challenges of a decolonizing methodology. In the process, they introduce readers to *Vistas: Visual Culture in Spanish America, 1520–1820*, a digital database that highlights how many colonial artifacts, in museums and elsewhere, are Indigenous. Zooming-in on an image of a feathered mosaic allows the viewer to see Indigenous handiwork and consider indigenous experience. At the same time, Mundy and Leibsohn remind us, we must consider that sight is historically situated, and today's visual accessibility should not allow us to forget the colonial past and present.

The book concludes with "Challenges and Possibilities in Digital Material Religion." Here, we reflect on future directions, challenges, and possibilities in the intersection of digital humanities and material religion. Additionally, we consider possible future avenues of research and the vitality of the field and reflect on what new questions and lines of inquiry "digital material" religion prompts us to ask.

References

Alvarado, Rafael C. "The Digital Humanities Situation." In *Debates in the Digital Humanities*. Matthew K. Gold, ed. Minneapolis: University of Minnesota Press, 2012.

Berry, David M. "Introduction: Understanding the Digital Humanities." *Understanding Digital Humanities*. David M. Berry, ed. New York: Palgrave MacMillan, 2012.

Brasher, Brenda. *Give Me That Online Religion*. New Brunswick, NJ: Rutgers University Press, 2004.

Burdick, Anne, Johanna Drucker, Peter Lunenfeld, Todd Presner, and Jeffrey Schnapp. *Digital_Humanities*. Cambridge: The MIT Press, 2012.

Busa, Roberto. "The Annals of Humanities Computing: The Index Thomisticus." *Computers and the Humanities* 14 (1980): 83 – 90.

Campbell, Heidi, ed. *Digital Religion: Understanding Religious Practice in New Media Worlds*. London: Routledge, 2012.

Cantwell, Christopher D. and Hussein Rashid. "Religion, Media, and the Digital Turn: A Report for the Public Sphere Program." whitepaper, December 2015; accessed 21 July 2019, https://s3.amazonaws.com/ssrc-cdn1/crmuploads/new_publication_3/religion-media-and-the-digital-turn.pdf

Clark, Emily. *A Luminous Brotherhood: Afro-Creole Spiritualism in Nineteenth-Century New Orleans*. Chapel Hill: University of North Carolina Press, 2016.

Crawley, Ashon. *Blackpentecostal Breath: The Aesthetics of Possibility*. New York: Fordham University Press, 2016.

Fitzpatrick, Kathleen. "Reporting from the Digital Humanities 2010 Conference." *ProfHacker*, 10 July 2010, https://www.chronicle.com/blogs/profhacker/reporting-from-the-digital-humanities-2010-conference/25473.

Hazard, Sonia. "The Material Turn in the Study of Religion." *Religion and Society: Advances in Research* 4 (2013): 58 – 78.

Hutchings, Tim. "Digital Humanities and the Study of Religion." in *Between Humanities and the Digital*. Patrik Svensson and David Theo Goldberg. Cambridge: MIT Press, 2015.

Kirschenbaum, Matthew. "What is Digital Humanities and What's It Doing in English Departments?" In *Debates in the Digital Humanities*. Matthew K. Gold, ed. Minneapolis: University of Minnesota Press, 2012.

Larsen, Elena. "Are Internet users singing out for that online religion?" Pew Internet & American Life Project, Pew Research Center. Last modified 23 December 2001, https://www.pewresearch.org/internet/2001/12/23/introduction-14/

Lindsey, Rachel McBride. *A Communion of Shadows: Religion and Photography in Nineteenth-Century America*. Chapel Hill: University of North Carolina Press, 2017.

Lofton, Kathryn. "Religious history as religious studies." *Religion* 42.3 (2012): 383 – 394.

Meyer, Birgit, David Morgan, Crispin Paine, and S. Brent Plate. "The Origin and Mission of *Material Religion*." *Religion* 40.3 (2010): 207 – 211.

Morgan, David. "Introduction: The matter of belief." In *Religion and Material Culture: The Matter of Belief*. Ed. David Morgan. New York: Routledge, 2010.

Primiano, Leonard. "Vernacular Religion and the Search for Method in Religious Folklife." *Western Folklore* 54 (Jan. 1995): 37 – 56.

Promey, Sally M. "Religion, Sensation, and Materiality: An Introduction." In *Sensational Religion*. Ed. Sally Promey. New Haven: Yale University Press, 2014.

Prown, Jules David. "The Truth of Material Culture: History or Fiction?" In *American Artifacts: Essays in Material Culture*. eds. Jules David Prown and Kenneth Haltman. East Lansing: Michigan State University Press, 2000.

Ramo, Joshua Cooper and Greg Burke. "Finding God on the Web," *Time*. December 16, 1996.

Schreibman, Susan, Ray Siemens, and John Unsworth. "The Digital Humanities and Humanities Computing: An Introduction." In *A Companion to Digital Humanities*. Susan Schreibman, Ray Siemens, and John Unsworth, eds. Malden, MA: Blackwell Publishing, 2004.

Supp-Montgomerie, Jenna. *When the Medium was the Mission: The Atlantic Telegraph and the Religious Origins of Network Culture*. New York: New York University Press, 2021.

Terras, Melissa, Julianne Nyhan, and Edward Vanhoutte. "Introduction," in *Defining Digital Humanities: A Reader*. Melissa Terras, Julianne Nyhan, and Edward Vanhoutte, eds. Farnham, Surrey: Ashgate, 2013.

Unsworth, John. 'What is Humanities Computing, and What is it Not?' In *Jahrbuch für Computerphilologie*. G. Braungart, K. Eibl and F. Jannidis eds. Paderborn: Mentis Verlag, 2002, 71–84.

Vanhoutte, Edward. "The Gates of Hell: History and Definition of Digital | Humanities | Computing." In *Defining Digital Humanities: A Reader*, Melissa Terras, Julianne Nyhan, and Edward Vanhoutte, eds. Farnham, Surrey: Ashgate, 2013, 119–157.

Vial, Theodore, Timothy Beal, Christopher Cantwell, Kristian Peterson, Jeri E. Weiringa. "Guidelines for Evaluating Digital Scholarship." *American Academy of Religion*, https://www.aarweb.org/AARMBR/AARMBR/About-AAR-/Board-of-Directors-/Board-Resolutions-/Guidelines-for-Evaluating-Digital-Scholarship.aspx, accessed December 22, 2020.

Winter, Thomas Nelson. "Roberto Busa, S.J., and the Invention of the Machine-Generated Concordance." *The Classical Bulletin* 75.1 (1999): 3–20.

Part 1 Emerging Frameworks of Digital Materiality

Suzanne van Geuns and Pamela E. Klassen
Chapter 2
Promiscuous Affiliation: Evangelical Women, Biblical Mediation and Digital Infrastructures of Conversion

Jenn's blog features many flowers, drawn in soft pinks and watercolor greens, with the occasional nightingale, and is framed by a header with a quote from the Epistle to Titus 2:4–5. These two verses from the New Testament show up on the blogs of conservative Christian women with some frequency, enjoining "young women to be sober, to love their husbands, to love their children, to be discreet, chaste, keepers at home, good, obedient to their own husbands, that the word of God be not blasphemed." In the sidebar, directly above various advertisements for candles and spa sets, Jenn's homemade daily Bible reading plans provide a guide for reading the entire Bible in one year. Jenn writes that she is "just your average Texan momma" blogging to "glorify God" and allow women to "find Biblical truths" as they read how Jenn herself applies the Scriptures to her life and circumstances.[1] What the flowers and the biblical citations do not directly reveal is that by visiting Jenn's blog and reading about her life, a user potentially also contributes to her bank account. Her blog has an "affiliate link" to Walmart embedded in the text, so that if anyone purchases something online from Walmart afterward, Jenn receives a small payment. Even if the purchase happens weeks afterward and the visitor never clicked anything on the blog, Jenn is paid by the companies of which she is an affiliate, as they reward her for bringing these customers, no matter what they purchase, into what is known in the online advertising industry as the "conversion funnel."

In this chapter, we take as our focus North American Evangelical Christian women's confessional production, by which we mean a wider Christian emphasis on testimonial witness as both a missionary and an entrepreneurial mode of address.[2] Jenn's blog is one of thousands of examples of white Evangelical wom-

---

1 Jenn, "Stuff About Me," *Is It Monday, Yet?* (blog), n.d., accessed April 16, 2017, https://mon dayfollowssunday.blogspot.com/p/blog-page_7.html. For blog posts that do not indicate a publication date, citations will include a 'accessed by' date.
2 Pamela E. Klassen, *The Story of Radio Mind: A Missionary's Journey on Indigenous Land* (Chicago: University of Chicago Press, 2018), 41–48; Kathryn Lofton, *Oprah: The Gospel of an Icon* (Oakland, CA: University of California Press, 2011).

https://doi.org/10.1515/9783110608755-003

en's online writing and self-presentation.[3] This chapter analyzes the blogs of more than thirty U.S. Christian women, published between 2008 and 2016. While the bloggers in our analysis generally do not mention any denominational affiliation, they claim an implicitly universal Christianity in which they—women who write about being wives, mothers, and being "sold out" for Christ—hold fast to the Bible in a culture that does not. Bloggers test "worldly philosophies" against the "real world of eternity" in homeschooling their children, lament "rudeness and misunderstanding" from people who do not see the blessing of having very large families, and reiterate that they are "set apart" or "pioneers" in a culture that rejects Christian values.[4] As a form of confessional production

---

3 It is impossible to estimate how many conservative Evangelical women's blogs exist online. We found the blogs in this chapter by looking at "link ups" on major conservative Christian blogging hubs: the Raising Homemakers link up, the Modest Monday link up, the Growing in Grace link up, and so on. When one blogger hosts a link up, other bloggers can post a link to their most recent post (formatted as a button) under it, creating a patchwork of links. Gathering these links rapidly yields hundreds of web addresses. The sheer amount of such link ups, and the fact that only bloggers who are actively marketing their blogs make use of them, hints at the large number of conservative Christian blogs online. For examples of link ups, see Caroline Allen, "Modest Monday and a Link Up!" *The Modest Mom* (blog), February 15, 2016, https://www.themodestmomblog.com/modest-monday-and-a-link-up-139/, Nicole Crone, "Growing in Grace Thursday Link Up #44," *Children Are a Blessing* (blog), February 4, 2016, http://childrenareablessing.org/2016/02/04/growing-in-grace-thursday-link-up-44/, June Fuentes, "Wise Woman Linkup!" *A Wise Woman Builds Her Home* (blog), February 9, 2016, http://proverbs14verse1.blogspot.nl/2016/02/wise-woman-linkup_9.html, Darlene Schacht, "Titus 2sDay Link-Up Party." *Time-Warp Wife* (blog), February 15, 2016. http://timewarpwife.com/7552-2/ (Archived here: https://web.archive.org/web/20160219071033/http://timewarpwife.com/7552-2/).

4 Grace Wheeler, "Our Family Mission Statement," *The Mommy On The Bus Says...* (blog), June 28, 2010, https://wheelsoffun.blogspot.com/2010/06/our-family-mission-statement.html; Kelly Crawford, "It's Normal to Have Babies. (That's Why I Look at You Weird When You Ask Me If I'm 'Done.')," *Generation Cedar* (blog), January 8, 2014, https://web.archive.org/web/20190103103642/http://www.generationcedar.com/main/2014/01/its-normal-to-have-babies-thats-why-i-look-at-you-weird-when-you-ask-me-if-im-done.html; Rebecca Jones, "Guarding the Heart – Part 2," *Leading Little Hearts Home* (blog), July 10, 2008, https://growingupgodskids.blogspot.com/2008/07/guarding-heart-part-2.html; Pam, "A Homemaker In All Seasons," *Where Your Treasure Is* (blog), November 2, 2015, https://treasureinanearthenvessel.blogspot.com/2015/11/a-homemaker-in-all-seasons.html; Erin Patrick, "When Life Isn't Fair," *My Nuggets of Truth* (blog), October 15, 2011, https://mynuggetsoftruth.blogspot.com/2011/10/when-life-isnt-fair.html; Holli, "A Rare Treasure...Seek One...or...Be One?," *Settled In My Home* (blog), June 2, 2008, https://settledinmyhome.blogspot.com/2008/06/rare-treasureseek-oneorbe-one.html.

at once intimate, material, and entrepreneurial, blogs reveal how Christian witness, digital infrastructure, and capitalist accumulation intersect.

Our chapter conjoins digital humanities and material religion through both theoretical critique and methodological practice. We take a rhetorical, intertextual, and infrastructural approach to gendered confessional production, through reading texts for their content and their coding. We understand digital humanities as a frame for theoretical analysis of how digital technologies facilitate and depend on cultural production. We deploy a method of looking under the hood of the internet, so to speak, to analyze how gendered, racialized, and commodified religious practices invoke coded tools of connection. Embedded in the infrastructure of the internet, "cookies" and "affiliate links" shape women's confessional production both with their knowledge and without it. When analyzing the modes of persuasion that Evangelical women use online, we pay attention to how and when they invoke the textual authority of the Bible, how they frame their words aesthetically, and how they make the digital infrastructure of the internet work for them as witnesses for God and as entrepreneurs.

Christian blogs do the work of the Church and the corporation, and Evangelical women have long stuck with the blogging format even as new social media platforms (Instagram, Snapchat, Twitter) rose in popularity. On one hand, these blogs are informed by biblically-rooted traditions of rhetoric and aesthetics in which missionaries witness to others as a profound responsibility. On the other, they are aligned by internet infrastructures both technical and corporate which seek to reach and influence as many people as possible. Engaging with the broader study of religion and mediation, our chapter brings to bear key concepts in digital studies, including affordances, aesthetic traps, and digital infrastructure, as well as widely used concepts in internet entrepreneurialism, such as affiliation and conversion. We use these terms to "undomesticate" Evangelical women's words and images at the same time that we highlight the testimonial fervor of internet "economies of salvation."[5] Grounding Evangelical women's blogs in personal and capitalist modes of affiliation called for by both Christian evangelism and digital infrastructures, we show the analytical benefits of bringing together the study of vernacular biblical exegesis and evangelical traditions of confessional production with digital tools for commercial success.

The devotional entrepreneurialism of the predominantly white Evangelical women we discuss here is a deeply material and gendered form of religious com-

---

5 Simon Coleman, "Materializing the Self: Words and Gifts in the Construction of Charismatic Protestant Identity," in *The Anthropology of Christianity*, ed. Fenella Cannell (Durham, NC: Duke University Press, 2006), 181.

munication. Women who may not consider themselves free to preach or speak in a church feel emboldened to circulate their biblical interpretations online in part because they are, quite literally, working from home. Evangelical bloggers are writers, designers, and creators of material religion. The women we discuss in this essay build and maintain digital infrastructures that anticipate and encourage the apprehensible and concrete effects (as conversion, as money) of the circulation they facilitate. They work within a Christian and online genre that is almost exclusively textual and visual; at the time of this analysis, this demographic of women had not made the transition to social media platforms that emphasize more audiovisual content, although many have expanded to Instagram and TikTok since 2016. Like the digital infrastructures through which the internet remains available, social media platforms and preferred content delivery methods shift constantly. That said, the infrastructures of these blogs remain alive. When readers today click on the affiliate links to Amazon or Walmart sprinkled through these blog posts, both blogger and reader are bound into commodified confessional production. These online infrastructures of circulation allow women to both sidestep and work within the contested terrain of their own gendered bodies as a containers of the sacred that may speak the word of the Lord from some places, and not others.

Jenn is an "influencer" who, like many other Evangelical bloggers, has varying capacity to incite purchasing action among her audiences and highlights her online contributions as a form of home-based Christian witness to other Christian women first and foremost. The wide broadcasting of these women's digital modes of address, however, means that they continue to grapple with the age-old tensions of confessional production, in which Christians worry that glorifying God through testimony often ends up glorifying the self along the way. Analysing not only their testimony but also the digital infrastructure coded below their words reveals a related tension: links of affiliation can be wildly "promiscuous," in the words of Wendy Chun, such that by sending users into internet conversion funnels where they may purchase any manner of product, Evangelical bloggers may end up serving "mammon" more than God (Luke 16:13).[6]

---

6 Wendy Chun, *Updating to Remain the Same: Habitual New Media* (Cambridge, MA: MIT Press, 2016), 58–60.

2.1 Biblical Mediation, Literalism, and the Affordances of Internet Witnessing

A verse from the Letter to Titus is a fitting epigraph for use on the internet, a medium of communication that increasingly acts as an affordance for duplicity in which people mask their identities in order to incite others. A text that, in the King James Version, enjoins "sound speech," "true witness," and sincerity, Titus also warns against liars and deceivers who will say anything in the pursuit of "filthy lucre." Along with its emphasis on wives' obedience to their husbands, it casts aspersions on Jews. But the Letter to Titus is itself a kind of lie. One of the so-called "Pastoral Epistles," the letter asserts the Apostle Paul as its author, which means that one of the most important founding figures of Christianity undergirds the doctrinal authority of the text. Biblical scholars, however, have long agreed that the Letter to Titus is "pseudepigraphical," meaning that it was not actually written by Paul, but by someone else seeking to ground his ideas in the authorial voice and influence of the apostle.[7] The Letter to Titus, then, is a text written in the first person that is replete with specific and confidence-inspiring detail of people and places, in which the pseudo-Paul commands that wives and servants be obedient to their husbands and masters. It is not too much of a leap to consider the Letter to Titus as an ancient precursor to the bots and web brigades of the twenty-first century, programmed to pretend to be real people or masking their online provocations in the identities of others.

Conservative Evangelical Christians such as Jenn, however, firmly believe that Paul is the author of all the New Testament epistles gathered in his name. Largely sharing a common denominator of biblical literalism in which the biblical text is held to be inerrant, these kinds of Christian readers privilege their understanding of the literal words of a Bible verse as they read them, concerned with the historical context of the text only insofar as it can be understood to confirm its transcendental legitimacy and power.[8] For them, approaching the biblical text as consisting of layered voices undercuts what is most important about it: its singularly clear truth, accessible to all. Transferring this hermeneutic of biblical literalism from the medium of the printed Bible to that of the internet,

---

7 John Marshall, "'I Left You in Crete': Narrative Deception and Social Hierarchy in the Letter to Titus," *Journal of Biblical Literature* 127.4 (2008): 781–803.
8 Vincent Crapanzano, *Serving the Word: Literalism in America from the Pulpit to the Bench* (New York: The New Press, 2000); Susan Friend Harding, *The Book of Jerry Falwell: Fundamentalist Language and Politics* (Princeton, NJ: Princeton University Press, 2000).

however, is a shift that is at once material, in terms of medium, and epistemic, in terms of presenting oneself as a "public" figure.

Writing as an American Christian woman in the nineteenth-century era of print required access to literacy, publishing networks outside the home (including church newspapers), and financial resources. While both race and gender limited women's access to public communication, there is a long history of both white and Black women who were public figures by virtue of their Christian witness. Such women stood out among their sisters, as women who communicated their vernacular biblical exegesis in a public realm both through writing and through public speaking.[9] Writing as an American Christian woman in the twenty-first century era of digital mediation and widespread literacy, however, the means of production may very well be located in one's kitchen or home office. As long as a woman has the money to purchase an internet connection and a suitable electronic device, she can address a public audience. No longer dependent on personal networks or church authorities, she relies on digital infrastructures and technical know-how to share her testimony.

Figuring out how to appropriately channel the home-based practices of biblical womanhood into an online world also involves quandaries of self-presentation in a very public medium. "Blogging ministries" like Jenn's stand in a long tradition of Christian women's confessional production framed as what Anthea Butler has pithily called "teaching not preaching."[10] Confessional production in which women detail how biblical truths have transformed them is predominantly instructional, in that it also details how the truths presented might transform the listener. Writing historically about Evangelical women's preaching in the US, Catherine Brekus points to how women justified their public preaching in churches, street corners, and camp meetings through personal testimony that they had been called to be an instrument for divine truth and biblical mediation.[11] Many eighteenth- and nineteenth-century varieties of Christianity were initially more open to women preachers than later battles over ordination might suggest. By the early twentieth century, however, most Protestant denominations

---

9 Katherine Bassard, *Transforming Scriptures: African American Women Writers and the Bible* (Athens: University of Georgia Press, 2010); Laurie Maffly-Kipp and Kathryn Lofton, eds., *Women's Work: An Anthology of African-American Women's Historical Writings from Antebellum America to the Harlem Renaissance* (New York: Oxford University Press, 2010); Catherine Brekus, *Strangers & Pilgrims: Female Preaching in America, 1740–1845* (Chapel Hill, NC: University of North Carolina Press, 1998).

10 Anthea Butler, *Women in the Church of God in Christ: Making a Sanctified World* (Chapel Hill, NC: University of North Carolina Press, 2007), 34–39.

11 Brekus, *Strangers & Pilgrims*, 15, 191–93.

restricted women's public preaching and writing, limiting them to more domes-
ticated and gendered terrain: teaching children about the Bible or writing for
the "Women's Page" of a church newspaper.[12] Overseas or home missions provided women with opportunities for testifying to their faith further afield, but
even those roles often kept women within domestic, women- and children-fo-
cused realms.[13] Conservative Evangelical women who felt themselves to be called
as instruments of God increasingly took up teaching as a vocation that fit within
the limits that patriarchal readings of the Bible and church regulations imposed
on them.[14] Similarly, the Evangelical women who publish their testimonies online today do so in an overtly instructional register, which allows them to affirm
patriarchal—literally, rule by the father—biblical interpretation even as they
claim space for their confessional productions in the public venue that is the internet.

Evangelical women's blogs draw inspiration from testimonial teaching and instructional traditions beyond (or adjacent to) Christian genres, including those of
therapeutic self-help. Many scholars have traced the crossover between Christian
and therapeutic genres in both Evangelical and liberal Protestant writing.[15] An especially important precursor to Evangelical women's blogging is the boom in
Christian women's self-help and marriage advice publishing during the 1970s
and 1980s, which Emily Suzanne Johnson argues was an integral part of the development of the religious right in the United States. Johnson's work shows that
Christian confessional self-help texts allowed women to teach other women by
channeling biblical truth—especially when such truths could be demonstrated
to pertain to problems specific to "feminine" occupations like being a wife, mother, or homemaker—thereby engaging in a genre of public address that did not
chafe at conservative Christian doctrinal bounds around gender roles.[16]

---

12 Brekus, *Strangers & Pilgrims*, 298–302.
13 Margaret Bendroth and Virginia Brereton, eds., *Women and Twentieth-Century Protestantism*
(Champaign, IL: University of Illinois Press, 2002).
14 Brekus, *Strangers & Pilgrims*, 305; Margaret Bendroth, *Fundamentalism and Gender, 1875 to
the Present* (New Haven, CT: Yale University Press, 1996), 84–91.
15 Amy DeRogatis, *Saving Sex: Sexuality and Salvation in American Evangelicalism* (Oxford: Oxford University Press, 2015); R. Marie Griffith, *God's Daughters: Evangelical Women and the
Power of Submission* (Berkeley: University of California Press, 2000); Pamela E. Klassen, *Spirits
of Protestantism: Medicine, Healing, and Liberal Christianity* (Berkeley: University of California
Press, 2011); Lofton, *Oprah*.
16 Emily Suzanne Johnson, *This Is Our Message: Women's Leadership in the New Christian Right*
(Oxford, UK: Oxford University Press, 2019), 25–31.

Even when a biblical text sanctions a woman's voice, whether as an early-twentieth-century preacher, a post-sixties self-help guide, or a twenty-first-century digital influencer, her female body remains an unstable mediator precisely because of doctrinal bounds about women's public speech.[17] In the digital realm, this instability becomes a particularly fascinating point of analysis, as conservative Evangelical women make themselves into mouthpieces for God in a public setting without ever leaving the sphere of the home or their commitment to marital obedience. Key to their ability to do so are the affordances of the internet that allow women to sanction their public address through biblical mediation based in the home. This biblical mediation is at once exegetical, aesthetic, and affiliative. They undergird their public confessional production with testimonial exegesis that cites and hyperlinks the biblical text as an actor in their lives. They aestheticize this scriptural connection by displaying, decorating, and hyperlinking biblical verses, such as from the Letter to Titus, in banners that convey their femininity and Christian devotion to home and family. They also make use of the internet as an affordance for webs of affiliation with other Evangelical women, their visitors, and corporations—bringing everyone into the funnel of conversion from their kitchen table.

2.2 Affiliation and Aesthetic Traps

Like their predecessors among nineteenth-century missionaries and twentieth-century Evangelical self-help writers, conservative Evangelical women's confessional production snugly intertwines Biblical references with commercialization efforts. They make careful use of what anthropologist Daniel Miller, inspired by Alfred Gell, has called the aesthetic traps of the web. Gell used the term in relation to captivation or enchantment, which he understood to arise when a viewer feels that an object has agentive abilities far beyond her own, as the object itself is laden with the networked agencies of all involved in its construction.[18] In the case of these blogs, this emphasis on the layering of agencies in the object in-

---

17 Pamela E. Klassen and Kathryn Lofton, "Material Witnesses: Women and the Mediation of Christianity," in *Media, Religion and Gender: Key Issues and New Challenges*, ed. Mia Lövheim (New York: Routledge, 2013), 52–65.
18 Alfred Gell, "The Technology of Enchantment and the Enchantment of Technology," in *Anthropology, Art, and Aesthetics*, ed. Jeremy Coote and Anthony Shelton (Oxford, UK: Clarendon Press, 1992), 40–63; Alfred Gell, *Art and Agency: An Anthropological Theory* (Oxford, UK: Clarendon Press, 1998), 69–72.

cludes both the agentive role of the Bible in Evangelical women's confessional production and their affiliations with corporations.

Writing about Trinidadian websites of the 1990s, Miller clarifies that "[t]he term aesthetic refers here not to some criterion of beauty but to the visual properties of sites as forms of social efficacy." (Gell would have glossed this as agency).[19] Miller insists that scholars pay close attention to the "particular materiality" of a website to gauge its attractions: while nightingales, rose petals, and biblical verses may deter some visitors from Jenn's blog, others are drawn to her blog precisely because of these aesthetic choices. Though Miller's use of the language of traps may seem overly dramatic, his insights from almost twenty years ago remain powerful for thinking about affiliate links as "aesthetic forms that [...] attempt to align web creator and potential surfer in time and space, so that each can, as it were, dock alongside the other in cyberspace."[20] Across genres and aesthetic choices, websites are traps for both like-minded visitors and for the scholarly analysts who visit them, "with their promise of insights into the intimacy of other people's sociality and revelations of the contradictions of the self."[21] The intimacy of online testimony is at once personal, public, and entrepreneurial. As John Durham Peters argues, Christianity can be seen as a doctrine of dissemination, in which Jesus is cast as a broadcaster, a sower who does not attend to where his seed lands.[22] In step with this call to spread the social efficacy of the Word, Evangelical blogs are promiscuously ready to entice a seemingly limitless audience.

Blogging, of course, is a skill, and it is not uncommon for bloggers to offer instructional posts meant to help instruct site visitors who might be thinking of starting a blog themselves, analogous to the more frequent topics of instruction, such as childrearing or housekeeping.[23] In the more detailed guides to Christian

---

19 Daniel Miller, "The Fame of Trinis: Websites as Traps," *Journal of Material Culture* 5.1 (2000): 16; Gell, *Art and Agency: An Anthropological Theory.*
20 Miller, "The Fame of Trinis," 17.
21 Miller, "The Fame of Trinis," 18–19.
22 John Durham Peters, *Speaking into the Air: A History of the Idea of Communication* (Chicago: Chicago University Press, 2011), 51–62.
23 See, for example, Stephanie Malcolm, "Mommy Blogger Series: For the Love of Writing," *Training Keepers of the Home* (blog), February 23, 2018, https://stephanieamalcolm.com/mommy-blog ger-series-keepers-home/ (Archived here: https://web.archive.org/web/20200928063907/https:// stephanieamalcolm.com/mommy-blogger-series-keepers-home/); Lydia Sherman, "Welcome to My Blog Home. Before Your Visit, Please Read This:," *Home Living: Quiet and Gentle Thoughts for Ladies at Home* (blog), August 1, 2014, https://homeliving.blogspot.com/2014/10/welcome-to-my-blog-home-before-your.html; June Fuentes, "Blogging to Advance the Kingdom of God," *A Wise Woman Builds Her Home* (blog), June 30, 2011, http://proverbs14verse1.blogspot.com/2011/06/

blogging that we found, the instructions for how to set up the website go beyond recommendations to highlight one's favorite biblical verses and flowers to explain how to include advertisements and build affiliate links.[24] These instructions show that some convincing is required to show that making money is not at odds with the higher purpose of glorifying God and encouraging others in their journey toward a biblical life. Sarah Hardee, who writes at *Christ-Centered Mama* and whose sidebar boasts a popular downloadable PDF guide to Christian blogging, offers the following explanation: "Your content is worth the same as secular content, and they get paid! No, I take that back… it's worth more!"[25] Some guides make the argument that laborers are worthy of their wages, usually with reference to 1 Timothy 5:18.[26] To be paid for godly activity is seen as preferable to being paid for work of a less noble character.

Far more common, however, are references to the "Proverbs 31 woman," whose "price is above rubies" and who is a strong, industrious, loving, virtuous wife and mother. Evangelical women rely specifically on Proverbs 31 to make the argument that making use of God-given talents (especially in handicrafts) is biblical. Internet platforms like blogs and Etsy make it possible to stay home while doing honorable work: a win-win.[27] That is not an uncomplicated conclusion, however. In a long post about the constant concern that her online photography work has come to stand in the way of giving God what is "rightfully his," Rachelle Chase concludes that she will accomplish what God wants ("praying, reading, spending quality time with my husband and kids") first and put "left over time" into photography. Articulating the explicit "goal" to become a Proverbs 31 woman, Chase writes that she feels calmer knowing that this "includes

blogging-to-advance-kingdom-of-god.html; June Fuentes, "New Blogging Series," *Raising Home-makers* (blog), July 2, 2011, http://raisinghomemakers.com/2011/new-blogging-series/.

24 Perhaps the most complete guide in the world of Christian blogging is *By His Grace We Blog*, which can be downloaded as a 64-page PDF (https://gumroad.com/l/MKRCm). It was written by Carmen Brown, whose blogging ministry heavily focuses on providing detailed instructions to prospective bloggers. See a list of resources and instructional posts under the "blogging as discipleship" category on her website. Carmen Brown, "Blogging: Discipleship in Writing," *Married by His Grace* (blog), n.d., accessed March 11, 2019, https://www.marriedbyhisgrace.com/category/tipsresources/.

25 Sarah Liberty Hardee, "Yes, Christian Mom, You Should Start a Christian Blog – 7 Reasons," *Christ-Centered Mama: Motherhood for the Glory of God* (blog), July 8, 2017, https://www.christcenteredmama.com/start-a-christian-blog/. See also Shanique, "Christian Affiliate Programs for Christian Bloggers," *Rock Solid Faith: Live With Intention Grow In Faith* (blog), May 11, 2018, https://www.rocksolidfaith.ca/christian-affiliate-marketing/.

26 Roberts, "A Christian Mom's Guide to Blogging."

27 Roxy, "A Homemakers Business…," *Living from Glory to Glory* (blog), January 29, 2014, https://livingfromglorytoglory.blogspot.com/2014/01/a-homemakers-buisness.html.

being a business woman as well as a mom!"[28] Other bloggers go further, noting that the Proverbs 31 woman is "industrious" and has "business sense," or even that she "fits into my business plan" because she "puts hard work in and is rewarded with profit."[29]

The limits of a virtuous woman's entrepreneurial ventures are a source of debate on Evangelical blogs, as according to some bloggers the use of the Proverbs 31 woman's linen- and tapestry-making to legitimate leaving the domestic sphere is something the Bible cannot abide. In a post responding to a dissident commenter, blogger Kelly Crawford forcefully writes that "[y]ou said she sells garments in the marketplace…no she doesn't. Read it again. She sells garments to the MERCHANTS. She is a wholesaler. THEY go to the marketplace. […] Her productivity flows outward from her home, not against it."[30] The home—where women's divinely ordained role plays out—must come first, not the use of talents on the internet.

References to biblical passages such as Proverbs 31 work both exegetically and aesthetically, frequently showing up in headers, "about" pages, or blog titles. Melissa Ringstaff, for example, writes from Kentucky, where she is homeschooling her nine children.[31] Her blog is called *A Virtuous Woman*, taken from Proverbs 31:10, a verse she has turned into a logo with cursive calligraphy. Explicitly offering to show other women how to become a "Proverbs 31 Woman today" through "spiritual and practical application," she also instructs site visitors how to design a blog without ever having to learn how to code, relying on templates and pre-made platforms. She notes that while "blogging is a great option for women who want to work at home," prospective bloggers will not make money unless they write with "passion." The examples Ringstaff offers of passionate writing include sharing "how God has transformed your life" and

---

28 Rachelle Chase, "Conflicted," *Rachelle Chase* (blog), September 8, 2011, http://rachellecha seblog.com/conflicted/.
29 Kristina Seleshanko, "What Is a Proverbs 31 Woman? (And a Bit About Me)," *Proverbs 31 Woman: Homesteading, Home Keeping, Family, & Faith* (blog), October 4, 2009, https://www. proverbs31homestead.com/2009/10/what-is-proverbs-31-woman.html; Nora Conrad, "How Proverbs 31 Fits Into My Business Plan," *Nora Conrad* (blog), November 23, 2015, https://www.nor aconrad.com/blog/proverbs31.
30 Kelly Crawford, "Proverbs 31…Surprising Her Day and Ours!," *Generation Cedar* (blog), May 9, 2008, https://web.archive.org/web/20120825012931/http://www.generationcedar.com/main/2008/ 05/proverbs-31surprising-her-day-and-ours.html. See also Lori Alexander, "A Stay-At-Home Wife Or Mom Is Unbiblical?," *The Transformed Wife* (blog), January 17, 2017, https://thetransformedwife. com/lies-of-the-proverbs-31-woman/.
31 Melissa Ringstaff, "About Melissa Ringstaff," *A Virtuous Woman* (blog), n.d., accessed July 29, 2019, https://avirtuouswoman.org/about-melissa-ringstaff/.

writing "Bible studies for young women."[32] As with earlier Evangelical traditions of making money with Christian purpose—and in line with Max Weber's theory of the Protestant ethic—the financial success of the Christian blogger is a reflection of her virtue and a sign of God's beneficence.[33] With all the hard work a profitable blog requires, the urge has to be strong: Ringstaff notes that although she was never good at writing or even housekeeping, she felt "in [her] heart this pull to teach other women. *Crazy, right?*"[34]

The tensions in this kind of confessional production, however, remain hard to shake. Jolene Engle, a woman who writes her glossy, flowered blog under the byline of "Mentoring Women & Wives Closer to Christ", focuses on biblical marriage advice, which her sidebar notes will enable her readers to have "a thriving relationship with God and your man." Like Ringstaff, Engle also understands her role to be instructional, and offers a post guiding her readers on how to start their own blogging ministry within the context of their home and the internet. She distinguishes her approach from that of more self-focused online entrepreneurs: "what I constantly hear is that we need to build *our* platforms. Well, this just rubs me the wrong way because it is not *my* platform I'm seeking to build."[35] Justifying her labor as a foray into devotional entrepreneurialism, she insists she is building a platform for God.

With an instructional precision, Amy Roberts, whose Christian convictions have inspired her to educate her nine children at home, offers a checklist of questions for prospective bloggers. Her list includes questions such as "Is there a financial need in your family that could be filled by blogging without taking away from the family?" and various others that address "aversion" to monetization as stemming more from seeing greed in others than from the Bible. Like Engle, however, Roberts' checklist underlines Christian priorities: "Do you have your husband's blessing? Do the things you make money from support the mission of your blog and the Word of God?"[36] Anchored by biblical references and templates with traditionally feminine designs, these women's blogging instructions insist that the internet offers a platform for biblical truth first and foremost. The money cannot be

---

32 Melissa Ringstaff, "How to Start Blogging as a Ministry," *A Virtuous Woman* (blog), May 9, 2016, https://avirtuouswoman.org/how-to-start-blogging-as-a-ministry/.

33 Heather D. Curtis, *Faith in the Great Physician: Suffering and Divine Healing in American Culture, 1860–1900* (Baltimore: Johns Hopkins University Press, 2010).

34 Ringstaff, "How to Start Blogging as a Ministry."

35 Jolene Engle, "How to Start an On-Line Ministry (Blog)," *Jolene Engle: Mentoring Women & Wives Closer to Christ* (blog), August 17, 2015, https://joleneengle.com/how-to-start-an-on-line-ministry-blog/.

36 Roberts, "A Christian Mom's Guide to Blogging."

the main point. Nevertheless, setting up infrastructures of commercialization is a key part of learning to be a Christian blogger: most guides address it explicitly, and even when they do not, they are themselves filled with advertisements and affiliate links that reach with a noticeable promiscuity into networks far beyond the homes or churches of the women who write them.[37]

2.3 Digital Infrastructures as Promiscuous Paths of Affiliation and Aspiration

Advertising, sponsorships, and more specifically digital modes of commercialization are not extraneous to the internet's technological development: they have deeply shaped the possibilities the internet offers its users since its earliest days. The internet was born at the intersection of military and academic interests during the Cold War, always embedded in religious imaginaries of utopia and apocalypse.[38] By every accounting, the internet has been a commercial realm shaped by countercultural vision from its inception. As Fred Turner has shown, it was countercultural Californians in the 1960s and 1970s who imbued Cold War technologies like the computer with ideological legitimacy, through the particularly commercial vehicle of the "Whole Earth Catalog", which included networked computers alongside ecological gardening equipment as tools for

---

37 For examples of guides to Christian blogging that explicitly explain how to set up advertisements, affiliate links, and sponsorships, see Lee, "The Complete Guide to Being a Successful Christian Blogger;" Hardee, "How to Make Money By Running a Christian Blog;" Roberts, "A Christian Mom's Guide to Blogging;" Titus, "My Story." For other instructional posts that instruct readers interested in blogging in how to launch a blog, choose designs, and start writing, see Allison Marie, "5 of the Best Resources for Christian Bloggers," *All Things Allison Marie* (blog), April 22, 2018, http://allthingsallisonmarie.com/5-best-resources-for-christian-bloggers/ (Archived here: https://web.archive.org/web/20180704232915/http://allthingsallisonmarie.com/ 5-best-resources-for-christian-bloggers/); Engle, "How to Start an On-Line Ministry (Blog)"; Hardee, "Yes, Christian Mom;" Ringstaff, "How to Start Blogging as a Ministry;" Sally Stunkel, "How to Start a Blog: The Ultimate Guide for Beginners," *Sweetly Sally* (blog), September 1, 2016, http://sweetlysally.com/how-to-start-a-blog-the-ultimate-guide/. All of these include affiliate links and advertisements in the instructions they offer readers.
38 Paul Edwards, *The Closed World: Computers and the Politics of Discourse in Cold War America* (Cambridge, MA: MIT Press, 1996); Bruce Sterling, "Short History of the Internet," *Magazine of Fantasy and Science Fiction*, February 1993, Internet Society, https://www.internetsociety.org/ internet/history-internet/short-history-of-the-internet/; Fred Turner, *From Counterculture to Cyberculture: Stewart Brand, the Whole Earth Network, and the Rise of Digital Utopianism* (Chicago: University of Chicago Press, 2006); John Naughton, *A Brief History of the Future: The Origins of the Internet* (London: Orion Books, 2000).

an incipient future.[39] As the network matured in the 1990s, the companies that had positioned themselves as subcultural pioneers were more openly negotiating the fact that they were, indeed, companies. Advertising has long been at the heart of Google as a search platform: 97% of the company's revenue comes not from the "technology" of search, but from its commercialization.[40] Along with its military and academic roots, profit and sales were always formative in internet development and use.

Initially, advertising models resembled those in use before the internet arrived. Early online commercialization models positioned the audience as a commodity to be sold to advertisers and reached through the aural effect of so-called banner ads. Online affordances, however, held the promise of surfacing the efficacy of such ads: now, it was possible to count how many site visitors had actually clicked through to purchase the advertised product. The costs of advertising, as a result, were based on "click through rates" rather than "page views," departing from an older tradition of paying to display. People largely ignore banner ads, it quickly turned out.[41] It was time for new strategies.

Coined in the early 2000s, the term "Web 2.0" describes the shift from broadcast models toward an emphasis on user-generated content, exchanged on platforms like Blogger, Facebook, YouTube, and so on.[42] The internet was no longer a place to passively receive content, and instead became the realm of "participatory culture"—a term that (like Web 2.0) arose in advertisement circles to articulate new models for harnessing people's behaviors for profit.[43] The notion of "viral" content, traveling across platforms rapidly because people cannot help but spread it to friends, stems from this period, as does the influencer, whose position on the platform is such that she can influence other users to spread content or indeed to make particular purchases.

Almost all guides to Christian blogging recommend Google advertisements. In a post that is frankly titled "How to Make Money Running a Christian Blog," Hardee explains that she adjusted Google Ads on her blog in accordance with

---

39 Edwards, *The Closed World*; Turner, *From Counterculture to Cyberculture*.
40 Ken Hillis, Michael Petit, and Kylie Jarrett, *Google and the Culture of Search* (New York: Routledge, 2013), 38.
41 Hillis, Petit, and Jarrett, *Google and the Culture of Search*, 39.
42 José van Dijck, *The Culture of Connectivity: A Critical History of Social Media* (Oxford, UK: Oxford University Press, 2013); Aaron Barlow, *Blogging America: The New Public Sphere* (Westport, CT: Praeger, 2007).
43 Henry Jenkins, Sam Ford, and Joshua Green, *Spreadable Media: Creating Value and Meaning in a Networked Culture* (New York: New York University Press, 2013); Henry Jenkins, *Fans, Bloggers, and Gamers: Exploring Participatory Culture* (New York: New York University Press, 2006).

the blog's Christian mission. To do so, she selectively opted into certain categories developed by Google, restricting her ads to "things that are strictly Christian, family, health, or counseling based" and blocking others.[44] Hardee writes
that the "spammy" ads resulting from opting into all categories did not fit the
"feel" of her *Christ-Centered Mama* blog. Both Hardee and Roberts underline
that they could potentially make much more money were they to opt into Google
Ads at odds with their mission.[45] Mitigating this problem is the array of companies—homeschooling publishers, accessories for long hair, essential oils—that
advertise primarily on Christian blogs. Through the use of such digital advertising infrastructure, the blogger becomes an influencer who tries on and reviews
different products, and bloggers like Hardee or Roberts (who primarily reviews
homeschooling curricula) point prospective bloggers toward advertising partners
that are aligned with the kind of influence a Christian would desire. Underneath
these more traditional advertisement models exists a much less visible but
equally important infrastructural outgrowth of ever-more sophisticated exploita-
tion models: affiliate marketing, which involves the use of site visitors' data.

If advertisements work by being visible to—and indeed seen by—site visitors, affiliate marketing operates without them noticing. Instead of paying for
every "click through" (as in the banner ad model), merchants instead only pay
when the customer encountering the advertisement on a blog has actually purchased something. Knowing whether a blog reader has become a customer on a
merchant's website is only possible through tracking the blog reader's data.
The means by which that data becomes available is the "cookie": a "technology
that enables a website to place data on a user's computer to recognize a user on a
later visit."[46] When a user visits the blog, she encounters the infrastructure the
blogger (who is "affiliated" with the merchant) has installed to make a bit of
code "stick" to that user as she goes on her way. Then when she visits the merchant's website and makes a purchase, the blogger receives a percentage (usually between 5 to 30%) of that purchase's cost.

Here promiscuity enters again. Affiliate payments do not depend on whether
the user bought something the blog recommended, nor does it matter whether
she clicked anything. She could read a post recommending Bible-based anti-
abortion pamphlets on Amazon, and go on to buy *Our Bodies, Ourselves*—a feminist, pro-choice "Bible" of women's health—and the blogger would still receive a
percentage of the Amazon purchase. Bloggers are generally intentional about

---

44 Hardee, "How to Make Money By Running a Christian Blog."
45 Hardee; Roberts, "A Christian Mom's Guide to Blogging."
46 Benjamin Edelman and Wesley Brandi, "Risk, Information, and Incentives in Online Affiliate
Marketing," *Journal of Marketing Research* 52, no. 1 (2015): 2.

the merchants, or the "affiliate networks" which bundle a group of merchants, with which they affiliate their blogs. The technological infrastructure, however, means that they cannot opt out of being compensated for purchases that are at odds with their beliefs. In light of this, it is not surprising that blogging instructions often suggest suitable affiliate networks, such as the homeschooling art company See the Light Art or HopeFuel's prayer journals, in the hope that it will be Christian—not "spammy"—linking that generates profits.[47]

That said, almost all bloggers affiliate with Amazon, which presents a wide range of products. Other frequently used affiliate networks, like RewardStyle and ShopStyle, focus on fashion. Pastor's wife, homeschooling mother, and modest fashion blogger Caroline Allen regularly posts pictures of her outfits, posing in ankle-length skirts in bright colors, pearly hair jewellery, and neutral t-shirts worn under clothing that would otherwise show bare arms or skin below the collar bone. In her "Modest Monday" outfit posts, Allen always includes links to her clothing or similar items, so that her readers know where they might acquire the same pieces.[48] Her affiliation with RewardStyle is inconspicuous, but can be traced nonetheless. When hovering the mouse on her "J.C. Penney" link, the browser shows the link as "rstyle.me/n/**ddunz3biwxf**". The "rstyle" in the url refers to RewardStyle, while the "affiliate ID" (in bold) is what lets the merchant know it was this *Modest Mom* post that made the referral. Clicking the link will open J.C. Penney's website as usual, but the browser's address bar shows Allen's referral (in bold): "https://www.jcpenney.com/?**cid=affiliate| RewardStyle|13419515|na&utm_medium=affiliate&utm_source=RewardStyle&utm_campaign**=13419515&utm_content=na&cjevent=5ae9d9ad442211e981-c200100a240612"[49] Depending on the expiry date of J.C. Penney's "cookies," a

---

47 Amy Roberts, "For Bloggers: Affiliate Ideas," *Raising Arrows* (blog), November 11, 2013, https://www.raisingarrows.net/for-bloggers-affiliate-ideas/; Shanique, "Christian Affiliate Programs for Christian Bloggers."
48 Caroline Allen, "Modest Monday and a Link Up!" *The Modest Mom*, December 24, 2018, https://www.themodestmomblog.com/modest-monday-and-a-link-up-251/.
49 In October 2009, the Federal Trade Commission updated its endorsement guidelines in light of online marketing. This means that bloggers have to disclose their use of affiliate links. The FTC has continued to update its guidelines with the rise of new social media platforms, now also mandating a #ad on Instagram and Snapchat videos, for instance. For bloggers, the disclosure is usually a statement in small print at the bottom of every post, or in the sidebar, in a manner analogous to the banner ad. The guidelines make it clear that any "material connection" between the blogger and the merchant needs to be disclosed, rendering the commission bloggers make by linking to products for online shopping as a tangible tie. See "Guides Concerning the Use of Endorsement and Testimonials in Advertising" (Federal Trade Commision, n.d.), 16 CFR Part 255, https://www.ftc.gov/sites/default/files/attachments/press-releases/ftc-publishes-final-

visit to J.C. Penney's website up to 60 days later could still show Allen's imprint, and put money in her bank account. Affiliate marketing is ubiquitous, woven into the material infrastructure of the web from its protocols and linking routes to every user's browser storage. Site visitors can look away from banners (and indeed frequently use browser extensions to block them altogether), but will find it much more difficult to shake off the sticky code of cookies.

Affiliate marketing is infrastructural work. Computer scientist Philip Agre helps bring into focus how this infrastructure works with his concept of the capture model, and how it differs from older models of surveillance. He explains that the capture model originated in computing, where "capture" refers both to acquiring data and modeling possible paths people take.[50] Tracking via cookie relies both on a monitoring technology and a grammar of action: the monitoring is triggered by the tracked person choosing a particular path, which is to say, the cookie tracks the user only when she purchases something from the merchant.[51]

While Agre and others have thought about such models primarily in terms of privacy, communication scholar Wendy Chun has theorized "capture" more broadly, in terms of habit. Her material analysis of the internet shows how networks depend on a combination of habits produced by actions, and storage produced through monitoring. Every connection in a network is fundamentally habitual, based on paths that have been walked before.[52] If a computer has never been connected to anything, it cannot be part of a network—networking is an impossibility without prior connection. Computers, Chun argues, are habitually "leaky", constantly connecting to maintain connectedness, to the point of being "promiscuous," in ways that generally escape users. If pathways and connections arise from the habitual leaking that software needs to function, data analytics track people's actions on these paths, storing and compiling this information to create histories and futures.[53]

The goal of digital infrastructures of affiliation are much like the goals of Christian bloggers: to re-orient habits. In order to steer people along desired routes, digital platforms record computers' habitual connectivity to amass infor-

---

guides-governing-endorsements-testimonials/091005revisedendorsementguides.pdf; "The FTC's Endorsement Guides: What People Are Asking," The Federal Trade Commission, n.d., https://www.ftc.gov/tips-advice/business-center/guidance/ftcs-endorsement-guides-what-people-are-asking.

50 Philip Agre, "Surveillance and Capture: Two Models of Privacy," *The Information Society: An International Journal* 10.2 (1994): 106.

51 Agre, "Surveillance and Capture," 113.

52 Chun, *Updating to Remain the Same*, 57.

53 Chun, *Updating to Remain the Same*, 58–60.

mation concerning the routes their users choose through the network enabled by this connectivity. Chun draws out the single-mindedness of this material infrastructure of tracking and storing: the person is defined through purchasing. The infrastructure renders moot everything outside the network, as only actions of clicking and purchasing can be captured, and only via paths already established in the intricacies of the software that allows us to go online in the first place. Cookie-planting thus commercializes a promiscuity that is integral to the internet's functioning, at the same time that it fits the habits it is seeking to change onto an existing grid of possible pathways.

These digital, infrastructural pathways map onto the instructional goals of much Christian confessional production. The purpose of conservative Evangelical women's blogging—and the phrasing used here is remarkably uniform—is to "share in the journey" and "encourage" others walking the same path.[54] This purpose calls into being a web of connections: paths along which the journey unfolds, and others who affirm and strengthen shared convictions. In his essay on the materialization of Christian transformation, anthropologist Simon Coleman lays out how believers externalize and objectify experiences of transformation in "containers of the sacred": words or things that make divine power and its transformative effects apprehensible for others.[55] Alongside speech or objects, modern media of communication also contain such force, and similarly participate in its (commodified) distribution. Coleman's research with charismatic Christians helps him identify an "economy of salvation" that is reliant on a shared "aesthetic sensibility" across conservative Protestantism.[56] An economy of salvation is a system of circulation in which Christians manifest the effect God's power has on them in order to see divine power as a transformative material force in the lives of others. This mediating activity then enables them to re-absorb that power as indeed materially transformative. Coleman notes that

---

54 See for example Caroline Allen, "About Caroline," *The Modest Mom* (blog), n.d., accessed July 28, 2019, https://www.themodestmomblog.com/about-caroline/; Kelly Crawford, "About," https://generationcedar.com/main/about, *Generation Cedar* (blog), April 24, 2010, https://generationcedar.com/main/about; Debbie, "About Me," *She Graces Her Home In God's Beauty* (blog), n.d., accessed July 28, 2019, https://shegracesherhome.blogspot.com/p/as-my-sister-said-five-years-ago-on-my.html, Jenn, "Stuff About Me"; Shelly, "About." *There's No Place Like Home: Homeschooling My Large, Crazy Family!* (blog), n.d., accessed April 16, 2017, https://redheadmom8.wordpress.com/about/, White Lace and Promises, "About Me," *The Upside of Down* (blog), n.d., accessed July 28, 2019, http://livinglifeupside.blogspot.com.
55 Simon Coleman, "Words as Things: Language, Aesthetics and the Objectification of Protestant Evangelicalism," *Journal of Material Culture* 1.1 (1996): 109; Klassen and Lofton, "Material Witnesses."
56 Coleman, "Words as Things," 108; Coleman, "Materializing the Self."

Christians have often depended on quantifiable numbers in the economy of salvation: the "effects of faith and correct practice" are to be "measured objectively."[57] The concept of economies of salvation underlines the importance of tangible transformation in the business of mediating the Bible.

The purpose Evangelical bloggers articulate for their blogs stems from Christian conviction: making available the effects of their conviction of Jesus's effects in their own lives so others can be picked up by the swirl of God's power and do the same. This means that there is, to stay in internet parlance, a certain virality to the economy of salvation. Jesus is the platform, and a blog that makes his transformative power tangible projects a specific journey through the network: from being a recipient of divine impact to being a channel it courses through, or from being affected by materializations of power to materializing power oneself. This is the aspiration underpinning the litany of blogging instructions available online: if the journey leads to everyone circulating the impact of biblical truths, it only makes sense to hand others the tools to contribute to that circulation. By setting aesthetic traps, and instructing others in how to build these on their own, a network buzzing with God's transformative efficacy can arise.

While Christian blogs imagine one web of connections through the network, monetization infrastructures construct another. A key term in the burgeoning field of electronic marketing is "conversion", with the "conversion rate" measuring whether people are impelled to act as a result of one's marketing, and the "conversion funnel" describing the journey the user takes before arriving at the intended destination, i.e. purchasing the product.[58] Conversion Rate Optimization (CRO) is the bread and butter of the online marketing industry, describing the effort to create websites that will ever more skillfully move users toward the desired actions—to be captured by cookies. Building again on Daniel Miller's description of personal webpages as "aesthetic traps" that serve as "conduits" sending users in particular directions,[59] Christian blogs can be seen to put in place a material infrastructure that lays a path between two states: the reader, converted, has become a customer. While the funnel built for affiliate marketing's conversion does not lead to the same destination as the journey that conservative Evangelical blogs project, the point is that success, in both cases, hinges on having moved the site visitor along in a circuit. Circulation is key for online

---

57 Coleman, "Materializing the Self," 177.
58 Bruce Brown, *The Complete Guide to Affiliate Marketing on the Web: How to Use and Profit from Affiliate Marketing Programs* (Ocala, FL: Atlantic Publishing Group, 2009); Khalid Saleh and Ayat Shukalry, *Conversion Optimization: The Art and Science of Converting Prospects to Customers* (Sebastopol, CA: O'Reilly Media, 2011).
59 Miller, "The Fame of Trinis."

marketeers as well as for bloggers. Where the worth of a node in a network depends on its ability to keep the flow going, money serves as an especially welcome index. As one blogger remarks, in between specific biblical justifications for the use of affiliate links, "it helps to have a little validation that what you are doing is making a difference."[60] The "what you are doing" in this statement deftly interlaces the circuits of salvation to which the blog links itself with the commercial circulation from which affiliate marketing draws its profits.

The transformation of the user or site visitor into customer leaves money as its material trace. While money and God-talk are no strangers in the history of American Evangelicalism,[61] the role of online money as an index of changed states also has its roots in the affordances specific to the internet. Even as the internet initially held the promise of paying only for measurably effective advertising, online marketeers quickly learned that measuring engagement online is exceedingly difficult.[62] On his personal blog, online marketing executive and self-declared "metrics man" Don Bartholomew continually emphasizes that determining "the return on investment of a social media initiative" is an "inexact science," since it is never quite possible to know for sure what brought the user to "complete the conversion funnel," especially when that completion occurs days or weeks after the initial site visit.[63] A 2018 *New York Magazine* article points out that recent technological developments have compounded this already difficult task: it is increasingly impossible to know whether actions like clicking and filling an online shopping cart are performed by people or by bots, and websites cannot meaningfully distinguish between them.[64]

---

60 Hardee, "Yes, Christian Mom."

61 William Connolly, *Capitalism and Christianity, American Style* (Durham, NC: Duke University Press, 2008); Kevin Kruse, *One Nation Under God: How Corporate America Invented Christian America* (New York: Basic Books, 2015); Bethany Moreton, *To Serve God and Wal-Mart: The Making of Christian Free Enterprise* (Cambridge, MA: Harvard University Press, 2010).

62 Scott Cotter, "Taking the Measure of E-Marketing Success," *Journal of Business Strategy* 23, no. 2 (2002): 30 – 37.

63 Don Bartholomew, "Social Media Measurement at a Crossroads," *Metrics Man* (blog), August 21, 2013, https://metricsman.wordpress.com/2013/08/21/social-media-measurement-at-a-crossroads-2/; Don Bartholomew, "Let's Play 20 Questions: Social Media Measurement Style," *Metrics Man* (blog), October 1, 2013, https://metricsman.wordpress.com/2013/10/01/lets-play-20-questions-social-media-measurement-style/.

64 Max Read, "How Much of the Internet Is Fake? Turns Out, a Lot of It, Actually," *New York Magazine* (blog), December 26, 2018, http://nymag.com/intelligencer/2018/12/how-much-of-the-internet-is-fake.html.

The sticky infrastructures of commercialized websites are built to capture the data trails left behind by human actions, so the flurry of data generated through the automated processes of bots misleads them. This is largely the merchants' problem: at the end of the conversion funnel, profits are affected by fakery.[65] Christian bloggers, however, sit at the beginning of the funnel, where the promiscuity of connection is less important than the mission to move the site visitor along in her journey. In his reflections on the parable of the sower, John Durham Peters notes that the story leaves "the harvest of meaning to the will and capacity of the recipient. The hearer must complete the trajectory begun with the first casting."[66] Who knows where the site visitor might head next? In this Christian model of communication, the important responsibility is to lay the first strands of the web, as Evangelical blogs do via aesthetic enticement and coded pathways.

2.4 Conclusion

The internet is a promiscuous network that connects devices and pages through a constant process of leaking. Devices and web pages may connect even prior to and without any deliberate connection being made. This chapter has traced some of these leakages and connections in conservative Evangelical women's confessional production online. Examining biblical mediation on Evangelical women's blogs reveals the Bible's centrality to their use of digital infrastructures. Blogging ministries are consistently presented as women's response to a call to be channels for biblical truths and applicability. Their blogs "encourage" by ensnaring site visitors in an aesthetic where God's power and women's skills bleed into each other. More than justification for making money "on the side," the Bible is the active force blogs mediate.

The very diversity of the possible steps available after visiting one place online and moving to another, and the uncertainty or ambiguity inherent in seeking to effect change in an unseen other, makes the entanglement of monetization and religious aspiration a sensible and material one. While there are many different paths that might make up a Christian's journey online, the money that trickles in when site visitors fill their online shopping carts and hit "order" reliably indexes the efficacy of referral. The amount—the fact of there being an

---

65 Edelman and Brandi, "Risk, Information, and Incentives in Online Affiliate Marketing"; Cotter, "Taking the Measure of E-Marketing Success."
66 Peters, *Speaking into the Air*, 52.

amount—shows that visitors *were* moved. Bloggers do not receive anything when their readers make a purchase on a site with which they are not affiliated: the money can only be the result of actions that users take when travelling along the hidden paths of affiliation between bloggers and businesses. When she builds an invisible infrastructure that tracks users' moves along commercial routes, the blogger builds a measurement of her ability to incite movement in the first place.

In both frameworks of the Evangelical and the entrepreneurial, the aspiration is to make a referral that has a noticeable impact, namely that readers of the blog will take their next steps within the network the blog opens up. In a digital register of affiliation, the less visible infrastructure of links and cookies entraps site visitors in sticky code that tracks their movement in the network. The aspiration that animates Evangelical blogs and online marketing is to exploit the leaky layers of online connection by harnessing people's reading and spending habits. Evangelical women bloggers thread together the biblical infrastructure to which they are so committed and the materiality of the digital in which they post, aspiring to encourage habits of journeying with the Bible. Through promiscuous affiliation, Evangelical bloggers operate as devotional entrepreneurs, in the business of making and anticipating connections.

Selective References

Agre, Philip. "Surveillance and Capture: Two Models of Privacy," *The Information Society: An International Journal* 10.2 (1994): 101–127.

Barlow, Aaron. *Blogging America: The New Public Sphere.* Westport, CT: Praeger, 2007.

Bassard, Katherine. *Transforming Scriptures: African American Women Writers and the Bible.* Athens: University of Georgia Press, 2010.

Bendroth, Margaret. *Fundamentalism and Gender, 1875 to the Present.* New Haven, CT: Yale University Press, 1996.

Bendroth, Margaret and Virginia Brereton, eds., *Women and Twentieth-Century Protestantism.* Champaign, IL: University of Illinois Press, 2002.

Brekus, Catherine. *Strangers & Pilgrims: Female Preaching in America, 1740–1845.* Chapel Hill, NC: University of North Carolina Press, 1998.

Brown, Bruce. *The Complete Guide to Affiliate Marketing on the Web: How to Use and Profit from Affiliate Marketing Programs.* Ocala, FL: Atlantic Publishing Group, 2009.

Butler, Anthea. *Women in the Church of God in Christ: Making a Sanctified World.* Chapel Hill, NC: University of North Carolina Press, 2007.

Chun, Wendy. *Updating to Remain the Same: Habitual New Media.* Cambridge, MA: MIT Press, 2016.

Coleman, Simon. "Words as Things: Language, Aesthetics and the Objectification of Protestant Evangelicalism," *Journal of Material Culture* 1.1 (1996): 107–128.

Coleman, Simon. "Materializing the Self: Words and Gifts in the Construction of Charismatic Protestant Identity," in *The Anthropology of Christianity*, ed. Fenella Cannell. Durham, NC: Duke University Press, 2006.

Connolly, William. *Capitalism and Christianity, American Style*. Durham, NC: Duke University Press, 2008.

Cotter, Scott. "Taking the Measure of E-Marketing Success," *Journal of Business Strategy* 23, no. 2 (2002): 30–37.

Crapanzano, Vincent. *Serving the Word: Literalism in America from the Pulpit to the Bench*. New York: The New Press, 2000.

Curtis, Heather D. *Faith in the Great Physician: Suffering and Divine Healing in American Culture, 1860–1900*. Baltimore: Johns Hopkins University Press, 2010.

DeRogatis, Amy. *Saving Sex: Sexuality and Salvation in American Evangelicalism*. Oxford: Oxford University Press, 2015.

Dijck, José van. *The Culture of Connectivity: A Critical History of Social Media*. Oxford, UK: Oxford University Press, 2013.

Edelman, Benjamin and Wesley Brandi, "Risk, Information, and Incentives in Online Affiliate Marketing," *Journal of Marketing Research* 52, no. 1 (2015): 1–12.

Edwards, Paul. *The Closed World: Computers and the Politics of Discourse in Cold War America*. Cambridge, MA: MIT Press, 1996.

Gell, Alfred. "The Technology of Enchantment and the Enchantment of Technology," in *Anthropology, Art, and Aesthetics*, ed. Jeremy Coote and Anthony Shelton. Oxford, UK: Clarendon Press, 1992, 40–63.

Gell, Alfred. *Art and Agency: An Anthropological Theory*. Oxford, UK: Clarendon Press, 1998.

Griffith, R. Marie. *God's Daughters: Evangelical Women and the Power of Submission*. Berkeley: University of California Press, 2000.

Harding, Susan Friend. *The Book of Jerry Falwell: Fundamentalist Language and Politics*. Princeton, NJ: Princeton University Press, 2000.

Hillis, Ken, Michael Petit, and Kylie Jarrett, *Google and the Culture of Search*. New York: Routledge, 2013.

Jenkins, Henry. *Fans, Bloggers, and Gamers: Exploring Participatory Culture*. New York: New York University Press, 2006.

Jenkins, Henry, Sam Ford, and Joshua Green, *Spreadable Media: Creating Value and Meaning in a Networked Culture*. New York: New York University Press, 2013.

Johnson, Emily Suzanne. *This Is Our Message: Women's Leadership in the New Christian Right*. Oxford, UK: Oxford University Press, 2019.

Klassen, Pamela E. *Spirits of Protestantism: Medicine, Healing, and Liberal Christianity*. Berkeley: University of California Press, 2011.

Klassen, Pamela E. *The Story of Radio Mind: A Missionary's Journey on Indigenous Land*. Chicago: University of Chicago Press, 2018.

Klassen, Pamela E. and Kathryn Lofton. "Material Witnesses: Women and the Mediation of Christianity," in *Media, Religion and Gender: Key Issues and New Challenges*, ed. Mia Lövheim. New York: Routledge, 2013, 52–65.

Kruse, Kevin. *One Nation Under God: How Corporate America Invented Christian America*. New York: Basic Books, 2015.

Lofton, Kathryn. *Oprah: The Gospel of an Icon*. Oakland, CA: University of California Press, 2011.

Maffly-Kipp, Laurie and Kathryn Lofton, eds., *Women's Work: An Anthology of African-American Women's Historical Writings from Antebellum America to the Harlem Renaissance*. New York: Oxford University Press, 2010.

Marshall, John. "'I Left You in Crete': Narrative Deception and Social Hierarchy in the Letter to Titus," *Journal of Biblical Literature* 127.4 (2008): 781–803.

Miller, Daniel. "The Fame of Trinis: Websites as Traps," *Journal of Material Culture* 5.1 (2000): 5–24.

Moreton, Bethany. *To Serve God and Wal-Mart: The Making of Christian Free Enterprise*. Cambridge, MA: Harvard University Press, 2010.

Naughton, John. *A Brief History of the Future: The Origins of the Internet*. London: Orion Books, 2000.

Peters, John Durham. *Speaking into the Air: A History of the Idea of Communication*. Chicago: Chicago University Press, 2011.

Sterling, Bruce. "Short History of the Internet," *Magazine of Fantasy and Science Fiction*, February 1993, Internet Society, https://www.internetsociety.org/internet/history-inter net/short-history-of-the-internet/.

Turner, Fred. *From Counterculture to Cyberculture: Stewart Brand, the Whole Earth Network, and the Rise of Digital Utopianism*. Chicago: University of Chicago Press, 2006.

Arjun Sabharwal

Chapter 3
Digital Scriptures, Material Religion, and the Digital Humanities: An Interdisciplinary Framework for Curating Digitized Sacred Texts Online

3.1 Introduction

Scriptures have long been central to formations of religious identity, communication, and heritage, and continue to occupy the same place in the digital environment with technologies utilized by religious institutions, communities, practitioners, and researchers. Information and communication technologies and computing devices emerging during the past few decades have opened new avenues to access sacred texts, share faith, discuss religion, educate, research, and provide access to heritage content. As such, these technologies have contributed to developing a new sense of community online, and have significantly ensured stability in the relationship between believers and religion.

The history behind sacred texts presents a critical backdrop for addressing the importance of digital technologies in religious communication. The clergy and literati had solely relied on oral and written transmission including manual scripting and manuscript copying before the sequential introductions of the printing press[1], typewriter, punch cards[2], and computers. In fact, Charles Ess has pointed out that religious scholars were pioneers in the exploration of computing technologies for textual analysis.[3] Together with photographing, record-

---

[1] For information on a global landscape of printing including the Chinese model from the 9th century predating Gutenberg's press from the 15th, see Theodore Low De Vinne, *The Invention of Printing: A Collection of Facts and Opinions, Descriptive of Early Prints and Playing Cards, the Block-Books of the Fifteenth Century, the Legend of Lourens Janszoon Coster, of Haarlem, and the Work of John Gutenberg and His Associates* (New York: Francis Hart & Co, 1876), https://www.gutenberg.org/files/51034/51034-h/51034-h.htm.
[2] See Arun Jacob, "Punching Holes in the International Busa Machine Narrative," *Interdisciplinary Engagement in Arts & Humanities* 1, no. 1 (2017/2018), https://doi.org/10.21428/f1f23564.d7d097c2.
[3] Charles Ess, "'Revolution? What Revolution?' Successes and Limits of Computing Technologies in Philosophy and Religion," chap. 12 in *A Companion to Digital Humanities*, Susan Schreib-

https://doi.org/10.1515/9783110608755-004

ing, broadcasting, and more recent imaging devices, these technologies have not only liberated religious communication from the physicality of the institution in favor of broader distribution but have gradually extended the spatial range and form of communication. As a result, localized events such as sermons, prayers, and recitations have grown into globally accessible events in recorded, streamed, and digitally reproduced forms. This has led to a greater flexibility in sharing and transferring textual and audiovisual data across devices, users, institutions, and computer networks. Additionally, digital technologies also enabled users to join networks and online communities focused on religious content.

The Internet and social networks have thus freed communities and members socially and geographically, as they could choose (and even create) their virtual communities based on interest. This development has been particularly significant to diaspora communities where the channels of communication were the only option for religious communication.[4] In fact, before the launching of the World Wide Web in 1994, smaller and marginalized communities had explored early social networking technologies such as bulletin boards, emails, and blogs, but access to these platforms has been limited.[5] Present-day virtual communities utilize a wide variety of technologies for religious communication, worship, and research.

The increased reliance on digital media in religious communication, however, poses important concerns about the long-term preservation of and meaningful access to digitized sacred texts. As with any digital content on the Internet, reliable access to sacred texts in digital formats will require a never-ending commitment to remediating, digitizing, and curating sacred texts on the Internet. With an increasing volume of digital content and variety of technologies in religious practices, research in the field of material religion may consider both the use of digital technologies in religious practice and the urgency to preserve and ensure long-term access to digital media. In fact, any new digital media, technology, and methods of curating born-digital content may also be of interest to material religion research just as ancient artifacts had been before the introduction of digital technologies. Alongside these technologies, standards for digital pres-

---

man, Raymond George Siemens and John M. Unsworth, eds. (Oxford: Blackwell, 2004), http://www.digitalhumanities.org/companion/.

4 Gwilym Beckerlegge, *From Sacred Text to Internet* (Aldershot, Hants, England: Open University, 2001), 22.

5 However, according to John Bruno Hare, very little of that data from the 1980s has remained accessible due to digital decay or incompatibility with newer software, hardware, and playback devices. John Bruno Hare, "About Sacred-Texts," *Internet Sacred Text Archive,* updated February 8, 2021, https://www.sacred-texts.com/about.htm.

ervation have also emerged in order to prolong access to digital content, but these have remained diverse albeit unique to the needs of religious institutions and communities. Religious edicts and preferences have also guided the creation of content on websites and social networking sites, and may override the capabilities of technologies; therefore, understanding the relationship of religious practices to digital technologies and nascent curatorial concerns may shed light on the dynamics driving the utilization of digital technologies in religious practice and communication.

3.2 Plan of Work and Methodology

This chapter focuses on the uses of digital technology in religious communities, practices, and methods of curating digital content used in religious communication, education, and research. Understanding how religious institutions have adopted technologies in the course of their unique histories—and how they continue to do so in the present—will point to two critical issues raised herein: the importance of community values in leveraging technology while communicating with remote followers through digital means; and the value of preserving community heritage through digital preservation. Three research questions emerge at this point: How can concerns of three disciplines—material religion, digital curation, and digital humanities—be represented in a framework for studying the effects of digital technology on religious life and practices? How can digital curation strategies ensure long-term access to digital data and media? What approaches have been taken by diverse religious institutions and communities that adopted digital technology?

This chapter combines exploratory research design and documentary evidence in order to investigate the relationship between religious communication and digital technologies. It utilizes an interdisciplinary framework for joining the interests of material religion with those of digital curation and digital humanities. In this context, material religion (rooted in study of material culture and religious studies) represents the disciplinary interest in understanding the role that digital technology plays in religious life and practices while digital curation (rooted in archival science and practice) spans interests in archiving and digital preservation of religious digital media including audio-visual and textual media based on ancient scriptures and artifacts. Digital humanities, in turn, focuses attention on scholastic practices such as textual analysis, text encoding, text mining, data visualization, and hypertext markup—all centered around the manipulation, presentation, and interpretation of sacred texts in the digital environment. More specifically, understanding the transformative and immersive nature of hypertext will underscore a faith community's relationship to its scriptures and artifacts to extents similar to the effects of the printing press, photography, filming, analog recording, and media broadcasting on religious communication at different stages of human history. In fact, one may regard present-day practices in social media and digital curation as direct outcomes of those transformative effects.

Next, the chapter turns attention to approaches in digital curation with a focus on remediation techniques (including digital imaging) and digital preservation. This approach aims to underscore the need to preserve digital media created through scanning, photographing, and audio-video conversions from analog to digital formats. The subsequent discussion on digital humanities addresses hypertextuality and related practices such as text encoding and data visualization. Although these techniques are used for scholarly purposes rather than everyday worship, they are vital to expanding religious scholarship in the digital environment.

Lastly, the chapter reviews diverse approaches to digital curation using digital repositories, hypertext archives, community portals, social media sites, and curation in hybrid spaces. Presented alphabetically, the examples of websites demonstrate unique curatorial approaches speaking to the relationship of faith communities to digital technologies. It becomes evident how technology and the various digital objects (media file, image, sound, and textual content) have entered religious life and practice of believers living independently and remotely from their home communities situated across a city, region, or the globe. The selection herein is both platform- and doctrine-agnostic for purposes of demonstrating the communities' independence in adopting technologies. This approach also highlights the effect of cultural practices (such as spiritualization) on technology use in both virtual and hybrid spaces combining technology uses in the physical architecture of a cathedral, mosque, synagogue, or temple. Cultural practices present a safe zone for worshippers to practice religion online without distraction and concerns about inappropriate content. However, the intent behind this approach is not prescriptive or exhaustive: while the aim behind this chapter is to demonstrate the extent to which religious communication has begun to incorporate a variety of technologies, emerging technologies continue to provide new and more immersive platforms for religious communication, education, and scholarship.

3.3 A Conceptual Framework

Sacred texts and objects used in religious practices and preserved in the archives of religious institutions attest to their importance in ritual contexts and everyday lives from the perspectives of material religion and curatorial studies. The successive introductions of technologies (from the printing press to the smartphones) into religious communication and daily practices have necessarily led to two related developments: the inclusion of analog and digital media for research within these fields and the expansion of humanistic practices related to sacred texts in digital form. With the rise of the digital humanities over the past few decades, it has become necessary to expand the focus of humanistic study of Classic literature to include digital manifestation of scriptures and relics. Hypertext markup, textual encoding and analysis, remediation and digitization, and text mining to enable scholars to perform qualitative and quantitative analysis of digital texts involving text mining. Moreover, the addition of digital repositories at some institutions also included the inclusion of sacred texts and descriptive metadata in curatorial practices. These developments bring religion, technology, and archives into an inseparable relationship and form a conceptual framework for interdisciplinary study bordering material religion, digital curation, and digital humanities.

3.3.1 Material Religion

The concept and understanding of *religion* frames the integration of technology into religious practices, communication, and education. Classical dictionary definitions like "particular system of faith and worship"[6] and "a personal set or institutionalized system of religious attitudes, beliefs, and practices"[7] because they underscore both the personal, collective, philosophical, and cultural dimensions of this concept. Clifford Geertz's definition for religion—that is, "a system of symbols which acts to establish powerful, pervasive, and long-lasting moods and motivations in men by formulating conceptions of a general order of existence and clothing these conceptions with such an aura of factuality that the moods and motivations seem uniquely realistic"[8]—has foundations in his definition of

---

6 *The Compact Edition of the Oxford English Dictionary* (1971), s.v. "religion."
7 *Merriam-Webster*, s.v. "religion," https://www.merriam-webster.com/dictionary/religion.
8 Clifford Geertz, *The Interpretation of Cultures: Selected Essays* (New York: Basic Books, 1973), 90.

culture—that is, "webs of significance [wherein analysis is] not an experimental science in search of law but an interpretive one in search of meaning."[9] Herein is evident the web-like networked nature of religion in the digital environment, which is also networked and full of cultural meanings associated with religion. In this context, it will be important to understand *material religion* as the study of "the relationship between religious belief and life in a material world and recognizes that human beings spend their lives creating, handling, and exchanging material objects."[10] This is because human beings use material things like mobile devices, desktop computers, and other recording devices to create digital content (blog posts, social media comments, and digital recordings) meaningful in religious communication and other practices.

Working definitions by S. Brent Plate for *material religion* are, "(1) an investigation of the interactions between human bodies and physical objects, both natural and man-made; (2) with much of the interaction taking place through sense perception; (3) in special and specified places and times; (4) in order to orient, and sometimes, disorient, communities and individuals; (5) towards the formal strictures and structures of religious traditions."[11] According to David Morgan, *material religion* also implies "feelings and ideas about things, the sensation of things, and the communal and interpersonal experience of things."[12] Matthew Engelke has pointed out that all religion is fundamentally material religion: "all religion has to be understood in relation to the media of its materiality. This necessarily includes a consideration of religious things, and also of actions and words."[13] Here, the relationship of sacred texts, artifacts, rituals, and utterances are integral to the materiality of religion.

In the digital environment, the discourse on material religion has extended to *digital religion,* which presents "a new frame for articulating the evolution of religious practice online, as seen in the most recent manifestation of cyber-churches, which are linked to online and offline contexts simultaneously. 'Digital religion' does not simply refer to religion as it is performed and articulated on-

---

9 Clifford Geertz, *The Interpretation of Cultures*, 5.
10 Daniel Sack, "Material Religion," in *Contemporary American Religion* (The Gale Group, 1999), https://web.archive.org/web/20180131223050/http://www.encyclopedia.com/religion/legal-and-political-magazines/material-religion.
11 S. Brent Plate, "Material Religion: An Introduction," in *Key Terms in Material Religion*, ed. S. Brent Plate (London: Bloomsbury Academic, 2015), 4.
12 Birgit Meyer et al., "Material Religion's First Decade," *Religion* 10, no. 1 (2014): 109.
13 Matthew Engelke, "Material Religion," in *The Cambridge Companion to Religious Studies*, ed. Robert A. Orsi (Cambridge University Press, 2012), 209.

line, but points to how digital media and spaces are shaping and being shaped by religious practice."[14] As a concept then, *digital religion* unites the human, cultural, intellectual, and technological dimensions of material culture into which digital curation fits well.

3.3.2 Digital Curation

The concepts of *curation*—that is, the guardianship in museums, galleries, libraries, and archives[15]—and *curate*—or "select, organize, and look after the items in (a collection or exhibition)" and "select, organize, and present (suitable content, typically for online or computational use)"[16]—provide a lexical framework for understanding *digital curation* as the extension of curatorial practices in the digital environment. Professional literature has defined *digital curation* as "the actions needed to maintain digital research data and other digital materials over their entire lifecycle and over time for current and future generations of users."[17] Christopher A. Lee and Helen Tibbo have added that "digital curation involves selection and appraisal by creators and archivists; evolving provision of intellectual access; redundant storage; data transformations; and, for some materials, a commitment to long-term preservation. Digital curation is stewardship that provides for the reproducibility and re-use of authentic digital data and other digital assets."[18]

The use of CMSs, databases, and catalogs in the libraries and archives of large religious institutions and governments underscores the administrative and educational use of digital content in religious environments. This is where the preservation of digital media and other archived data takes place under the care of professional curators who themselves are ordained ministers or highly respected figureheads. The *Digital Vatican* presents an eminent model for preserving sacred texts, but the curation of scriptures is not limited to such large

---

14 Heidi Campbell, *Digital Religion: Understanding Religious Practice in New Media Worlds* (London: Routledge, 2013), 1.

15 *The Compact Edition of the Oxford English Dictionary* (1971), s.v. "curation."

16 *Oxford English Dictionary* (n.d.), s. v. "curate." http://www.oxforddictionaries.com/us/definition/ american_english/curate.

17 Neil Beagrie, "The Digital Curation Centre," *Learned Publishing* 17, no. 1 (January 2004): 7, http://dx.doi.org/10.1087/095315104322710197.

18 Christopher A. Lee, and Helen Tibbo, "Digital Curation and Trusted Repositories: Steps toward Success," *Journal of Digital Information* 8, no. 2 (2007), https://journals.tdl.org/jodi/ index.php/jodi/ article/view/229.

institutions. In fact, public libraries like the British and Huntington Libraries have participated in (if not led) the digitization of such canonic works as the *Gutenberg Bible* and the *Dead Sea Scrolls*. The *Internet Sacred Text Archive* was an early and independent undertaking to preserve religious texts and medium uploaded on the Internet before the launching of the World Wide Web. These examples—and discussed in detail in this chapter—demonstrate how religious digital texts and media have reached a stage for inclusion in material religion research.

3.3.3 Digital Humanities

Digital humanities has been defined as "the use of digital media and technology to advance the full range of thought and practice in the humanities, from the creation of scholarly resources, to research on those resources, to the communication of results to colleagues and students."[19] As the framework for holding material religion and digital curation together for purposes of the present study, including the digital humanities is necessary to address such textual practices such as hypertext markup, text encoding, text and data mining, and data visualization. On both practical and theoretical levels, digital humanities joins both the academic and spiritual aspects of religious scholarship, faith curation, and technology. Religious scholars may use technology for hermeneutic purposes focused on messages in sacred texts and further explore scriptural intertextuality.[20] Other digital humanities approaches may use similar technologies for purposes of mining texts and image data in geospatial, linguistic, literary, and historical research.

3.4 Approaches to Digital Curation

Depending on the unique needs of religious institutions and followers, digital curation may involve diverse strategies and approaches. Professional curators at formal archival facilities typically begin the process by preserving (including conserving and stabilizing) the original collection in physical or born-digital

---

19 Daniel J. Cohen, Federica Frabetti, Dino Buzzetti and Jesus D. Rodriguez-Velasco, "Defining the Digital Humanities," *Interviews*, Columbia University Academic Commons, mp4 video, 1:50:22, https://academiccommons.columbia.edu/doi/10.7916/D8MS41Z1.
20 See Christine Mitchell, "Review of John C. Reeves, ed., Bible and Qur'an: Essays in Scriptural Intertextuality," *Journal of Hebrew Scriptures*, 5 (2005), https://www.jhsonline.org/index.php/jhs/ article/view/5789.

forms.[21] In regard to digitization, sacred texts are particularly interesting because copious reprints and recordings have survived prior to the arrival of digital technology. Curating them will require documentation regarding provenance and preservation—information in the ownership of religious institutions. Knut Lundby has labeled digital texts as "visual and multimodal documents"[22] that have to comprise a significant subset of digital media used in religious communication mostly in the form of sermons, prayers, recitations, and performances. As visual documents, digitally reformatted sacred texts have become accessible as scanned page images, electronic texts, and hypertextual documents on Websites, blogs, social media, and digital repositories. The recorded versions of prayers (and calls to prayers), sermons, recitations, and other religious performances including chanting, dancing, instrumentals, and visual space are available via audio and video files. Digitization efforts during the past four decades have yielded large volumes of digital surrogates including preservation and public-access copies, and native project files—these are "[digital copies] of a record on any analog medium, such as paper, parchment, motion-picture film, analog audio, and analog video.[23] However, born-digital collections created with computers, digital cameras, recorders, and smartphones do not generate print or analog originals; therefore, the urgency to preserve them in their original digital formats is significantly greater because—in many cases—the only available copies may be those Web-accessible copies that have been saved in the original low-resolution and lossy (e. g., JPEG) formats with no native project files or high-resolution preservation (TIFF or JPEG2000) copies. Digital decay in low-resolution and lossy files occurs sooner than it does in preservation copies.[24] Digital curation spans several approaches: remediation (photographing, filming, scanning, and hypertextual conversion), text encoding, data visualization, social curation, and spatialized curation (requiring the use of specific architectures). For religious pur-

---

21 For a study on processing diverse collections, see Dorothy Waugh, Elizabeth Russey Roke, and Erika Farr, "Flexible processing and diverse collections: a tiered approach to delivering born digital archives,"*Archives and Records* 37, no. 1 (2016): 3–19, https://doi.org/10.1080/23257962.2016.1139493.

22 Knut Lundby, "Theoretical Frameworks for Approaching Religion and Media," in *Digital Religion: Understanding Religious Practice in New Media Worlds*, ed. Heidi Campbell (London: Routledge, 2013), 225.

23 In archival practices, a surrogate is *Dictionary of Archives Terminology,* s.v., "digital surrogate," https://dictionary.archivists.org/entry/digital-surrogate.html.

24 Digital Preservation Coalition, "File formats and standards," in *Digital Preservation Handbook*, 2nd ed, https://www.dpconline.org/handbook/technical-solutions-and-tools/file-formats-and-standards.

poses in some communities and activities, spiritualization of virtual spaces may pose additional requirements prior to making selected contents accessible.[25]

3.4.1 Remediation

Bolter and Grusin have defined *remediation* as "the representation of one medium in another [and is] a defining characteristic of new digital media."[26] Despite the relative recency of their definition, the practice of remediation has roots in the history of books and other forms media used for writing, recordkeeping, and graphic representations. The introduction of each new media from clay tablets and papyrus scrolls to present-day digital formats have necessitated iterative efforts, as each new technology has prompted massive conversions to emerging media formats as seen in the cases of paper, microfilm, and (more recently) digital media.[27] The practice of conversion from print into analog and subsequently into digital formats attests to the survival of remediation in present-day practices.

In explaining remediation, Bolton and Grusin have echoed Marshall McLuhan[28] who described the transition of film from a mechanized and industrialized environment into the electronic age dominated by TV. When TV began replacing film, viewers regarded the film "old" and TV became the imperceptible lens through which they accessed old content. As film, print, and analog media transitioned into digital media, personal computers and mobile technologies have become those new imperceptible lenses to access old content in new formats. Present-day remediation is a curatorial strategy aiming to convert original materials in paper- and film-based and analog media into current digital formats. With the constant development of computing hardware and software, operating systems, storage mechanisms, digital media, and file formats, remediation has become a perpetual pursuit of industrial developers, technologists,

---

25 See Heidi Campbell, "Spiritualising the Internet: Uncovering Discourses and Narratives of Religious Internet Usage," *Online – Heidelberg Journal of Religions on the Internet* 1, no. 1 (2005), https://doi.org/10.11588/rel.2005.1.381.

26 Jay David Bolter and Richard Grusin, *Remediation: Understanding New Media* (Cambridge, Mass.: MIT Press, 1999), 45.

27 For a comprehensive history on books, see "History of Books," in *Understanding media and culture: an introduction to mass communication* (Minneapolis, MN: University of Minnesota Libraries Publishing, 2016).

28 Marshall McLuhan, *Understanding Media: The Extensions of Man* (New York: McGraw-Hill, 1964), 3.

curators, and scholars alike. It may particularly interest material religion research because of the use of various media equipment and content in religious practice over time. In the digital environment, remediation techniques include digital imaging (scanning and photography) and hypertextual reformatting—an extension of text-based work with scriptures, classical literature, and other cultural heritage materials. From a techno-cultural viewpoint, digital technology—and social media in particular—has become that "imperceptible lens" in believers' relationship to sacred texts in ways that the TV occupied that spot much beforehand.

3.4.2 Digital Imaging

As a method of remediation, digital imaging has relied on the use of scanners and digital cameras, which transformed photographs on paper and film into digital images. The first scanner was invented in 1957 by Russell Kirsch, and in 1975, Ray Kurzweil created Optical Character Recognition (OCR) to recognize texts in image form on scanned photographs, which has led to the concept of searchable images.[29] These developments have set the stage for present-day digitization projects, which began in the late 1990s, as it took another forty to fifty years of developments on computers, scanners, storage media, and digital file types to facilitate mass digitization projects beginning in the 1990s and well into the present.

Most historic scriptures including the Old and New Testaments of the *Bible*, *The Dead Sea Scrolls*, and *Quran* had passed through decades of successive remediation (from print to photographs and/or electronic texts and analog recordings, and then to digital media and/or hypertext) before becoming accessible on the Internet in electronic text or page-image versions.[30] Leslie Johnston's chronology[31] places the beginning of text digitization in 1971 with the beginning of

---

29 Nathan Brewer, "Your Engineering Heritage: Scanners and Computer Image Processing," *Insight* (February 8, 2016), https://insight.ieeeusa.org/articles/your-engineering-heritage-scanners-and-computer-image-processing.

30 See Jeffrey S. Siker, "Digital Bibles and Social Media," in *Liquid Scripture* (Minneapolis: Augsburg Fortress Publishers, 2017); Siker, "A Brief History of Digital Bibles," in *Liquid Scripture* (Minneapolis: Augsburg Fortress Publishers, 2017); and Muhammad Khurram Khan, and Yasser M. Alginahi, "The Holy Quran Digitization: Challenges and Concerns," *Life Science Journal* 10, no. 2 (2013), 156-64

31 Leslie Johnston, "Before You Were Born: We Were Digitizing Texts," *The Signal* (blog), December 19, 2012. https://blogs.loc.gov/thesignal/2012/12/before-you-were-born-we-were-digitizing-texts/.

Project Gutenberg (the first hypertext archive)[32] followed by two decades of successive projects before the launch of the Web. Photographing the *Dead Sea Scrolls* in 1981 at the Huntington Library had eventually set the stage for digitizing that collection much later in 2010.[33] Digitizing the *Gutenberg Bible* began soon after the founding of the Humanities Media Interface Project at Keio University in Japan in 1996 became accessible online by 2008.[34]

The digitization of the *Quran* and the development of Quranic software for CD-ROM began in the 1990s for eventual hosting of Quranic texts on Islamic Websites in the 2000s.[35] The present-day digitized recitations and calls to prayer for access on computers and smartphones underscore the role of audiovisual media in religious practice.[36] In India, over 1,600 hours of endangered Vedic performances have been recorded between 1960 and early 2000s with a portion of that material released in DVD form.[37] The use of three-dimensional X-ray based imaging similar to those used in hospitals to scan the charred scrolls of the 2000-year-old *Book of Leviticus* in the Hebrew Bible[38] marks one of the latest developments in remediation techniques. These developments illustrate the use of digital media for spiritual, informational, and educational purposes. With the commitment to convert them digitally comes the commitment to preserve them for long-term access, but the role of digital curation in these areas of religious

---

32 Marie Lebert, *The eBook is 40 (1971–2011)*, Gutenberg Project, 2011, https://www.gutenberg.org/cache/epub/36985/pg36985.html.

33 Russell Chandler, "Library Lifts Veil on Dead Sea Scrolls: Antiquities: The Huntington Breaks Four Decades of Secrecy Surrounding Biblical Texts," *Los Angeles Times*, September 22, 1991, https://www.latimes.com/archives/la-xpm-1991-09-22-mn-4145-story.html.

34 "The HUMI Project," *Gutenberg Bible*, Morgan Library and Museum, 2010, https://www.themorgan.org/collections/works/gutenberg/humi.

35 Micro Systems International, *Al-Qur'an Al-Kareem: A Multimedia Presentation of Islam's Holy Book*. V.4.0 on CD-ROM. https://web.archive.org/web/19961219062154/http://www.quran.com/; see also Muhammad Taqi-ud-Din Al-Hilali & Muhammad Muhsin Khan, *The Noble Qur'an* (English), *Muttaqun Online* (2000), https://web.archive.org/web/20001007041829/http://muttaqun.com/quran/.

36 Gary R. Bunt, "'Rip.Burn.Pray.': Islamic Expression Online," in *Religion Online: Finding Faith on the Internet*, ed. Lorne L. Dawson and Douglas E. Cowan (New York: Routledge, 2004), 124; see also Keith Anderson, *The Digital Cathedral: Networked Ministry in a Wireless World* (New York: Morehouse Publishing, 2015), 6.

37 "'Digitised' Vedas Released," *The Hindu*, November 19, 2015. https://www.thehindu.com/news/national/andhra-pradesh/digitised-vedas-released/article7893801.ece.

38 Andrew Griffin, "Scientists finally read the oldest biblical text ever found," *Indy/Life* (blog), *The Independent* (September 22, 2016), https://www.independent.co.uk/life-style/gadgets-and-tech/news/scientists-finally-read-the-oldest-biblical-text-ever-found-a7323296.html.

life would also aim to reserve the knowledge of texts, rituals, and religious identity.

3.4.3 Digital Preservation

The preservation of religious canon has extensively relied on memory as well as archives for millennia throughout human history, and religious institutions have relied on archives to preserve heritage and memory. Kenneth Foote has emphasized that archives have played a crucial role in preserving culture and collective memory through the "collections of documents and material artifacts as means of extending the temporal and spatial range of communication.[39] Digital archives have begun to play a vital role in an environment where technology has become the connecting bridge between religious communities and their collective memories.

Digital preservation—defined as "the series of managed activities necessary to ensure continued access to digital materials for as long as necessary"[40]—extends this association of memory, culture, and archives into the digital environment where archivists deploy technologies to ensure access to information and knowledge while also protecting professionally stored physical originals from excessive handling and environmental effects.[41] In William Y. Arms' definition, the digital library is a "managed collection of information, with associated services, where the information is stored in digital formats and accessible over a network."[42] Emphasis falls on the managed nature and systematic organization of information, which area critical aspects of trustworthy digital repositories. Lee and Tibbo point out that the "development of trustworthy and durable digital repositories; principles of sound metadata creation and capture; use of open

---

39 Kenneth E. Foote, "To Remember and Forget: Archives, Memory, and Culture," *The American Archivist* 53, no. 3 (1990): 378. http://www.jstor.org/stable/40293469. For connections between religion, archives, memory, commandment, and commencement—all associated with the Greek word *arkhé*—see Jacques Derrida, *Archive Fever: a Freudian Impression*, trans. Eric Prenowitz (The University of Chicago Press, 1996).
40 Maggie Jones and Neil Beagrie, "Definitions and Concepts," in *Preservation Management of Digital Materials: A Handbook* (London: The British Library for Resource, the Council for Museums, Archives and Libraries, 2001), 10. Accessible online via the Digital Preservation Coalition. https://www.dpconline.org/docs/digital-preservation-handbook/299-digital-preservation-handbook/file.
41 "Standard Enclosures," Storage and Handling, Smithsonian Institution Archives, n.d., https://siarchives.si.edu/what-we-do/preservation/storage-handling.
42 William Y. Arms, *Digital Libraries* (Cambridge, MA: MIT Press, 2000), 2.

standards for file formats and data encoding; and the promotion of information management literacy are all essential to the longevity of digital resources and the success of curation efforts."[43] However, the level of commitment and expertise at religious institutions, faith communities, and among individual followers may have contributed to varying results with respect to digital preservation, which have ranged from producing large and richly described digital archival materials to scantily curated collections.

Digital curation aims to prolong access to electronic data and digital media by way of remediating and digitizing them, as hardware and software used to produce those contents may no longer be functioning. Content migration and digital reformatting are critical parts of the process to ensure access to born-digital and digitized content in their new environments (e. g., websites, digital repositories, and databases) where users can access them for worship, education, or research.

3.5 Digital Humanities Practices

3.5.1 Hypertextuality

The transfer of printed and scribed texts into computer-generated format does not constitute digital imaging but nonetheless falls under digitization though different processes. In fact, the remediation of texts did not begin with scanning but manual entry of texts into electronic format, which has evolved over time into a hypertext markup language (i.e., HTML) format using the American Standard Code for Information Interchange (ASCII) and Unicode Transformation Format (UTF) code languages for machine readability. Over time, hypertext has become as transformative and immersive as other forms of digital remediation, and has enabled curators to preserve textual structures using navigational links.

Jeffrey Siker's chronological overview from 1949 to the 1990s follows developments in hypertext to convert historic religious works in print form into electronic text. These early projects include Busa's work with IBM starting in 1949 to create the *Index Thomisticus*, A.Q. Morton's entering Greek text in the New Testament for statistical calculations in 1964 similar to present-day text mining, and other computer-based studies of the Bible in a manner similar to Yehuda Radday's application of computing to the Hebrew Bible in 1970.[44] At this time, Robert

---

43 Lee and Tibbo, "Digital Curation and Trusted Repositories."
44 Siker, "A Brief History of Digital Bibles," 36, 37, and 40.

Kraft worked on processing Hebrew and Greek texts, David W. Packard built the IBYCUS machine capable of processing Greek texts in 1972. Religious texts appeared to be among the earliest works to be digitized, according to Siker.[45] While Busa's pioneering work began in 1949, it was not until the 1980s when digitization finally translated into portability between PCs and reading devices such as Bible Reader and CDWord on CD-ROMs.

Successive remediation of electronic texts have impacted the development of plain text using ASCII characters into the Standard Generalized Markup Language (SGML) in 1986, the Text Encoding Initiative (TEI), HTML, and XML by 1994.[46] A critical backdrop to these developments was the transition in network architectures from the U.S. Defense Department's Advanced Research Projects Agency Network (ARPANET) in 1969 through the Internet in 1983 and the World Wide Web in 1994.[47] The first scanning of scriptures waited until after 2000, which is when the full-scale release of Optical Character Recognition (OCR) allowed the production of searchable page-image PDF scans of those texts.[48]

With early roots in Vannevar Bush's Memex, which was a desktop interactive device using a heuristic approach to discovery,[49] the conversation began with Theodore Holm Nelson's definition of on *hypertext:* "a body of written or pictorial material interconnected in such a complex way that it could not conveniently be presented or represented on paper."[50] Other works have built on this definition, combining the ideas of open text by poststructuralists with Barthes' concept of *lexia* [51]—that is, interlinked textual blocks are basic elements forming hypertextual networks.[52] The role of hypertextuality in digitization did not focus

---

45 Siker, "A Brief History of Digital Bibles."

46 Text Encoding Initiative, History, Updated June 2, 2021. https://tei-c.org/about/history/.

47 Barry M. Leiner, et al. "Introduction," Brief History of the Internet, Internet Society, 1997. https://www.internetsociety.org/internet/history-internet/brief-history-internet/.

48 Nathan Brewer, "Your Engineering Heritage: Scanners and Computer Image Processing" *Insight* (February 8, 2016). https://insight.ieeeusa.org/articles/your-engineering-heritage-scanners-and-computer-image-processing.

49 Vannevar Bush, "As We May Think," *The Atlantic* (1945, July). https://www.theatlantic.com/magazine/archive/1945/07/as-we-may-think/303881/.

50 Theodore Holm Nelson, "Complex Information Processing: A File Structure for the Complex, the Changing and the Indeterminate," ACM '65: Proceedings of the 1965 20th national conference (Cleveland, Ohio, August 1965): 96.

51 See Roland Barthes and Honoré de Balzac, *S/Z* (Paris: Editions de Seuil, 1970).

52 See Jay David Bolter, *Writing Space: The Computer, Hypertext, and the History of Writing* (Hillsdale N.J.: Erlbaum, 1991); Jay David Bolter, "Literature in the Electronic writing space," in *Literacy Online: The Promise (and Peril) of Reading and Writing with Computers*, edited by Myron C. Tuman (Pittsburgh: University of Pittsburgh Press, 1992), 19–42; George P. Landow, *Hypertext:*

on representing texts as digital images; rather, the aim was to create a form of linked ext that could be used to navigate across infinite bodies of texts and media, which has directly shaped the development of present-day websites and social media content. It has, in George P. Landow's view, lead to the democratization of digital technology,[53] and religious institutions, communities and individual followers have embraced the transformative and immersive nature of hypertextuality for purposes of religious communication, education, worship, and research.

3.5.2 Text Encoding

Text encoding is a significantly different approach to curating texts, but it extensively relies on hypertext. Unlike HTML used for Website development and social media content, TEI has proved to be most suitable for scholarly purposes mainly in the digital humanities. Introduced by the Text Encoding Initiative (TEI) consortium in 1987[54] as a standard for representing texts in digital form, this method presents a different curatorial strategy. It was largely utilized by literary scholars for textual analysis in scholarly editions; text encoding supported the annotation of texts with visible editing remarks, deletions, additions, strikeouts, and other modifications. Among the TEI standard's capabilities are adding hypertext references to other texts and other information (such as biographical, historical, geospatial, and other sources of data), but not all the projects utilize the entire gamut of the TEI code library. Text encoding offers a variety of curatorial possibilities for religious uses; through this method, theologians, educators, and curators can encode transcribed scriptures with references to authors, locations, other religious texts, corrections, additions, and interpretive remarks[55] with the help of metadata fields formatted for TEI work.

Regarding the preservation of endangered Tibetan cultural and religious heritage, Linda E. Patrik has pointed out three reasons for using text encoding: First, digital technology provides the large Tibetan diaspora without a central-

The Convergence of Contemporary Critical Theory and Technology (Baltimore: Johns Hopkins University Press, 1992); and Jakob Nielsen, *Multimedia and Hypertext: The Internet and Beyond* (Boston, Mass.: AP Professional, 1995).

53 See George P. Landow, *Hyper/Text/Theory* (Baltimore: Johns Hopkins University Press, 1994).
54 "History," Text Encoding Initiative, updated June 2, 2021, https://tei-c.org/about/history/.
55 "History," Text Encoding Initiative.

ized official support structure.[56] The growing Buddhist Tibetan community in exile has come to use digital technologies to communicate with others and reach out to newcomers to Buddhism. Another reason for using text encoding is that such sacred texts provide an opportunity for international scholarship to build scholarly discourse around these texts and create a better understanding of the meanings behind them and associated practices. A global undertaking of a project of this magnitude, however, extensively relied on the TEI standard. This applies to all digitally curated scriptures as well. Finally, the third reason for using digital technologies is that it can incorporate visual and aural dimensions of Buddhist practice and not just the textual aspects, thus bringing text encoding into the combination of various technologies to enhance Buddhist religious experience.

TEI projects have included literary, historical, scientific, and religious (Buddhist, Christian, and Jewish) texts.[57] Among the notable projects involving religious texts are the Chinese Buddhist Electronic Text Association's Electronic *Tipitaka Collection*, the University of Tokyo's *Digital Dictionary of Buddhism*, the *Open Siddur Project* archive containing transcribed, scanned, and translated prayers and such compilations as the *Siddurim* and *Haggadot* with interactive functions.[58] The archive also features tags and categories to show topical and other logical arrangements of texts. A noteworthy collection of text-encoded Koran projects is available via *The Digital Walters* manuscript repository—a resource of *The Walters Art Museum* in Baltimore, Maryland.[59] It contains scanned images of the Koran, prayers, and other manuscripts related to Islamic history from all over the Middle East. In addition to metadata presented in TEI-XML format, the scanned manuscripts are available via download. Text encoding, therefore, offers curators additional channels for preserving and making available historic texts.

---

56 Linda E. Patrik, "Encoding for Endangered Tibetan Texts," *Digital Humanities Quarterly* 1, no. 1 (2007), http://www.digitalhumanities.org/dhq/vol/1/1/000004/000004.html.
57 Projects Using the TEI, "Text Encoding Initiative," updated August 29, 2020, https://tei-c.org/Activities/Projects/.
58 Projects Using the TEI.
59 Walters Ms. W.554, Koran, *Digitized Walters Manuscripts*, https://www.thedigitalwalters.org/Data/WaltersManuscripts/html/W554/description.html.

3.5.3 Data Visualization

Data visualization has become a significant part of curatorial practice in heritage organizations and has remained so in the digital environment where curation is no longer restricted to museum and archival work. Scientists, digital humanists, digital archivists, data librarians alike are now employing advanced methods in curating data through diverse data visualization methods. Abe has addressed the dual nature of the association between curation and visualization: "A part of general curation in (art) museum is of course visualization in the real world. Curators select and arrange the placement of works according to the theme of exhibition or museum and their philosophy. Their philosophy is visualized as an exhibition."[60] However, this is only one side of the relationship since the exhibition is predominantly educational—that is, programmed with lost opportunities for chance discoveries and deep learning for exhibition visitors. Secondly, Abe points out that as part of holistic communication chance discovery (without too much guidance) can promote "active visualization" with a freedom to think deeply.[61] This conceptual relationship between visualization and curation is vital to understanding theological programming in religious communication. While religious institutions would want followers to apply independent thinking in terms of interpreting scriptures and applying them towards their personal lives, they would need to adhere to a theological framework to publish content on their portals and social media sites in order to stay connected with followers. Hence, religious communication on the Internet involves theologically oriented (programmed) curation and visualization leading to varying results in discoveries. However, it is evident that data visualization offers as much an opportunity for religious scholars as it does for digital humanists in disciplines beyond comparative religion and theology.

Digital technologies have facilitated the visualization of data using maps, timelines, network charts, word clouds, and other techniques. These approaches are especially helpful in merging the humanities and science with information from sacred texts; examples could be the temporal and spatial representations of historical events and locations in the Old and New Testaments as well as the Quran. For instance, the use of concept map visualization has aimed to pre-

---

60 Akinori Abe, "Visualization as Curation with a Holistic Communication." (Paper presented at the 2012 Conference on Technologies and Applications of Artificial Intelligence, Tainan, Taiwan, 16–18 Nov. 2012): 269.
61 Abe, "Visualization as Curation," 269.

sent historical data from the Quran.[62] In her article, Caroline Bruzelius has described the use of visualization and animations in reconstructing space over time at religious institutions such as the Franciscan convent of Piacenza.[63]

An association between visualization and digital data curation was the focus of a report on the use of archaeological heritage data in relation to a site in Çatalhöyük, Turkey,[64] bringing these two practices into a tangible relationship. Elsewhere, the UNESCO map showing the distribution (and listing) of world heritage sites can help heritage preservationists identify religious sites in dire predicament (due to conflicts or neglect).[65] Geospatial and other data on this site can help worshippers locate religious sites for spiritual as well as curatorial purposes. Religious institutions pursuing educational outreach to the community can use visualization tools such as historical timelines and charts to present the history of the community. For instance, the Association of Religious Data Archive (Founded in 1997) publishes data (including interactive maps and timeline visualizations) in supporting public inquiries of academic, socio-political, administrational, and personal nature.[66] Faith communities can use historical data in order to validate their legacy in communicating faith to followers and potential members. While these types of visualizations are not representations of sacred texts *per se*, they are a form of curation of information based in religion, mythology, folklore, and history.

Visualization can also facilitate research into the usage of words in sacred documents—a curation approach that can visually present vocabularies in sacred texts while also bringing worshippers face to face with the meanings of words. Flerlage has demonstrated that textual analysis and visualization using the Tableau program can effectively work across the board for multiple sacred texts.[67] The visualizations include sigmoid curves, bubble charts, and world

---

62 Raja-Yusof Raja-Jamilah, Akmal Jananatul, and Jomhari Nazean, "Information Visualization Techniques for Presenting Qur'an Histories and Atlas," *Multicultural Education & Technology Journal* 7, no. 4 (2013): 305, https://doi.org/10.1108/METJ-03-2013-0011.

63 Caroline Bruzelius, "Teaching with Visualization Technologies," *Material Religion: The Journal of Objects, Art and Belief* 9, no. 2 (2013): 248.

64 Nicola Lercari, Emmanuel Shiferaw, Maurizio Forte, and Regis Kopper, "Immersive Visualization and Curation of Archaeological Heritage Data: Çatalhöyük and the Dig@IT App," *Journal of Archaeological Method and Theory* 25, no. 2 (2018), https://doi.org/10.1007/s10816-017-9340-4.

65 "World Heritage List," UNESCO World Heritage Centre, updated August 22, 2021, https://whc.unesco.org/en/list/.

66 "Quality Data on Religion," Association of Religious Data Archive, updated August 17, 2021, https://www.thearda.com/.

67 Ken Flerlage, "Word Usage in Sacred Texts," *Dataviz* (July 2017), *The Flerlage Twins*, https://www.flerlagetwins.com/2017/07/word-usage-in-sacred-texts_4.html.

clouds with the former linking shared words in textual pairs such as Upanish-ads and *Bhagavad Gita*; *Bible* and *Quran*; *Dhammapada* and *Tao Te Ching*. In contrast, the bubble charts and word clouds demonstrate the frequency, usage, and ranking of selected words such as "Lord," "Allah," "Tao," "world," "mind," and "nature" in selected sacred texts.[68] The findings may support a va-riety of interpretations depending on the purpose of inquiry such as scholarly research or religious communication. Although not directly related to the topic of archival preservation—but considerably more to digital curation—visualiza-tion and textual analysis facilitate research and religious communication and re-lated hermeneutic work by digital humanists researching sacred texts.

3.6 Curating Scriptures in Digital Repositories and Hypertext Archives

Digital representations of sacred texts come in three familiar forms: electronic text (or hypertext), visual data (or page-image/PDF files), or digitized audiovisual media containing recitations, prayers, sermons, and other performances. Larger institutions have organized these media files in digital repositories, databases, hypertext archives, but most virtual communities, social networking sites pro-vide the means for establishing any semblance of a digital archive for regular religious uses. The following selection exemplifies the diversity of curatorial ap-proaches illustrating the uses of technologies primarily for purposes of scholarly research and religious communication. However, the curation of these works for long-term access is an essential part of faith formation curation, and the use of digital media as such remains of interest to the field of material religion and par-ticularly to those taking a historical perspective.

3.6.1 Buddhist Digital Resource Center (BDRC)

Founded in 1999, the mission of the BDRC has been to preserve, organize, and make available endangered Buddhist literary heritage to researchers, religious leaders and communities, Tibetan scholars, and interested visitors around the

---

68 Flerlage, "Word Usage in Sacred Texts."

globe.[69] Digitization of the material has involved scanning and photographing fragile manuscripts, cataloguing, and archiving and ensuring long-term storage at Harvard University's Digital Repository Service. Originals form private and public collections are first digitized, cataloged, archivally processed, annotated, and described before digital dissemination. The website also contains preservation eleven case studies in PDF format discussing the preservation and conservation of endangered Buddhist sacred texts. One such case study was about the re-discovery and scanning *of The Ragya Kangyur* consisting of woodblock prints carved at Ragya Monastery in Eastern Tibet between 1814 and 1820. These artifacts were believed to have been destroyed during China's Cultural Revolution until they were re-discovered in 2013 by Jigme Gyaltsen. The scanning of this 104-volume collection has produced 66,156 pages.[70] These and other scanned texts are accessible via the BRDC's digital library containing the collections organized by works, outlines, places, and topics. There is offline access to these collections on hard drives made for monasteries in remote locations.

The digital library provides access to core text collections, selected works, print masters, and resources for translators. The catalog is searchable by author, subject, and title. The texts are presented in Tibetan and transliterated into Latin script with hyperlinks to black-and-white scans of original manuscripts. The user interface allows navigating the document and downloading a small segment of the manuscript, as user account id required to access complete manuscripts. The full-text searchable library allows searching and browsing e-texts and collections with faceted browsing on the left. The purpose of hypertext in this curatorial approach was to enable users to move between transliterated and original versions of these scanned canonical texts.

3.6.2 DharmaNet

DharmaNet is a hypertext archive of learning resources that include self-didactic materials, audio recordings, and lesson plans.[71] The Learning Resource Center provides materials through a network of interlinked resources on Buddhist traditions, meditations, fundamentals, and a library of texts and sutras of the Ther-

---

69 "Buddhist Digital Resource Center," Buddhist Digital Resource Center, 2017, https://www. tbrc.org/#!footer/about/newhome; see also "The Buddhist Digital Archives," Buddhist Digital Resource Center, 2019. https://library.bdrc.io/.
70 "The Ragya Kangyur," in *Preservation Case Studies,* Buddhist Digital Resource Center, n.d., http://www.tbrc.org/docs/case/W2PD17098.pdf.
71 "Learning Resource Center," DharmaNet, updated March 13, 2021, https://dharmanet.org/.

avada, Mahayana, and Tibetan branches of Buddhism. The text has been transcribed and translated into English with links to updated—and possibly corrected—versions with links to the recorded chanting, instructions (e. g., when to bow), glossary, and links to external resources such as the BDRC described in this chapter. Unlike the BDRC, however, DharmaNet does not offer a searchable library of texts; instead, the organization of texts is by the branch of Buddhism, followed by groupings according to principles. The approach to curating aims to integrate these prayers into daily mediations and rituals of ordained monks, nuns, as well as private worshippers. Some of the links have ceased to work, which demonstrates that curation of hypertext archives must also include the preservation of the entire site and the hyperlinks holding the content together —in other words, the information architecture.

3.6.3 Digital Bible Library

United Bible Societies is one of many faith communities partnering with the library is a member of a network of Bible societies in over 200 countries focusing on providing access to the Bible.[72] This is an important part of curating the Bible and scriptures, as UBS aims to unite member communities through the texts and teachings in the Bible. Digital Scriptures are not merely curated for preservation but also shared through social media to foster sharing, dialog, and human connection in the digital environment.

This global digital library maintains a detailed curation program description including information on content and software updates, metadata management. While text-based resources (digital scriptures) dominate the holdings, the catalog shows a growing collection of digital audio and video content. Their curation approach extends to identifying the relationship between text entries and related publication entries. The metadata for each catalog record includes the title, country, language, and copyright holder information. A simple search box supports searching by keyword in any of the visible fields. Clicking the title opens the text, but access to the digital scripture is restricted to membership and subscription and login is required.

The extended curation program features five activities: digital asset management, publishing, connecting, reporting, and translation. Data from the Digital Bible Library feeds into the Global Bible Catalogue used for publishing, which

---

[72] "The Digital Bible Library," United Bible Society, Updated May 17, 2021. https://thedigitalbiblelibrary.org/.

feeds data into the Scripture Progress system for reporting purposes.[73] The Translation component presents the text in multiple languages and feeds into the Scripture progress system. This curation architecture focuses on scripture process for meaningful access to hundreds of language communities.

3.6.4 Digital Vatican Library

The Digital Vatican Library contains religious heritage materials such as artifacts, graphic and selected printed materials including a selection of digitized manuscripts from 80,000 codices in the Vatican Library established in 1450. The Archivist and Librarian of the Vatican shares authority with the Council over the collections and their curation. Started in 2010, the digitization project has applied open standards for metadata and interoperability by adopting the International Image Interoperability Framework in order to provide access to scholars and the global public easy access to the library's collections.[74]

The user interface provides access to featured collections, archives, searchable authority files. Digital images in the collection are in JPEG file formats at a 72 ppi (pixel per inch) resolution, which is the commonly used file format for contents on the Web. Searching the database is possible with faceted browsing and navigation bar on the left to expand choices or limit by formats, dates, names, languages (including Ancient Greek, Arabic, Hebrew, and Latin). The hypertext presentation of the collection preserves the hierarchical structure of manuscripts, allowing readers to move between pages (also possible with the thumbnails) and across the entire document. A commitment to preserving this resource will also include preserving the information architecture.

3.6.5 The Internet Sacred Text Archive

Launched in 1999, this website presents an example of Web-based curation with original content migrated from earlier FTP archives and bulletin boards. Many files are in earlier digital file formats that have eventually become unusable or disappeared altogether; hence was the need to place them on a permanent website[75] in e-text form using Hypertext Markup Language (HTML) as well as

---

73 "The Digital Bible Library."
74 "Digital Vatican Library," Vatican Library, updated February 10, 2021, https://digi.vatlib.it/.
75 Hare, "About Sacred-Texts."

PDF file format currently in use for digital preservation. Along with scriptures from the major religions—Buddhism, Christianity, Hinduism, Islam, and Judaism, there are scanned copies and transcriptions of books on tribal traditions, folklore, mythology, and native religions from non-Western cultures. Although Hare warns about representational bias in the transcribed books, he acknowledges the wealth of first-person accounts.[76] The hypertext structure of the e-text version has aimed to represent the original text but adds polyglot presentations and transliterations, which enables readers to view earlier versions of the texts and in multiple languages. The footnotes allow readers to read cross-references, thus presenting opportunities for interpretive and discursive activity.

3.6.5 Jewish Virtual Library

The Jewish Virtual Library began in 1998 as a "source for information about Jewish history, Israel, U.S.-Israel relations, the Holocaust, anti-Semitism and Judaism" with 25,000 articles and 10,000 images.[77] The broadly conceived resource devotes significant space to presenting Jewish history, culture, politics, biography, religion, and many other topics. The page titled "Religion Wing" contains links to resources on Judaism, heritage, and scriptures including the *Tanakh* (written law), *Talmud* (oral law), and the King James Version of the *New Testament* which presenting the texts in numbered lines with hyperlinks connecting readers with chapter indices and other related texts.[78] The hypertext presentation uses HTML supplied with pop-up texts explaining underlined concepts, terms, names, and places, demonstrating a concept-level curation approach. The translated version of the *Talmud* from 1918 is accessible in PDF format with a table of contents and helpful navigational features allowing readers to move across the textual landscape of scriptures. Aside the one-person curatorial staff, there is no description of digital preservation by archival staff.

---

76 Hare, "About Sacred-Texts."
77 "Jewish Virtual Library," American-Israeli Cooperation Enterprise (AICE), updated August 13, 2021, https://www.jewishvirtuallibrary.org/.
78 "Jewish Virtual Library."

3.6.6 Panjab Digital Library

Started in 2003, the objective behind the Panjab Digital Library was to preserve surviving Panjab's regional (including Sikh) cultural heritage including the region's literary traditions, manuscripts, architecture, collective memory, and other endangered treasures.[79] Descriptions of the curation process provide significant detail on the preservation of content. The collections include manuscripts, books, magazines, newspapers, and photographs. Curators perform assessment of the original documents' physical characteristics and condition, sacredness of religious texts (which will require proper treatment), age, and historical value for research purposes. The PDL contains 1,967 manuscripts, most of which are sacred writings by revered spiritual leaders. The *Rig-Veda-Sanhita*, *Bhagavad Gita*, and *Upanishads* are also accessible in digital form.

In terms of hypertextual approaches to curation, the connections are most obvious between the website and the Facebook site. The individual records are not interlinked—that is, the PDL does not offer hyperlinks to visual (PDF or image) representations of the *Rig-Veda*. The metadata, however, offers hyperlinks via indexed fields such as script, custodian (curator) in order to allow researchers to view records in selected fields. It is important to notice the field related to paper material with essential data for researchers of material culture and material religion.

The digitization project has followed internationally supported benchmarking and preservation standards as a means of preserving and providing access to digitally reformatted originals. The standards involve creating digital copies of original texts in RAW, TIFF, JPEG formats, searchable PDF images (scanned with OCR), and Dublin Core metadata schema. In addition to the copies accessible online, the curators have also retained master copies on hard drives and DVDs with the archiving process generating five backups in three file formats for safety reasons. Upon accessioning, the curators prepare metadata and complete the digitization process. The curators also prepare exhibitions of the original materials for educational purposes, and online exhibitions are accessible to view digitized materials. The site offers space for commenting, a discussion forum, and a Facebook site, inviting visitors into a participatory curation network. PDL also allows registered users to add descriptions and keywords, which can enrich discourse on the subject of the PDL collections and exhibitions.

---

79 "Panjab Digital Library," Panjab Digital Library (PDL), updated June 18, 2021, http://www. panjabdigilib.org/webuser/searches/mainpage.jsp.

3.6.7 Quran Explorer

The *Quran Explorer* was launched in Orlando, Florida in 2005, with the aim to reach out to all audiences regardless of racial, ethnic, age, or religious background.[80] The authors have consulted Muslim scholars to proofread and certify the content for accuracy, authority, and reliability of the original and translated material. The site presents three ways of accessing the text of the *Quran:* mobile version; classic and full-text searchable presentation that allows faceted browsing by chapter, verse, script (Indo-Pakistani/Urdu and Usmani), language (there are 15), and reciter (with a choice of 20; and 3) simple hypertext each of which enables site visitors to access audio version of the texts. There is a *surah* (chapter) index where each link opens a verse in multiple interpretations. Visitors can hear the audio version of highlighted passages, which facilitates learning, practicing, and memorizing. Curation of the *Quran* at the verse level suggests that in addition to preserving the text and the hypertext structure, there is a commitment to preserving the audio files as well. There is also a blog aiming to engage visitors to discuss methods to learn the *Quran* via Facebook, Twitter, Disqus, and Google Plus. The community-based participatory curation not only aims to help learners but also to enrich discussions about the meaning of the *Quran.*

3.6.8 Social Media

Religious communication on the Internet had gained considerable momentum well prior to the launching of the World Wide Web in 1994. Among the pioneers were marginalized New Age and pagan groups followed by the mainstream Buddhist, Christian, Hindu, Jewish, and Muslim communities.[81] As the early bulletin boards and chat rooms eventually faded, these groups migrated to social media, mobile technologies, and new digital media formats. Prayers, sermons, discussions, personal interpretations, event announcements, and quotations from scriptures supplemented with photographs of religious texts, artifacts, places, and events continue to dominate these sites. This form of curation—or social curation—enables institutions and other organizations to engage members and followers in deeper discussion on faith and other aspects of religion. There is an interesting parallel between leaders of these virtual communities and muse-

---

80 "Quran Explorer," Quran Explorer.com, updated August 19, 2021. https://www.quranexplor er.com/quran/.
81 Charles Ess, "'Revolution? What Revolution?'"

um curators. Roberto calls these leaders faith formation curators who do more than merely provide religious content; he writes, "a content curator [such as those in museums as well as archives] continually finds, groups, organizes, and shares the best and most relevant content on a specific subject to match the needs of a specific audience."[82] The transformation of the sacred text in terms of media format is a noteworthy effect of curation on the forms of sacred texts emerging in the digital environment. Digital contents have become a part of the material world for religious organizations and worshippers. With respect to the forms of content, Siker writes

> The Bible in digital social media is where we can best see what I am calling the liquid character of the Bible, the way in which the Bible gets transformed from solid text to image and sound. The ability to change shapes and mediums across digital platforms has been one of the most important ways in which the Bible has been adapted to the digital age, especially in the form of mobile social apps. [83]

What early chat rooms and bulletin boards have started in terms of faith formation curation continues in present-day websites and social media. Facebook pages aim to curate passages from sacred texts as exemplified by the "My Bible" page seeking to integrate Bible verses, quotations of Jesus, and passages from Genesis and other parts of the Bible into daily life. My Bible.com[84] posts verses in a call-and-response manner whereby Facebook users respond with "Amen" often followed by (or following) other supportive comments. Another religious site on Facebook titled "Holy Quran, A Complete code of Life"[85] adheres to Islamic tradition of presenting verses from the *Quran* in Arabic while also offering English translations. The same site also engages visualization through the still image or video display of the Kaaba in Mecca along with a translated quotation from Book 10, Haith 117 of the *Quran* in a November 18 posting.

Blogging and vlogging activity also represents a high level of popularity of social media in religious groups. Siker has cited multiple data sources indicating a steep rise in the number of blogs (from 23 to 150 million) between 1999 and 2010 with over 16 million hits on "bible blogs" in Google searches.[86] The text-heavy nature of both blogging and tweeting provides an ideal medium for

---

82 John Roberto, "Becoming a Faith Formation Curator," *Lifelong Faith* (Spring 2011): 20.

83 Siker, "Digital Bibles and Social Media," 183.

84 My Bible. "Write AMEN If This Is True Of You!" Facebook, November 18, 2018. https://www.facebook.com/pg/MyBibleVerses/posts/.

85 Holyquran.Islam77, "Build your House in Paradise," Facebook, September 15, 2018. https://www.facebook.com/pg/Holyquran.Islam77/posts (site discontinued).

86 Siker, "Digital Bibles and Social Media," 187.

faith formation curation via discussions of scriptures, and this is not limited to Christians. Siker writes, "Patheos.com also hosts blogs aimed at Roman Catholics, Eastern Orthodox, Evangelical Christians, Progressive Christians, Mormons, Jews, Muslims, Buddhists, Hindu, Pagan, Atheist, Spirituality, Politics Blue, Politics Red, Entertainment, and many more audiences."[87] Alas, the overall popularity of blogs has declined in favor of microblogging in social media (e.g., Facebook, Twitter) and the adaptability of these platforms for smart phones and apps.

3.6.9 Community Portals, Spiritualization, and Other Culturally Aligned Approaches

The selection of appropriate materials is a core objective of curatorial activity, which shapes faith formation in the present context. The spiritualization of the internet in Jewish communities "involves identifying the common discourses employed by religious users that conceptualize the Internet for acceptable use, and the narratives of use that emerge from these discourses. This process is defined as the 'spiritualising of the Internet,' [which means] the Internet is seen as technology or space that is suitable for religious engagement, whereby allowing users to include Internet-based activities into rhythm of their spiritual lives."[88] Social shaping of technology (SST) is a related concept that illustrates how communities of technology users shape the internet for their specific purposes. The selection of material takes place with regards to Jewish cultural and religious preferences, and in some communities, this process is under the supervision of individuals who themselves have professed Judaism as is evident in the case of Chabad[89] and Aish websites.[90] The reliance on curators with rabbinical training results in the selection and even preservation of religious media including sacred textual materials.

Launched in 2000, the Aish website has become a leading community portal to address all aspects of Jewish culture and traditions.[91] All members of the cu-

---

87 Siker, "Digital Bibles and Social Media," 188.
88 Campbell, "Spiritualising the Internet."
89 Menahem Blondheim and Elihu Katz, "Religion, Communications, and Judaism: The Case of Digital Chabad, "*Media, Culture & Society* 38, no. 1 (2016), https://doi.org/10.1177/016344371 5615417.
90 Heidi Campbell and Wendi Bellar, "Sanctifying the Internet: Aish Ha Torah's Use of the Internet for Digital Outreach," in *Digital Judaism: Jewish Negotiations with Digital Media and Culture*, ed. Heidi Campbell (London: Routledge, 2014), 74–75.
91 "Aish," updated August 11, 2021, https://www.aish.com/.

ratorial team have earned rabbinical ordination with the editor-in-chief being himself a rabbi, which is in line with efforts to spiritualizing the Internet for the Aish audience. The site provides a live feed of the Western (or Wailing) Wall, which a holy site for devout Jews as it had once formed a part of the Second Temple destroyed by Romans in 70 BCE. The "Torah Study" tab offers links to hypertext segments from the Torah for basic and advanced study and for parents and kids. Site visitors can also consult the "Ask the Rabbi" page on the Bible, History, traditions, language, Israel, and other topics. "Blogging the Bible" is a social curation feature that allows viewers to leave comments and discuss the contents of the videos on this site. The site also features an audio library of recorded Torah portions that members can access.[92]

The Chabad.org site is a community portal focused on Judaism and has stood out as a leading proponent of using technology.[93] In addition to information on religious matters, Jewish culture, community, it provides a library of hypertext and audio collections of scriptures, performances, prayers, and other transliterated and translated sacred texts. Members of the organization can comment on the texts some of which come with instructions for movements during the recitation of prayers. The site provides hypertext versions of sacred texts such as the *Tanakh*, *Talmud*, *Torah* portions, *Kabbalah*, and others. The *Tanakh* appears to be text-encoded with toggling enabled between texts or without commentaries.[94] Chassidic texts are also included since the Chabad community has Hasidic history rooted in Eastern Europe where adversity and lack of technology has led to creative approaches to religious communication.[95]

In the Muslim communities, it is commonplace to observe similar culturally aligned approaches to integrating technology into religious life. Bunt has addressed the issues with integrating hypertexts into Islam: "The question is whether the translation of Islam and the *Quran* into hypertext facilitates a clearer understanding of the religion in its myriad forms and dimensions, both for Muslims and other travelers in cyberspace."[96] The sacredness of the *Quran* also raises the question whether the hypertextual forms of the *Quran* are respected as equal to the manuscript originals or the page-image scanned (PDF/A) versions, which retain the original appearance of the sacred text. In addition to the digitized versions, recordings of prayers and Quranic recitations, scans of religious calligraphies are also regarded as religious expressions. The multi-lingual

---

92 "Aish."
93 Chabad-Lubavitch Media Center, updated July 5, 2021, https://www.chabad.org/.
94 "Tanakh," https://www.facebook.com/Tanakh.HebrewBible/.
95 Blondheim and Katz, "Religion, Communications, and Judaism," 95.
96 Bunt, "Rip.Burn.Pray," 124.

Quran Explorer website clearly illustrates at least one of many approaches to integrating technology into religion.

Access to the *Quran* in the digital environment signals the emergence of a new concern—that is, the need for preserving the master audio digital files as well as analog recordings made available on cassettes. Archives are the appropriate facilities to conserve and preserve such media. However, the cultural perspectives on sacredness are crucial because in order for digitized versions or texts and recordings to be relevant to the faith community, the digital masters and surrogates of ancient sacred texts and recently produced analog media recordings must first be accepted and integrated into worship. Svensson has also raised an important issue surrounding the sacredness of the *Quran* and the issue of ritual purity, as there are edicts (or *fatwas*) declaring the suitability of the location as well as the person in various stages of ritual purity handling such texts.[97]

3.7 Hybrid curation spaces

The combination of architecture and interior of religious structures (such as churches, mosques, synagogues, temples, etc.) comprise unique culturally coded spaces for immersion and religious communication. Through displays of sacred texts, artifacts, and (where acceptable) graphic visualizations of deities and their stories can communicate significantly about community identity and religious values. In the digital environment, the design of websites plays that same crucial role because websites contain a variety of media, texts, and other information posted for worshippers and potential members. There is a metaphorical relationship between the information architecture of websites and the physical structure where the former is a metaphoric representation (and extension) of the latter.[98] In the case of a religious institution, both serve as semiotic frameworks for religious communication and expression. In both the physical and virtual environments, faith formation curation goes beyond sacred texts, artifacts, images, and sounds; some elaborate architectures (and their digital representations) become integral to the framework for religious immersion. Curators of digital content used in these settings must also document structural context of the digital files

---

97 Jonas Svensson, "Relating, Revering, and Removing: Muslim View on the Use, Power, and Disposal of Divine Words," in *The Death of Sacred Texts: Ritual Disposal and Renovation of Texts in World Religions*, ed. Kristina Myrvold (Farnham, England: Ashgate, 2010), 40.
98 Louis Rosenfeld and Peter Morville, *Information Architecture for the World Wide Web*, 2nd ed. (Cambridge, Mass.: O'Reilly, 2002).

just as archival finding aids show the location and context of records in a collection. For digital curators, the preservation of the entire website as a disk (ISO) image would be an effective approach to preserve these contextual relationships of media to texts and other media within the information architecture of the website.

3.7.1 Digital Cathedral

In *The Digital Cathedral*, Anderson focuses on the immersive aspect of St. Patrick's Cathedral in New York—the seat of the Roman Catholic Archdiocese:

> This cathedral approach to faith formation lends itself to our digitally integrated environment, which is itself ubiquitous, immersive, and highly visual...We begin to see that faith formation is not something that happen solely within the confines of the church or cathedral building [but] everywhere and at all times—in the precincts, the town, and today, the globe, both online and off.[99]

Social media thus becomes an integral part of this digital environment in which people seek access to the Bible, the Gospel, psalms, hymns (or canonical texts), and other materials. Websites and social media are no longer and extension but integral parts of the information architecture for faith curation. The *Lent Madness* website provides both educational and immersive experience through participatory activities revolving around the traditions and history of the Catholic Church and its notable candidates for sainthood and others recognized for martyrdom and other deeds. These activities do not merely include previously posted images of saints and other icons but encourage participants also to share their own photographs on social media.[100] While hashtags may be words that participants use to describe and interpret thoughts, they are also micro-ontologies—and, thus, a tool in curation—with participation and communication organized around them.

---

99 Keith Anderson, *The Digital Cathedral: Networked Ministry in a Wireless World* (New York: Morehouse Publishing, 2015), 167.
100 "Lent Madness," updated May 31, 2021, https://www.lentmadness.org/.

3.7.2 Digital Mosque

The digital mosque exemplifies how the mosque architecture serves as a setting for virtual services. In this particular case, information architecture aims to represent goals for Islamic religious communication in the digital environment. Imdat As writes, "Digital media technologies can generate new means for a mosque more in line with the times. The mosque of the information age can function as a 'village well,' and, theoretically, the entire Islamic community can be brought around it, in ways that could not have been imagined prior to the digital age."[101] He discusses the essence of the mosque of the twenty-first century where digital media and technologies transform the mosque into a new architecture following four principles: 1) correspondence of form and function focusing on *adhan* (call for prayer); ablution, preaching, praying, learning; and socializing; 2) customization of virtual convergent space—a personal profile created upon joining the mosque—featuring a digital version of the *Quran,* a resource library, and means of remote access to this content; 3) the integration of hardware and software into the physical architecture to converge physical and virtual spaces; and 4) the visualization of users in a virtual socialization process that is integral to attending services at mosque.[102]

The digital mosque presents a unique approach to curating content and faith in customized solutions. Key functions include access to the digitized version of the *Quran* as well as social media space, access to other visual religious media, remediation, and projection of the Kaaba complex—which reinforces the logic of immediacy[103]—and the visualization of a user community that reinforces user identity and faith formation through participatory curation. As noted earlier, a curation approach would need to include the preservation of digital files and present the records in a manner that would reinforce the contextual relationships between content, religion, and religious uses of that digital content.

---

101 Imdat As, "The Digital Mosque: A New Paradigm in Mosque Design," *Journal of Architectural Education* 1 (2006): 54.
102 As, "The Digital Mosque."
103 Jay David Bolter and Richard Grusin, *Remediation: Understanding New Media* (Cambridge, Mass.: MIT Press, 1999), viii.

3.8 Conclusion

Digital technologies emerging since the middle of the twentieth century have significantly shaped religious communication from the earliest bulletin boards to present-day social media, enabling faith communities and religious institutions to connect with members. The digital curation of scriptures held sacred in various religions has relied on remediation techniques, enabling institutions to convert (and thus preserve) print materials into analog and ultimately digital format. Not only could these remediation efforts facilitate the preservation of rare and important materials, but also opened up new channels of communication via Websites, social media, and streaming (not covered in this chapter) as result of these technological advancements. New as these alternatives may be in religious communication, the digital preservation of scriptures, manuscripts, and other textual material is an extension of venerated traditions of archiving and preserving community heritage, identity, and memory in faith communities and religious institutions. Digital technology has significantly shaped religious scholarship with a focus on texts. The role of computing and punch cards in the 1940s has laid the foundation for textual practices that would eventually fall in the purview of digital humanities scholars. Textual mining and analysis have eventually led to textual encoding (TEI) and hypertext (SGML, HTML, and XML) markup practices, lending a fully digital framework for creating and disseminating scriptures for scholarly purposes, and this has set the stage for most current trends in social media where all but photographed texts were digitally produced and shared among followers.

Cultural perspectives and practices—such as spiritualization—have also influenced the acceptance of digital technologies in religious practices and rituals, and there were requirements for ordained and venerated leaders to establish some parameters for access and use of webs content during religious practices. Ancient edicts about who can touch a sacred book and who should abstain have been place for millennia in many civilizations; some of these edicts are still in force as a compromise between moving forward in a digital age while maintaining community identity and heritage as defining aspects of humanity in those communities. These cultural attitudes towards technology reinforce identity while facilitating the use of technology in places without a faith community and leader to guide believers in traditional ways. This close association with digital technology among followers, faith communities, and religious institutions reinforces the use of technology as object in religious practice, and the field of material religion the among the disciplines most interested in how religious practitioners use technologies that are new and foreign albeit familiar important at the same time because of the connection to sacred texts.

In order to bring the disparate practices of preservation, textuality, and faith formation, this chapter has presented a triadic interdisciplinary framework comprised of material religion, digital curation, and digital humanities. This approach was most instrumental because religious institutions had devoted significant energies on preserving manuscripts, codices, and artifacts—hence, objects —in archives for safety, longevity, and prospect for future uses. The digital environment has democratized access to data, media, and knowledge, which has made it possible for remote followers to stay in touch with their chosen faith communities. Digital humanities scholars have developed new techniques for research using digitized texts and media. At the same time, the realization that digital media deteriorates has prompted media experts, archivists, and data scientists to raise flags about data loss and preservation.

The framework in this chapter suited the present approach but interdisciplinary—and for that matter, cross-, multi- and transdisciplinary[104]—research may consider different disciplinary boundaries to include (as needed) other areas such as cultural anthropology, semiotics, other areas of information science, linguistics, and literary and media studies. Revisiting seminal works focusing on signs, symbols, language, intertextuality, and other critical themes amidst a perpetually evolving relationship between humans, religion and technology may be difficult without a supportive interdisciplinary framework. Given the specific framework, this chapter has explored the need to preserve heritage content created with digital technology because there is so much more to lose than just a file.

References

Abe, Akinori. "Visualization as Curation with a Holistic Communication." Paper presented at the 2012 Conference on Technologies and Applications of Artificial Intelligence, Tainan, Taiwan, 16–18 Nov. 2012.

"Aish" (website). Aish.com. Updated August 11, 2021. https://www.aish.com/.

Al-Hilali, Muhammad Taqi-ud-Din, and Muhammad Muhsin Khan. "The Noble Qur'an (English)." *Muttaqun Online*, October 7, 2000. https://web.archive.org/web/20001007041829/http://muttaqun.com/quran/.

---

104 For a more extensive discussion of integrative, see Julie Thompson Klein, *Interdisciplinarity: History, Theory, and Practice* (Detroit: Wayne State University Press, 1990), 55–73.

Anderson, Jon W. "The Internet and Islam's New Interpreters." In *New Media in the Muslim World: The Emerging Public Sphere*. Edited by D. F. Eickelman and J. W. Anderson. 45–60. Bloomington: Indiana University Press, 2003.

Anderson, Keith. *The Digital Cathedral: Networked Ministry in a Wireless World*. New York: Morehouse Publishing, 2015.

Arms, William Y. *Digital Libraries*. Cambridge, MA: MIT Press, 2000.

As, Imdat. "The Digital Mosque: A New Paradigm in Mosque Design." *Journal of Architectural Education* 1 (2006): 54–66.

Barthes, Roland and Honoré de Balzac. *S/Z*. Paris: Editions de Seuil, 1970.

Beagrie, Neil. "The Digital Curation Centre." *Learned Publishing* 17, no. 1 (January 2004): 7–9. https://doi.org/10.1087/095315104322710197.

Blondheim, Menahem, and Elihu Katz. "Religion, Communications, and Judaism: The Case of Digital Chabad, "*Media, Culture & Society* 38, no. 1 (2016). https://doi.org/10.1177/0163443715615417.

Beckerlegge, Gwilym. *From Sacred Text to Internet*. Aldershot, Hants, England: Open University, 2001.

Bolter, Jay David. *Writing Space: The Computer, Hypertext, and the History of Writing*. Hillsdale N.J.: Erlbaum, 1991.

Bolter, Jay David. "Literature in the Electronic Writing Space." In *Literacy Online: The Promise (and Peril) of Reading and Writing with Computers*. Edited by Myron C. Tuman. Pittsburgh: University of Pittsburgh Press, 1992.

Bolter, Jay David, and Richard Grusin. *Remediation: Understanding New Media*. Cambridge, Mass.: MIT Press, 1999.

Brewer, Nathan. "Your Engineering Heritage: Scanners and Computer Image Processing." *Insight*, IEEE-USA February 8, 2016. https://insight.ieeeusa.org/articles/your-engineering-heritage-scanners-and-computer-image-processing.

Bruzelius, Caroline. "Teaching with Visualization Technologies." *Material Religion: The Journal of Objects, Art and Belief 9*, no. 2 (2013): 245–253.

"The Buddhist Digital Archives." Buddhist Digital Resource Center, 2019. https://library.bdrc.io/.

Bunt, Gary R. "'Rip.Burn.Pray.': Islamic Expression Online." In *Religion Online: Finding Faith on the Internet*. Edited by Lorne L. Dawson and Douglas E. Cowan. New York: Routledge, 2004.

Bush, Vannevar. "As We May Think." *The Atlantic* (1945, July). https://www.theatlantic.com/magazine/archive/1945/07/as-we-may-think/303881/.

Campbell, Heidi. "Spiritualising the Internet: Uncovering Discourses and Narratives of Religious Internet Usage." *Online – Heidelberg Journal of Religions on the Internet* 1, no. 1 (2005). https://doi.org/10.11588/rel.2005.1.381.

Campbell, Heidi. *When Religion Meets New Media*. London; New York: Routledge, 2010.

Campbell, Heidi. *Digital Religion: Understanding Religious Practice in New Media Worlds*. London: Routledge, 2013.

Campbell, Heidi, and Wendi Bellar. "Sanctifying the Internet: Aish Ha Torah's Use of the Internet for Digital Outreach." In *Digital Judaism: Jewish Negotiations with Digital Media and Culture*, edited by Heidi Campbell, 74–90. London: Routledge, 2014.

"Chabad.org" (website). Chabad-Lubavitch Media Center. Updated July 5, 2021. https://www.chabad.org/.

Chandler, Russell. "Library Lifts Veil on Dead Sea Scrolls: Antiquities: The Huntington Breaks Four Decades of Secrecy Surrounding Biblical Texts." *Los Angeles Times,* September 22, 1991. https://www.latimes.com/archives/la-xpm-1991-09-22-mn-4145-story.html.

Cohen, Daniel J.; Frabetti, Federica; Buzzetti, Dino; and Rodriguez-Velasco, Jesus D. "Defining the Digital Humanities " *Interviews.* Columbia University Academic Commons 2011, mp4 video, 1:50:22. https://academiccommons.columbia.edu/doi/10.7916/D8MS41Z1.

De Vinne, Theodore Low. *The Invention of Printing: A Collection of Facts and Opinions, Descriptive of Early Prints and Playing Cards, the Block-Books of the Fifteenth Century, the Legend of Lourens Janszoon Coster, of Haarlem, and the Work of John Gutenberg and His Associates.* New York: Francis Hart & Co, 1876. https://www.gutenberg.org/files/51034/51034-h/51034-h.htm.

"The Digital Bible Library." United Bible Society. Updated May 17, 2021. https://thedigitalbiblelibrary.org/.

Digital Preservation Coalition. "File Formats and Standards." In *Digital Preservation Handbook,* 2nd ed. https://www.dpconline.org/handbook/technical-solutions-and-tools/file-formats-and-standards.

"Digital Vatican Library." Vatican Library. Updated February 10, 2021. https://digi.vatlib.it/.

"'Digitised' Vedas Released." *The Hindu.* November 19, 2015. https://www.thehindu.com/news/national/andhra-pradesh/digitised-vedas-released/article7893801.ece.

Ehrenkranz, Melanie. "How Ancient Religious Texts Went Digital." *Firsts Week* (blog). *Gizmodo,* January 3, 2019. https://gizmodo.com/how-ancient-religious-texts-went-digital-1831241832.

Engelke, Matthew. "Material Religion." In *The Cambridge Companion to Religious Studies.* Edited by Robert A. Orsi (Cambridge University Press, 2012): 209–229.

Ess, Charles. "'Revolution? What Revolution?' Successes and Limits of Computing Technologies in Philosophy and Religion." Chap. 12 in *A Companion to Digital Humanities.* Edited by Susan Schreibman, Raymond George Siemens and John M. Unsworth. Oxford: Blackwell, 2004. http://www.digitalhumanities.org/companion/.

Flerlage, Ken. "Word Usage in Sacred Texts" *Dataviz* (blog). *The Flerlage Twins.* July 2017. https://www.flerlagetwins.com/2017/07/word-usage-in-sacred-texts_4.html.

Foote, Kenneth E. "To Remember and Forget: Archives, Memory, and Culture." *The American Archivist* 53, no. 3 (1990): 378–392. http://www.jstor.org/stable/40293469.

Geertz, Clifford. *The Interpretation of Cultures: Selected Essays.* New York: Basic Books, 1973.

Griffin, Andrew. "Scientists Finally Read the Oldest Biblical Text Ever Found." *Indy/Life* (blog). *The Independent,* September 22, 2016. https://www.independent.co.uk/life-style/gadgets-and-tech/news/scientists-finally-read-the-oldest-biblical-text-ever-found-a7323296.html.

Hare, John Bruno. "About Sacred-Texts." *Internet Sacred Text Archive.* 2010. Updated February 8, 2021. https://www.sacred-texts.com/about.htm.

"History." Text Encoding Initiative Consortium. Updated June 2, 2021. https://tei-c.org/about/history/.

Holyquran.Islam77. "Build your House in Paradise." Facebook, September 15, 2018. https://www.facebook.com/pg/Holyquran.Islam77/posts (site discontinued).

"The HUMI Project." *Gutenberg Bible.* Morgan Library and Museum. 2010. https://www.themorgan.org/collections/works/gutenberg/humi.

Jacob, Arun. "Punching Holes in the International Busa Machine Narrative." *Interdisciplinary Engagement in Arts & Humanities* 1, no. 1 (2017/2018). https://doi.org/10.21428/ f1f23564.d7d097c2.

"Jewish Virtual Library." American-Israeli Cooperation Enterprise (AICE). Updated August 13, 2021. https://www.jewishvirtuallibrary.org/.

Johnston, Leslie. "Before You Were Born: We Were Digitizing Texts." *The Signal* (blog). *The Library of Congress.* December 19, 2012. https://blogs.loc.gov/thesignal/2012/12/before- you-were-born-we-were-digitizing-texts/.

Jones, Maggie and Neil Beagrie. "Definitions and Concepts." In *Preservation Management of Digital Materials: A Handbook.* London, England: The British Library for Resource, the Council for Museums, Archives and Libraries, 2001. Accessible online via the Digital Preservation Coalition. https://www.dpconline.org/docs/digital-preservation-handbook/ 299-digital-preservation-handbook/file.

Khan, Muhammad Khurram and Yasser M. Alginahi. "The Holy Quran Digitization: Challenges and Concerns." *Life Science Journal* 10, no. 2 (2013): 156–164.

Klein, Julie Thompson. *Interdisciplinarity: History, Theory, and Practice.* Detroit: Wayne State University Press, 1990.

Landow, George P. *Hypertext: The Convergence of Contemporary Critical Theory and Technology.* Baltimore: Johns Hopkins University Press, 1992.

Landow, George P. *Hyper/Text/Theory.* Baltimore: Johns Hopkins University Press, 1994.

Lee, Christopher A., and Helen Tibbo. "Digital Curation and Trusted Repositories: Steps toward Success." *Journal of Digital Information* 8, no. 2 (2007). https://journals.tdl.org/ jodi/index.php/jodi/ article/view/229.

"Learning Resource Center." DharmaNet. Updated March 13, 2021. https://dharmanet.org/.

Lebert, Marie. *The eBook is 40 (1971–2011).* Gutenberg Project, 2011. https://www.gutenberg. org/cache/epub/36985/pg36985.html.

"Lent Madness" (website). Updated May 31, 2021. https://www.lentmadness.org/.

Lercari, Nicola, Emmanuel Shiferaw, Maurizio Forte, and Regis Kopper. "Immersive Visualization and Curation of Archaeological Heritage Data: Çatalhöyük and the Dig@IT App." *Journal of Archaeological Method and Theory* 25, no. 2 (June 27, 2017): 368–392. https://doi.org/10.1007/s10816-017-9340-4.

Leiner, Barry M., Vinton G. Cerf, David D. Clark, Robert E. Kahn, Leonard Kleinrock, Daniel C. Lynch, Jon Postel, et al. "Introduction." *Brief History of the Internet.* Internet Society, 1997. https://www.internetsociety.org/internet/history-internet/brief-history-internet/.

Lundby, Knut. "Theoretical Frameworks for Approaching Religion and Media." In *Digital Religion: Understanding Religious Practice in New Media Worlds.* Edited by Heidi Campbell, 225–237. London: Routledge, 2013.

McLuhan, Marshall. *Understanding Media: The Extensions of Man:* New York: McGraw-Hill, 1964.

Meyer, Birgit, David Morgan, Crispin Paine, and S. Brent Plate. "Material Religion's First Decade." *Material Religion* 10, no. 1 (2014): 105–111. https://doi.org/10.2752/ 175183414X13909887177628.

Micro Systems International. *Al-Qur'an Al-Kareem: A Multimedia Presentation of Islam's Holy Book.* V.4.0 on CD-ROM. https://web.archive.org/web/19961219062154/http://www. quran.com/.

Mitchell, Christine. Review of *Bible and Qur'an: Essays in Scriptural Intertextuality*, edited by John C. Reeves. *Journal of Hebrew Scriptures* 5 (December 31, 2005). https://doi.org/10.5508/jhs5789.

My Bible. "Write AMEN If This Is True Of You!" Facebook, November 18, 2018. https://www.facebook.com/pg/MyBibleVerses/posts/.

Nelson, Theodore Holm. "Complex Information Processing: A File Structure for the Complex, the Changing and the Indeterminate." Paper presented at the ACM '65: Proceedings of the 1965 20th national conference, Cleveland, Ohio, August 1965.

Nielsen, Jakob. *Multimedia and Hypertext: The Internet and Beyond*. Boston, Mass.: AP Professional, 1995.

"Panjab Digital Library." Panjab Digital Library (PDL). Updated June 18, 2021. http://www.panjabdigilib.org/webuser/searches/mainpage.jsp.

Patrik, Linda E. "Encoding for Endangered Tibetan Texts." *Digital Humanities Quarterly* 1, no. 1 (2007). http://www.digitalhumanities.org/dhq/vol/1/1/000004/000004.html.

Pearce-Moses, Richard. *A Glossary of Archival and Records Terminology*. Chicago: Society of American Archivists, 2005. https://files.archivists.org/pubs/free/SAA-Glossary-2005.pdf.

Plate, S. Brent. "Material Religion: An Introduction." In *Key Terms in Material Religion*. Edited by S. Brent Plate, 1–8. London: Bloomsbury Academic, 2015.

"Projects Using the TEI." Text Encoding Initiative Consortium. Updated August 29, 2020. http://www.tei-c.org/activities/projects/.

"Quality Data on Religion." Association of Religious Data Archive. Updated August 17, 2021. https://www.thearda.com/.

"Quran Explorer." QuranExplorer.com. Updated August 19, 2021. https://www.quranexplorer.com/quran/.

"The Ragya Kangyur." Preservation Case Studies. Buddhist Digital Resource Center, 2017. http://www.tbrc.org/docs/case/W2PD17098.pdf.

Raja-Yusof, Raja-Jamilah, Akmal Jananatul, and Jomhari Nazean."Information Visualization Techniques for Presenting *Qur'an* Histories and Atlas." *Multicultural Education & Technology Journal* 7, no. 4 (November 2013): 301–316. https://doi.org/10.1108/METJ-03-2013-0011.

Roberto, John. "Becoming a Faith Formation Curator." *Lifelong Faith* (Spring 2011): 20–25. https://www.lifelongfaith.com/uploads/5/1/6/4/5164069/becoming_a_faith_formation_curator.pdf.

Rosenfeld, Louis, and Peter Morville. *Information Architecture for the World Wide Web*. 2nd ed. Cambridge, Mass.: O'Reilly, 2002.

Sack, Daniel. "Material Religion." In *Contemporary American Religion*. Gale Group, 1999. https://web.archive.org/web/20180131223050/http://www.encyclopedia.com/religion/legal-and-political-magazines/material-religion.

Siker, Jeffrey S. "A Brief History of Digital Bibles." In *Liquid Scripture* (Minneapolis: Augsburg Fortress Publishers, 2017): 35–56.

Siker, Jeffrey S. "Digital Bibles and Social Media." In *Liquid Scripture* (Minneapolis: Augsburg Fortress Publishers, 2017): 183–208.

"Standard Enclosures." Storage and Handling. Smithsonian Institution Archives, n.d. https://siarchives.si.edu/what-we-do/preservation/storage-handling.

Svensson, Jonas. "Relating, Revering, and Removing: Muslim View on the Use, Power, and Disposal of Divine Words." In *The Death of Sacred Texts: Ritual Disposal and Renovation of Texts in World Religions.* Edited by Kristina Myrvold, 31–54. Farnham, England: Ashgate, 2010.

"Tanakh." https://www.facebook.com/Tanakh.HebrewBible/.

Walters Ms. W.554, Koran. Digitized Walters Manuscripts. Walters Art Museum. https://www.thedigitalwalters.org/Data/WaltersManuscripts/html/W554/description.html.

Waugh, Dorothy, Elizabeth Russey Roke and Erika Farr. "Flexible Processing and Diverse Collections: A Tiered Approach to Delivering Born Digital Archives." *Archives and Records* 37, no. 1 (2016): 3–19, https://doi.org/10.1080/23257962.2016.1139493.

"World Heritage List." UNESCO World Heritage Centre. Updated August 22, 2021, https://whc.unesco.org/en/list/.

Part 2 **How the Material Becomes Digital:
Methods in Digital Material Religion**

Emily C. Floyd and Meg Bernstein

Chapter 4
Visiting Religious Spaces in the Digital Realm: The MAVCOR Digital Spaces Project in Historical Context

Medieval and early modern Christians in Europe wishing to experience the holy sites in Palestine first-hand were presented with substantial barriers to their journeys: cost, family obligations, and distance made it difficult for many people—particularly for the poor, for cloistered religious, and for women—to make the long and arduous trip from their homes in Europe. In the fifteenth century real and perceived Ottoman hostility towards travelers traversing their territories rendered it even more challenging to reach the Holy Land.[1] Although there were many popular pilgrimage shrines on European soil (for example, Santiago de Compostela and Canterbury Cathedral), no true substitute existed for travel to the holy sites of Palestine, both in terms of spiritual formation and in the plenary nature of the indulgences offered. Fifteenth-century Europeans responded to the challenges confronting them by developing "virtual" substitutes—mental pilgrimage using books and the imagination, and pilgrimage to artificial landscapes imitating the Holy Land in northern Italy. Today, religious practitioners and scholars of material religion have produced a wide range of digitalizations and virtual experiences of religious spaces that, similar to fifteenth-century virtual Holy Land pilgrimages, provide access to places that are otherwise inaccessible to their viewers.

   This article considers contemporary efforts to produce virtual experiences of spaces meaningfully considered to be religious within the context of historical practices of proxy pilgrimage, while also addressing the unique ethical and practical implications of photographic documentation. Virtual experiences of religious spaces offer scholars and religious practitioners visual access to sites otherwise inaccessible due to distance or other practical barriers. They may fruitfully be understood in parallel to medieval proxy pilgrimage as an acceptable alternative in lieu of physical presence when physical presence is unavailable as an option. At the same time, we emphasize the ways in which digital experi-

---

1 David Leatherbarrow, "The image and its setting: A study of the Sacro Monte at Varallo," *RES: Anthropology and Aesthetics* 14 (1987): 107. See also M. Cecilia Gaposchkin, *Invisible Weapons: Liturgy and the Making of Crusade Ideology* (Ithaca: Cornell University Press, 2017), 226–255.

https://doi.org/10.1515/9783110608755-005

ences of religious spaces privilege certain aspects of these buildings: the visual over the tactile, aural, or olfactory; solitude rather than community; pixels rather than practice.

4.1 When Material Religion Scholarship becomes Material Religion

In 2017, the authors traveled with fellow art historian James Alexander Cameron to the Fens in southern Lincolnshire, England, to photograph a series of medieval parish churches as part of the Center for the Study of Material and Visual Cultures of Religion (MAVCOR—mavcor.yale.edu)'s Digital Spaces Project; Floyd is MAVCOR Editor and Curator. The MAVCOR Digital Spaces Project produces high-resolution giga-pixel, drone, and 360º photography of religious spaces. Over the course of a week, we flew a DJI Phantom 4 Pro drone high above these medieval structures in order to document their location within the landscape and photograph details of their exterior architecture, in particular elements of the roof and higher elevations of the building **[fig. 1].** Floyd used a tripod with a Nodal Ninja M2 Giga w/RD8-II tripod head to take as many as 250 individual exposures per panorama that she later stitched together into 360º panoramas in post-processing.[2] The tripod head allows for manual movement of the camera in precise increments around a central base so as to ensure coverage of the entire 360º space. These images document the current interior and exterior appearance of these medieval structures and allow viewers to understand the location of liturgical objects and both historical and contemporary artworks within the space. For example, many of the churches bear witness to the English custom of displaying poppies in commemoration of World War I during the month of November **[fig. 2].** The photographs also record other dimensions of community engagement with the edifices, including children's artworks, book and craft sales, and other assorted ephemera of the daily life of the congregation.

The purpose of these photographs was to support Cameron and Bernstein's research into the medieval use of these churches by their parishioners and clergy. The buildings selected all feature a transept, a north-south extension to

---

2 For post-processing we use Adobe CameraRaw, PTGui Pro, Adobe Photoshop, and Pano2vr. All photos are shot on a Sony a7rII camera with a wide-angle lens. Photographing in HDR (high definitive range) allows for capture of the full range of light and dark tones available within the architectural space.

Figure 1: Parish church of St. Mary, Sutterton (Lincolnshire), drone image. Photograph: Emily C. Floyd.

Figure 2: Parish church of St. Mary, Sutterton (Lincolnshire), nave and south arcade facing southwest, with Remembrance Day poppies. Screenshot of MAVCOR site. Original photograph: Emily C. Floyd.

a church building that makes its ground-plan cruciform, mirroring the central symbol of Christianity. Transepts are common in cathedrals and large monasteries. However, within the context of smaller parish churches, they are a rarity.

Scholars frequently assume that, before the development of the parish system of pastoral care, parish churches with transepts were minsters, large churches housing a community of clerics who went out to rural villages to say Mass and administer sacraments. We selected this particular group of churches in Lincolnshire because they are located in a small, defined area and all include (or included) transepts, yet we know they could not have all been minsters.[3] These sites suit the purview of the MAVCOR Digital Spaces Project because the 360º images enable a view of all four major volumes of a cruciform church (the nave, chancel, and north and south transepts) when photographed from the crossing **[fig. 3]**. The 360º panoramas also allow the viewer to compare the four different approaches to transeptal space.

Figure 3: Parish church of St. Mary, Sutterton (Lincolnshire), panoramic image photographed from the crossing. Photograph: Emily C. Floyd.

Visitors to the MAVCOR website are able to access a virtual tour of these images, uniting the Lincolnshire churches into a single experience. Viewers are able to shape their experience of the churches, choosing the order in which to view the images and lingering on certain features while ignoring others. Although visitors are inherently limited by the locations from which we chose to produce the photographs, we do not wish to prescribe a single viewing experience, but rather

---

3 By the twelfth century when at least three of these churches were probably built, the minster system was defunct. Two of these churches may have served as minsters, but the marshy Fens where the Lincolnshire churches were built were not drained until the mid-twelfth century and thus the ground did not allow for construction.

allow users to navigate diverse routes through these spaces led by individual interest or curiosity. This content was not specifically produced for devotional use, but we allow for the possibility that visitors may experience these tours within that framework.

4.2 Historical Context: Medieval proxy pilgrimage

Early modern and medieval proxy pilgrimages typically took one of two different approaches. They are either texts, often illustrated, which guide the reader in a mental journey to otherwise inaccessible holy sites, or they are physical structures that, while not necessarily reconstructing the optical appearance of the original buildings they "reproduce," allowed for a sensory, tactile, and embodied experience of pilgrimage in a location more geographically convenient for the individual participant. The MAVCOR Digital Spaces Project parallels these proxy pilgrimages in that they all grant access to holy sites in a manner more geographically accessible to their viewers. The Digital Spaces Project also parallels these proxy pilgrimages insofar as by their very nature their creators were forced to choose which aspect of the original experience to prioritize as essential, and which dimensions to elide or eclipse. As with MAVCOR's photographic reproductions, the form of early modern proxy pilgrimages, be it textual or architectural, prescribed certain ways of interacting with the holy sites, and limited others.

Textual proxy pilgrimages, in a mode reminiscent of the early modern prayer movement *devotio moderna*, frequently employed rich description in order to encourage readers and listeners to develop mental sensescapes, using the imagination to transport them to distant lands.[4] Francesco Suriano's early-sixteenth-century *Treatise on the Holy Land* is an example of such a text. Suriano was a Venetian Franciscan friar who was the sometimes head of the Custodia Terrae Sanctae in the Holy Land.[5] He wrote his *Treatise on the Holy Land* at the request

---

4 On devotio moderna, see for example John Van Engen, *Sisters and Brothers of the Common Life: The Devotio Moderna and the World of the Later Middle Ages* (Philadelphia: University of Pennsylvania Press, 2013). For more on religion and the senses, see Sally M. Promey, ed. *Sensational Religion: Sensory Cultures in Material Practice* (New Haven: Yale University Press, 2014).
5 Leigh Ann Craig, *Wandering Women and Holy Matrons: Women as Pilgrims in the Later Middle Ages* (Leiden: Brill, 2009), 243–244; Tsafra Siew, "Translations of the Jerusalem Pilgrimage Route at the Holy Mountains of Varallo and San Vivaldo," in *Between Jerusalem and Europe*, ed. Renana Bartal and Hanna Vorhold (Leiden: Brill, 2015), 113.

of his sister, a cloistered Franciscan nun in Perugia, so that she and her community could reap the spiritual benefits of a journey to the Holy Land from within their convent.[6] The treatise lists the significance of the various shrines frequented by pilgrims and the indulgences each offers to its visitors. It overflows with sensory accounts of Suriano's own experiences in Palestine. Suriano's text is filtered through an imaginary dialogue with his sister, Sixta, who asks questions about each of the sites.

The author seems acutely aware that his experience in the Holy Land is not one to which his cloistered sister and her fellow nuns would ever have direct access. Suriano framed Sixta as a devoutly curious nun who requested "detailed information about each step of the pilgrims' route, including details about churches, relics, geography, and peoples."[7] Historian Leigh Ann Craig argues that the "love of seemingly irrelevant pragmatic detail was intended for the nuns' benefit, not as invitation or direction, but as meditative aid."[8] That is to say, Suriano's text was not intended as a guide for physical travel, but as a prompt for mental imagination. Details, including the cost of pilgrimage and the physical fabric of various churches, evoke a vivid reading experience. Because Suriano's intended audience was never expected nor intended to corporeally visit the Holy Land, he imbues the text with sensory metaphors to aid the nuns' comprehension of what he describes, and to enhance the spiritual journey that relies on the imagination to succeed. At one point, Suriano writes:

> I wish you to know that the great sanctity of Christ and its fragrance and odor, with which all of the region is redolent, has increased and multiplied, not only in the primitive church, but also at the present time it is diffused throughout the world, so that it never ceases to attract itself to men and women.[9]

Suriano may have intended this level of evocative sensorial detail to craft a spiritually edifying experience for the nuns, and hoped that a mental pilgrimage could be a reasonable substitute for the actual event. In his *Treatise,* the limitations of the textual format encourage its author to focus on just those aspects most difficult to access via proxy: the scents, sounds, tastes, tactile elements, as well as visual descriptions, within which pilgrims who traveled physically to the Holy Land would be immersed. As we will discuss, the non-visual dimen-

---

6 Craig, *Wandering Women and Holy Matrons*, 244.
7 Craig, *Wandering Women and Holy Matrons*, 245.
8 Craig, *Wandering Women and Holy Matrons*, 252.
9 Francesco Suriano, *Treatise on the Holy Land*, trans. Theophilus Bellorini and Eugene Hoade (Jerusalem: Franciscan Printing Press, 1949), 29.

Figure 4: Sacred Mountain of Varallo, chapels. (Flickr marcofluens, CC BY 2.0) https://www.flickr.com/photos/marcofluens/5014327504.

sions of distant sites, described so evocatively by Suriano, are precisely the sensorial experiences lost to viewers of the Digital Spaces Project. As is so often the case with virtual reality, our digital recreations privilege the visual over the other senses.

If Suriano's *Treatise* emphasized rich sensorial detail for nuns who would never leave the walls of their convent, other early modern proxy pilgrimages took a more physical approach to immersing visitors within the sensory experience of the distant Holy Land, creating a substitute, more conveniently-located built environment in lieu of the churches and shrines of Jerusalem **[fig. 4]**. The Sacro Monte di Varallo, conceived of in 1481 by the Franciscan friar Bernardino Caimi, is the first of nine such "sacred mountains" in Italy. In an era when pilgrimage travel to the holy sites of Christianity in the Middle East was rendered impossible by the expense of the journey and the dangers travelers faced en route, the Franciscans sought to create a site for pilgrimage in Italy itself by imitating the sacred sites of the Holy Land. Fra Bernardino thus initiated the building of a New Jerusalem in Italy where religious people could go on a pilgrimage without the difficulties of traveling through hostile territories. On the mountain at Varallo, pilgrims stopped at sites inspired by the actual holy spots in Jerusalem, which were constituted of small chapels furnished with artistic representations. These representations became increasingly elaborate over time, ultimately including polychromed sculptures arranged in elaborate vignettes of biblical events. The chapels were intentionally spaced in a way that replicated the distance between the actual pilgrimage stops in Jerusalem. Unlike a textual account, Varallo allowed for more choice on the part of the visitor as to how they might circumambulate, where to linger and for how long, and from which angle to experience the chapels. Like the holder of the mouse navigating the Digital Spaces Project images and choosing where to pause and what to examine, the Varallo pilgrim was freed from the linear narrative that characterized Suriano's text.

Though the Italian sites do not bear direct resemblance to their prototypes, they meet the criteria of the copy as laid out by Richard Krautheimer in "Introduction to an 'Iconography of Medieval Architecture.'" In this article, Krautheimer discusses a class of centrally-planned medieval buildings that declare themselves to be imitations of the Holy Sepulchre. These buildings vary substantially in appearance among themselves and differ significantly from the dimensions and actual floor plan of the prototype. Krautheimer addresses the formal differences between copy and prototype in relation to their declared mimetic qualities, noting that "the only justifiable conclusion seems to be that the medieval conception of what makes one edifice comparable to another was different from our own."[10] Few characteristics link the four imitative edifices presented by Krautheimer as examples (which range from the ninth through twelfth centuries) together save for a round or octagonal shape. Though there are some similarities between the five structures, he argues that they "seem to be rather vague to the modern eye."[11] Similarly, to the modern eye the structures at Varallo may lack clear linkages to the originals in Palestine. For early modern viewers, particularly given the fact that most would never see the originals in person, the buildings at Varallo were *plausibly* similar to their prototypes, in the same way that the buildings described by Krautheimer were capable of evoking the Holy Sepulchre without precisely reproducing its exact forms. Jonathan Z. Smith has referred to these kinds of connections between structures as "relations of equivalence" resulting from the confluence of ritual and architecture.[12] As we will demonstrate below, similar relations of equivalence arguably underly the Digital Spaces Project images.

---

10 Richard Krautheimer, "Introduction to an 'Iconography of Mediaeval Architecture,'" *Journal of the Warburg and Courtauld Institutes* 5 (1942): 3.
11 Krautheimer, "Introduction," 5.
12 Jonathan Z. Smith, *To Take Place: Toward Theory in Ritual* (Chicago: University of Chicago Press, 1987), 86–87.

There is nothing intrinsically holy about Varallo or other early modern Italian sacred mountains; the site borrowed meaning from elsewhere (in this case, Jerusalem), and applied onto a more accessible landscape. The illusions were apparently successful perhaps due to early modern understandings of relations of equivalence as alluded to by Smith and Krautheimer. Giralamo Morone, a learned pilgrim who visited the site in 1507, wildly praised the site. He writes:

> I was met by a priest, a leader of [the Franciscan order], a man both religious and most experienced with the site where the body of Jesus was actually buried. Leading me across neighboring hills—one moment by climbing, the next moment with an easy descent—he brought me into individual chapels in which images are exhibited, just as the mysteries of the passion of the Lord are narrated in successive order in the gospel and just as it is related that Christ himself was taken to many places among many people and endured diverse humiliations and torments. And he kept assuring me that all these things have been made like the place of the real Sepulchre with the same proportions, the same architecture, and with the same paintings and shapes. Truly, my Lancino, I have never seen anything more religious, more devout. I have never seen anything that could pierce the heart more, which could compel one to neglect everything else and follow Christ alone. This new and pious work repeats everything, and by the very simplicity of the craft and the artless architecture, the ingenious site surpasses all antiquity.[13]

This letter provides some indication of the impact Varallo had on at least some of the people who visited it. In it, Giralamo describes the experience as mediated by a knowledgeable friar who interpreted the chapels in a set order structured according to the chronology of Christ's final days and Passion. This experience moved the Giralamo, who mentioned having "never seen anything more religious, more devout." He also refers to the "simplicity of the craft" and the "artless architecture," indicating that he found the setting to be authentic to reality rather than the product of artifice. Although the letter seems to imply he had not visited the holy sites of Palestine, he writes that the site "surpasses all antiquity." From his perspective, in fact, Varallo is preferable to the real thing, perhaps because it allowed for a more focused piety.

It may have been that Giralamo felt more comfortable within the cultural context of Varallo, unconfronted by the diversity of ethnicities and religious traditions that characterized Jerusalem in his time.[14] Annabel Wharton has de-

13 Girolamo Morone, "Lettre Ed Orazioni Latine Di Girolamo Morone," in Miscellanea Di Storia Italiano, ed. Giuseppe Müller, vol. 2 (Turin: Stamperia Reale, 1863), translation by Annabel Jane Wharton, see *Selling Jerusalem: Relics, Replicas, Theme Parks* (Chicago: University of Chicago Press, 2006), 97–98.
14 On this, see for example Palmira Brummett, *The 'Book' of Travels: Genre, Ethnology, and Pilgrimage, 1250–1700* (Leiden: Brill, 2009), 18–19.

scribed the architecture at Varallo as "a particular historical mix of the Herodian, Franciscan, and Mamluk."[15] As she notes, however, "its living occupants were exclusively pious Christians."[16] Caimi designed the buildings at Varallo incorporating a range of architectural traditions drawn from his knowledge of Jerusalem. The visitors to the site, however, were substantially less diverse. In Palestine, the presence of non-Western, non-Christian subjects could complicate the pilgrim's singular focus on the life of (an apparently fair-skinned European) Christ; many pilgrim accounts narrating journeys to Jerusalem describe Islam and Muslims and, to a lesser extent, Jews and Judaism with derision and even repugnance.[17] At Varallo, no such disambiguation occurred.

Of course, in spite of the apparent feeling of authenticity provided by Varallo, early modern devout Christians still valued experience of the genuine place. Giralamo explicitly notes that his Franciscan guide had spent significant time in Jerusalem, thus privileging it over the copy. Varallo was, after all, an imitation of a holy site, and its mere existence was predicated on the sanctity of Jerusalem. The Varallo pilgrim could not claim to have literally walked in Jesus' footsteps. The sensory experiences would be unavoidably distinct between these two geographically distant locales with corresponding differences in climate, populace, and cuisine. Varallo was a locus for the fulfillment of European desires for a homogeneously Christian holy land, familiar yet sacred, but it still relied on the existence of the original site for its authority. As with the Digital Spaces Project photos, the experience of the copy may be perceived as authentic and satisfying, but the existence of the copy never fully eclipses the power and authority of the original.

4.3 Pixels and pilgrimage

None of the sites photographed in Lincolnshire are cult sites for pilgrimage. Instead, these five churches were and continue to be parish churches, which is to say gathering spaces for local communities to engage in religious worship. Both today and historically these churches permit outside visitors to enter, worship, and explore the space; in the twenty-first century, some of these churches have applied for and received government funding to provide heritage-based historic interpretation for visitors. These churches did not, however, originally func-

---

15 Wharton, *Selling Jerusalem*, 105.
16 Wharton, *Selling Jerusalem*, 105.
17 See Nicole Chareyron and W. Donald Wilson, *Pilgrims to Jerusalem in the Middle Ages* (New York: Columbia University Press, 2005), especially pages 111–126.

tion as outwardly directed spaces, aiming to attract pilgrims, nor did they promise the kinds of spiritual benefits available at pilgrimage sites, such as plenary indulgences or access to famous saints' relics. Nonetheless, MAVCOR's Digital Spaces Project parallels the medieval creation of physical and textual aids to virtual pilgrimage by enabling the non-physical experience of religious sites. These two kinds of experiences raise similar questions about authenticity, potential spiritual benefits, and relationship of reproduction to original.

A common response of first-time viewers of the Digital Spaces Project is to remark on the realism of the images, voicing a sensation of being transported to the represented space: "It's just like I'm there!" This response mirrors Giralamo's effusive description of the perceived authenticity and veracity of his experience at Varallo. Indeed, this seems to be a common response to a variety of forms of "virtual" tours, spaces, or visits. Perhaps one of the best examples of this is the series of hyperreal giga-pixel panoramas of spaces within the Vatican, notably of the Sistine Chapel, produced by Villanova University's Computer Science and Communications departments' internship program in collaboration with the Vatican. As Frank Klassner, one of the project leaders, explained to Floyd, the Villanova project used a telephoto lens and electronic gigapan mount to take the thousands of individual photographs of each Vatican space over the course multiple days prior to stitching them together in post-processing.[18] The result is an unprecedented degree of detail and precision that allows the viewer to feel immersed in the reproduced spaces while simultaneously conveying a sense of wonder and awe at the sharpness and clarity of both detail and light, and remarkable emptiness of this usually bustling room, crowded with tourists. The Vatican giga-pixel panoramas grant a viewing experience impossible outside of the virtual realm. When physically present in the chapel in Rome, our eyes enable us to focus only on small areas of detail at a time, and certainly cannot zoom in to see Michelangelo's brushstrokes on the ceiling. Within the giga images all information is equally clear and simultaneously accessible, projecting on the screen a more perfect image than the human eye is capable of. Delight in artifice seems to be a powerful reason for enjoying a virtual experience.

Alison Griffiths has explored alternate forms of spectatorship (beyond the passive spectatorship of the cinema viewer) within the frame of what she terms "immersive" experiences. She writes, "I use the term immersion ... to explain the sensation of entering a space that immediately identifies itself as somehow separate from the world and that eschews conventional modes of spectatorship in favor of a more bodily participation in the experience, including allowing the spectator to

---

18 Personal communication, 28 October 2016.

move freely around the viewing space (although this is not a requirement)."[19] She includes here the architectural space of medieval cathedrals, nineteenth-century panoramic viewing experiences, iMAX, and modern museums, but this same framework might fruitfully be applied to early modern proxy pilgrimages and to the panoramas of the MAVCOR Digital Spaces Project. Griffiths writes, "A defining characteristic … [of these experiences] is the sense of being present in a scene, the cognitive dissonance that comes from feeling like you're elsewhere while knowing that you haven't moved and forgetting for a moment about the mediating effects of the technology."[20]

The immersive feeling of the Digital Spaces Project panoramas is the result of a combination of techniques that the project shares with earlier "lower tech" approaches to panoramic viewing. As Griffiths describes, in the nineteenth century, specially constructed viewing platforms for observing massive panoramic paintings created the uncanny sensation of being spontaneously transported geographically and temporally to distant lands and historical moments. The MAVCOR photographs function around a similar principle: in creating composite images that allow the viewer to rotate 360º within the photographed space, the viewer gains the sensation of being surrounded by and immersed within the reproduced building. The high resolution at which MAVCOR produces these images helps contribute to this feeling of presence within the building as the sharpness of detail and seemingly precise capture of the range of light and dark lend a sense of heightened realism. Depending on the size of the screen on which the panoramas are viewed, and particularly with the use of Virtual Reality glasses, the represented space can fill and come to dominate the field of vision. In contrast, for users observing the panoramas on the reduced screen of their smartphones, the sensation can be one of holding the interior space of a building within the palm of the hand.

If the images of the MAVCOR Digital Spaces Project have the potential to immerse the viewer within the photographed religious building, how might this sensation of immersion impact the devout viewer witnessing such a reproduction? Early modern visitors to Varallo could expect to receive concrete spiritual blessings in the form of indulgences as well as the sense of visiting Jerusalem by proxy. In contrast, the conventual readers of Suriano's treatise likely did not receive the indulgences available at the shrines of the Holy Land simply by envisioning the shrines in their meditation on Suriano's descriptions. This

---

19 Alison Griffiths, *Shivers Down Your Spine: Cinema, Museums, and the Immersive View* (New York: Columbia University Press, 2008), 1.
20 Griffiths, *Shivers Down Your Spine*, 4.

is not to say that the nuns did not benefit from their practices, but they did so in an unofficial rather than an officially sanctioned manner. The virtual experience of religious spaces similarly need not be approved by members of the religious hierarchy in order to shape a valid encounter for the devout individual.

Indeed, the internet has become a central space for proxy religious experiences, often of spaces geographically distant to the devotee. As early as 2002 Mark W. MacWilliams documented the presence of diverse forms of virtual pilgrimage on the internet. As he punningly noted, the internet had become home to many "sacred 'sites.'"[21] In the little over a decade and a half since MacWilliams's article, religion on the internet has only increased in volume and diversity. In 2016, for example, the *New York Times*'s Virtual Reality Project, in collaboration with the photographer Luca Locatelli, produced a virtual reality film of the photographer's pilgrimage to Mecca and Medina.[22] Some Hindu temples offer livestreams of cult objects for religious adherents to practice *darshan*, the ritual relationship of "seeing and being seen by" a holy person or image; some religious practitioners report using these strategies in addition to weekly devotion at a physical temple.[23] Adarsh Mitra Mandal, co-founder of universalganesha.com notes that one of the motivations for launching the website was "to make Ganesh darshan possible for the handicapped and old citizens."[24] The reasons cited by Mandal accord with the motivations for medieval and early modern people who took advantage of alternative pilgrimage opportunities: logistical or physical ability may have been impediments for making the journey to Jerusalem, rendering other options desirable. Some Hindu websites and cellphone content companies even offer virtual pilgrimage experiences, which may rely on maps, photographs, and/or videos to grant the viewer access to the distant holy location.[25]

---

21 Mark W. MacWilliams, "Virtual Pilgrimages on the Internet," *Religion* 32 (2002): 316.

22 "Pilgrimage: A 21st-Century Journey to Mecca and Medina," *The New York Times*, July 21, 2016, https://www.nytimes.com/2016/07/22/world/middleeast/pilgrimage-virtual-reality-in-mecca-and-medina.html.

23 Phyllis K. Herman, "Seeing the Divine Through Windows: Online Darshan and Virtual Religious Experience," *Heidelberg Journal of Religions on the Internet* 4, no. 1 (2010): 157. For more information on darshan, see Diana L. Eck, *Darśan: Seeing the Divine Image in India*, 3rd edition (New York: Columbia University Press, 1998). See also Lawrence Babb, "Glancing: Visual Interaction in Hinduism," *Journal of Anthropological Research* 37, no. 4 (1991): 387–401.

24 Shweta Nair, "How about a Virtual Darshan?," *Femina* (blog), September 21, 2012, https://www.femina.in/lifestyle/in-the-news/how-about-a-virtual-darshan-528.html.

25 Natalie R. Marsh, "Online Puja, Digital Darshan, and Virtual Pilgrimage: Hindu Image and Ritual," Dissertation, The Ohio State University, 2007, 34.

These Hindu virtual religious experiences come in a variety of forms, created by a range of individuals, and possessing varying degrees of official credentials —some digital darshan sites are produced by the temples that house the corresponding cult images, other virtual Hindu religious projects are produced by private individuals. Virtual proxy pilgrimage has in some instances been affiliated with highest of religious authorities. The Vatican was engaged with virtual pilgrimage relying on reproduced imagery at the turn of the twenty-first century. As MacWilliams describes, in 2000, Pope John Paul II made a pilgrimage to the Holy Land. The pope had hoped to begin his pilgrimage at the ancient city of Ur in present day Iraq, which is believed to be the birthplace of Abraham, but then-Iraqi president Sadaam Hussein refused to grant the required permission. Rather than give up and begin the pilgrimage at the second site in Egypt, the pope conducted a virtual pilgrimage from the Vatican: a ceremony which relied on Middle East-inspired decor, a reproduction of a fifteenth-century Russian icon, incense, and a small screen on which images were projected (the same images were shown on a larger screen to Vatican visitors).[26]

As with fifteenth-century pilgrims for whom political tensions and safety concerns prevented pilgrimage to the Holy Land, the pope's virtual pilgrimage responded to the political imbroglios of the turn of the twenty-first century. To what extent, could such a virtual pilgrimage stand in for the physical journey? MacWilliams usefully establishes a number of ways in which virtual pilgrimage differs from the "real thing": it is instantaneous; it "takes place figuratively not literally"; and it is potentially discontinuous rather than inherently sequential as are physical pilgrimages.[27] MacWilliams goes on to address at length the question of *communitas,* the sense of shared humanity described by Victor and Edith Turner as one of the primary raisons d'être and results of physical pilgrimage.[28] As MacWilliams points out, the centrality of communitas to physical pilgrimage has been challenged by numerous scholars, nonetheless, the experiences of virtual vs. physical pilgrimage are fundamentally divergent in the nature of the embodied experience of the pilgrim: both as far as movement and sensory stimuli are concerned and in terms of interaction with other pilgrims.[29]

---

26 Alessandra Stanley, "Pope Makes Virtual Visit To Iraqi Site He Must Skip," *The New York Times*, February 24, 2000, National edition, sec. A, https://www.nytimes.com/2000/02/24/world/pope-makes-virtual-visit-to-iraqi-site-he-must-skip.html; MacWilliams, "Virtual Pilgrimages on the Internet," 319–320.
27 MacWilliams, "Virtual Pilgrimages," 326.
28 MacWilliams, "Virtual Pilgrimages," 326. See also Victor W. Turner and Edith L. B. Turner, *Image and Pilgrimage in Christian Culture* (New York: Columbia University Press, 2011).
29 MacWilliams, "Virtual Pilgrimages," 327–328.

We have already discussed Giralamo's experience of Varallo and the possible benefit of visiting the Sacro Monti versus journeying to Palestine as represented by Varallo's homogenous and familiar cultural milieu. Early modern proxy pilgrimage allowed for a certain control over the experience and mitigation of potentially unpleasant or unexpected dimensions of the contemporary reality in Jerusalem. This kind of proxy pilgrimage nonetheless still allowed for physical exertion and bodily movement within the substitute holy space. In contrast, virtual religious experiences like that of the nuns reading Suriano's text or those of potential devout viewers of the Digital Spaces Project, engage the body and the senses in a very different manner.

The average viewer of the Digital Spaces Project panoramas is seated before a computer screen or smartphone, using a mouse, keyboard, or finger on a touchscreen to change the position of the panorama. The body is more static than would be required to actually visit one of the Lincolnshire churches, and the panoramas privilege the experience of the eye, unable to convey, for example, the profound chill and damp that pervaded the stone buildings in November when we took the photographs. The majority of Digital Spaces Project viewers are also likely observing the panoramas in solitude, or at least this is the imagined experience generally envisioned of internet users. If nothing else, the Digital Spaces Project allows for a kind of isolated, individual experience of religious spaces that is unusual when physically present in such locations. This experience is enhanced by the exclusion of human figures within the Digital Spaces Project images, an effect produced by deliberately avoiding photographing visitors, community members, worshippers, and members of the photography team who were present at the moment of the photography. This is a choice made in order to limit distracting elements in the photographs and enable the best possible view of the space. The Digital Spaces Project is generally more concerned with religious architecture, liturgical furnishing, and decorative ornament, than with human presence. Furthermore, by avoiding including people in the photographs, we endeavor to respect the privacy and personal spiritual experiences of individuals who might prefer to retain their anonymity.

4.4 Devout Viewers and the Digital Spaces Project

As we have established, the initial intent of the Digital Spaces Project photography was not primarily to create virtual religious experiences for a devout audience but rather to further scholarly inquiry into material religion. Users are not precluded from viewing Digital Spaces Project images from a devotional perspective, however, and it is possible that pious viewers may find these images useful to their devotional practices. Such devotional use of the Digital Spaces Project images would presumably exist as an extension of existing religious or meditative practices, rather than as part of an emergent one. Heidi A. Campbell's formulation of "digital religion" characterizes a blend of online and offline religious spheres. She writes: "This merging of new and established notions of religious practice means digital religion is imprinted by both the traits of online culture (such as interactivity, convergence, and audience-generated content) and traditional religion (such as patterns of belief and ritual tied to historically grounded communities."[30]

What is the relationship between the MAVCOR Digital Spaces Project and the church communities whose buildings have been photographed? In most cases, it was not necessary to gain explicit permission to photograph in the Lincolnshire churches. Some of them are open for public visitors on a daily basis. Others are kept locked due to fear of theft or vandalism, and thus require the assistance of a keyholder to open the buildings. In the open churches, we often met members of the parish or clergy within the buildings; in general, these people ranged from mildly curious to enthusiastic about our project, and were pleased to share a cup of tea and their knowledge about the building and its community. Some were eager to take us up on an offer to share the high-quality images with them.

Although we shared the Lincolnshire photographs with some of the parishioners, we have little knowledge as to how they ultimately used them, and it is challenging to prove whether or not they may have engaged with the panoramas as displayed on the MAVCOR site. In contrast, we do have some information about the use of an earlier group of churches included in the Digital Spaces Project, photographed for MAVCOR by photographer Raúl Montero Quispe in the area around Cuzco, Peru in collaboration with the Society of Jesus in Cuzco. These seven churches are all rural parish churches built in the colonial period (sixteenth-early-nineteenth centuries) for indigenous villages, with a single exception, the principal Jesuit church of Cuzco, called La Compañía. To photograph the rural churches, Montero, Floyd, and Montero's assistants drove into the countryside around Cuzco, sometimes traveling for several hours through steep mountains, before reaching small towns where the *ecónomos* (churchwar-

---

30 Heidi A. Campbell, "Introduction: The Rise of the Study of Digital Religion," in *Digital Religion: Understanding Religious Practice in New Media Worlds*, ed. Heidi A. Campbell (London: Routledge, 2013), 4.

dens) awaited us, unlocking the buildings and allowing us to enter and take the photographs.

The Peruvian parish churches, like the Lincolnshire churches, are actively used by their communities as places for prayer and worship. Even as we photographed, parishioners entered to pray the rosary and light candles before holy images; while we were photographing inside the church of Marcapata, perched at the skirts of the Mt. Ausangate at the edge of the Amazon rainforest, funeral bells began to toll and a funerary procession wound its way around the church towards the cemetery at the back. Traces of the ongoing devotional practices of Peruvian parishioners appear in the Digital Spaces Project photographs taken by Montero. Frozen flames of votive candles, caught flickering before images of the Virgin, Christ, and the saints, gleam in the panoramas; flowers stand in vases on altars; linens embroidered with the date they were donated drape over tables [fig. 5].

Figure 5: Candles before a side altar at the Church of San Pablo de Ocongate, Peru. Screenshot of MAVCOR site. Original photograph: Raúl Montero Quispe.

Having finalized the photography and completed the post processing, Montero sent the panoramas to MAVCOR where Floyd added them to the Digital Spaces Project of the site. Montero and Floyd also shared the photographs with the Cusco Jesuits who had facilitated the photography. We also wanted to share the photographs with the communities who worshipped in the documented churches and so, on the recommendation of Montero, Floyd launched a Facebook page for MAVCOR on which she posted links to some of the Digital Spaces

Project images. The warmth and enthusiasm of Spanish-language commentators on these posts frequently reflected national pride or aesthetic admiration, but in some cases went beyond these sentiments. Williams Baca wrote, for example, "A beautiful gift ... now I view it daily and I am delighted by so much art in our beloved land."[31] Others shared fond childhood memories of visiting a particular church. None of these comments explicitly expressed religious sentiments, but instead, in ruminating on their experiences of viewing the photographs, tended to reveal a nationalistic identification with the religious heritage of Peru.

Although we have generally envisioned the potential religious viewer of the Digital Spaces Project images as a single devout individual engaged in pious meditation, the kind of communal identity as expressed by Spanish-language viewers on the MAVCOR website parallels the local pride of Lincolnshire church parishioners who opened the doors of churches for us and welcomed us and our cameras. Religious identity as a locus for the creation of community may be what is best expressed in the Digital Spaces Project images. Community members, be they in rural England or rural Peru, seem to appreciate when their homes and places of worship are recognized as sites of art historical and cultural interest. These images then become opportunities for celebration of local and regional identities as embodied in religious cultural heritage sites.

4.5 Conclusion

In our twenty-first-century pursuit of the new and the innovative, at times we neglect to recognize the historical trajectories that undergird our current reality. Virtual records like the Digital Spaces Project present experiences that seem inherently new. Their detailed, high-resolution photographic capture of architecture creates a sense of immersion within the virtual space that simultaneously diverges from prior virtual experiences and builds on them. The digital virtual experience is, nonetheless, in many ways a continuation of earlier proxy approaches to accessing distant spaces. Considering those proxy experiences can help us understand the appeal and function of these new ways of acquiring virtual access.

Historical practices of proxy pilgrimage to Palestine relied on a range of descriptive and physical tools to evoke the absent geography of the holy land in ways that were sensorily rich and compelling for contemporaneous individuals. They granted access to these distant spaces to devout participants who would

---

31 "Excelente regalo mi querido Rubén, ahora la veo diariamente y me deleito con tanto arte en nuestra querida tierra."

have been otherwise unable to experience them. The ways in which viewers responded both to these early modern proxy experiences and to more recent online virtual religious spaces demonstrates the diverse ways in which people recognize authenticity in reproduction—not depending solely on perfect digital capture, but also on more intangible factors such as the pope's use of incense, icon, and Middle Eastern decor to evoke the city of Ur.

As we have established over the course of this essay, the primary purpose of the Digital Spaces Project is not to offer virtual religious experiences, but in documenting religious spaces we are aware such a possibility exists. Thus, the panoramas we have created offer devout viewers access to spaces that may carry a religious charge. We hope that the photographs we have produced allow for devotional as well as academic interaction in a way that is respectful and ethical. As we and other scholars move forward into the digital in support of our research we believe it is important to consider the diverse ways in which viewers may engage with the work we produce, and to acknowledge the rich historical grounding in which such projects are based.

References

Babb, Lawrence. "Glancing: Visual Interaction in Hinduism." *Journal of Anthropological Research* 37, no. 4 (1991): 387–401.

Brummett, Palmira. *The 'Book' of Travels: Genre, Ethnology, and Pilgrimage, 1250–1700.* Leiden: Brill, 2009.

Campbell, Heidi A., "Introduction: The Rise of the Study of Digital Religion," in *Digital Religion: Understanding Religious Practice in New Media Worlds*, ed. Heidi A. Campbell. London: Routledge, 2013.

Craig, Leigh Ann. *Wandering Women and Holy Matrons: Women as Pilgrims in the Later Middle Ages.* Leiden: Brill, 2009.

Chareyron, Nicole and W. Donald Wilson. *Pilgrims to Jerusalem in the Middle Ages.* New York: Columbia University Press, 2005.

Eck, Diana L. *Darśan: Seeing the Divine Image in India*, 3rd edition. New York: Columbia University Press, 1998.

Gaposchkin, M. Cecilia. *Invisible Weapons: Liturgy and the Making of Crusade Ideology.* Ithaca: Cornell University Press, 2017.

Griffiths, Alison. *Shivers Down Your Spine: Cinema, Museums, and the Immersive View.* New York: Columbia University Press, 2008.

Phyllis K. Herman, "Seeing the Divine Through Windows: Online Darshan and Virtual Religious Experience," *Heidelberg Journal of Religions on the Internet* 4, no. 1 (2010): 151–178.

Krautheimer, Richard. "Introduction to an 'Iconography of Mediaeval Architecture." *Journal of the Warburg and Courtauld Institutes* 5 (1942). 1–33.

Leatherbarrow, David. "The image and its setting: A study of the Sacro Monte at Varallo," *RES: Anthropology and Aesthetics* 14 (1987): 107–122.

MacWilliams, Mark W. "Virtual Pilgrimages on the Internet," *Religion* 32 (2002): 315–335.

Marsh, Natalie R. "Online Puja, Digital Darshan, and Virtual Pilgrimage: Hindu Image and Ritual," (PhD diss., The Ohio State University, 2007).

Morone, Girolamo "Lettre Ed Orazioni Latine Di Girolamo Morone," in *Miscellanea Di Storia Italiano*, ed. Giuseppe Müller, vol. 2 (Turin: Stamperia Reale, 1863).

Nair, Shweta. "How about a Virtual Darshan?," *Femina*, September 21, 2012, https://www.femina.in/lifestyle/in-the-news/how-about-a-virtual-darshan-528.html.

"Pilgrimage: A 21st-Century Journey to Mecca and Medina," *The New York Times*, July 21, 2016, https://www.nytimes.com/2016/07/22/world/middleeast/pilgrimage-virtual-reality-in-mecca-and-medina.html.

Sally M. Promey, ed. *Sensational Religion: Sensory Cultures in Material Practice*. New Haven: Yale University Press, 2014.

Siew, Tsafra. "Translations of the Jerusalem Pilgrimage Route at the Holy Mountains of Varallo and San Vivaldo," in *Between Jerusalem and Europe*, ed. Renana Bartal and Hanna Vorholt. Leiden: Brill, 2015.

Smith, Jonathan Z. *To Take Place: Toward Theory in Ritual*. Chicago: University of Chicago Press, 1987.

Stanley, Alessandra. "Pope Makes Virtual Visit To Iraqi Site He Must Skip," *The New York Times*, February 24, 2000, National edition, sec. A, https://www.nytimes.com/2000/02/24/world/pope-makes-virtual-visit-to-iraqi-site-he-must-skip.html.

Suriano, Francesco. *Treatise on the Holy Land*. Translated by Theophilus Bellorini and Eugene Hoade. Jerusalem: Franciscan Printing Press, 1949.

Turner, Victor W. and Edith L. B. Turner. *Image and Pilgrimage in Christian Culture*. New York: Columbia University Press, 2011.

Van Engen, John. *Sisters and Brothers of the Common Life: The Devotio Moderna and the World of the Later Middle Ages*. Philadelphia: University of Pennsylvania Press, 2013.

Wharton, Annabel Jane. *Selling Jerusalem: Relics, Replicas, Theme Parks*. Chicago: University of Chicago Press, 2006.

Urmila Mohan
Chapter 5
Balinese Religio-cultural Imaginaries and Rituals of Digital Materiality

5.1 Introduction

Bali is the only Hindu island in the predominantly Islamic nation of Indonesia, and its religious customs and beliefs have been of much interest to scholars and artists over the twentieth and twenty-first centuries[1]. The great extent to which Bali has fascinated the West has led to the island being called the "imaginary museum"[2]. In studying the island, we find ourselves unpacking images of a tropical paradise long mediated by Dutch colonial agents, tourists, artists, and anthropologists[3]. Further, these imaginaries are affected by tourism *(Bahasa Indonesia: pariwisata)*, supported initially by Dutch colonial policies, and, later, by the Indonesian Republic, as well as the accompanying creation of Balinese 'heritage' as the object of cultural tourism. Indeed, the idea of Balinese culture as a "timeless, harmonious synthesis of religion, custom and art"[4] is testimony to the work done by religio-cultural imaginaries—co-produced by foreigners and Balinese—for nearly a century.

Bali's culture draws from a mixture of Javanese, Indic and Chinese influences as well as strong underlying beliefs in animism, common to other parts of the archipelago. It is believed that the island is inhabited by spirits who have lived there from the earliest times, and most of the Balinese I interacted with perceived negative incidents in their daily lives as either immanent spirit activity or the effects of black magic *(ilmu hitam)*. They searched for underlying causes and solutions for their problems in the intangible, spirit world *(niskala)* as well as

---

1 James Boon, *The Anthropological Romance of Bali, 1597–1972: Dynamic Perspectives in Marriage and Caste, Politics and Religion* (Cambridge: Cambridge University Press, 1977).
2 Michael Hitchcock and Lucy Norris, *Bali, the Imaginary Museum: The Photographs of Walter Spies and Beryl de Zoete* (Kuala Lumpur: Oxford University Press. 1995). For Bali's importance in exhibits curated by anthropologists Margaret Mead and Gregory Bateson, see Urmila Mohan, "The Indonesian Alcove at the American Museum of Natural History: Art, Culture Areas and the Mead-Bateson Bali Project," *Museum Anthropology* 44.1–2 (2021): 11–23.
3 Adrian Vickers, *Bali: A Paradise Created* (Ringwood: Penguin, 1989/2009), 4–9.
4 Mark Hobart, "Bali is a Battlefield: Or the Triumph of the Imaginary over Actuality," *Jurnal Kajian Bali* 7 (2017): 187.

https://doi.org/10.1515/9783110608755-006

tangible, human world *(sekala)*. Propitiatory rituals and a calendrical cycle of ceremonies were, and still are, ways for them to access, connect and manipulate these realms.

Against this backdrop, this chapter explores several examples to understand how digital media is used in a culturally-specific manner to make images and imaginaries as part of Balinese heritage and identity. How do some Balinese—in contexts ranging from ethnographic studies in the 1930s to contemporary re-enactments of colonial photographs—use digital media to create imaginaries that help sustain beliefs in *niskala* and *sekala,* the push towards "Ajeg Bali"[5] or Balinese self-assertion, and notions of heritage? How does digital materiality as the intersection between the digital and visual/material, influence the social and cultural impetus to believe, act and think a certain way in order to be (perceived as) suitably 'Balinese'? What kinds of new rituals and practices are created in the process?

In discussing the historiographic production of the subject by narrative, the French philosopher Michel De Certeau[6] argued that the "believer" is more or less compelled to comply with the 'real' of institutionalized images through the efficacy of an 'imaginary' which is, in turn, created by practices, involving bodies and materials. By exploring digital media and images, this chapter proposes that Balinese imaginaries transform bodies, objects and ideas into something real for the faithful to coalesce around. The Real that is invoked in this case could range from the existence of invisible spirits to ideas of what constitutes heritage. In any case, in order to be perceived as an authentic and/or appropriate religio-cultural subject the Balinese believer has an obligation "to make certain gestures, to relate to certain substances and objects, and to experience certain perceptions and emotions."[7] Using De Certeau's idea of the imaginary as that which moves and shapes people towards a real, I will proceed to explore digital materiality as the transmedia flow of beliefs across the analog and virtual

---

5 *Ajeg Bali,* a term that arose in the early 2000s, refers to the politics of Balinese identity and power. For the various meanings of the term, see Allen and Palermo (2005).

6 See Michel De Certeau, *Histoire et psychoanalyse entre science et fiction* (Paris: Gallimard Press, 1987), 57, and Urmila Mohan and Jean-Pierre Warnier, "Editorial: Marching the Devotional Subject: The Bodily-and-Material Cultures of Religion," *Journal of Material Culture* 22 (2017): 373. In the original French: *'C'est toujours au nom d'un réel qu'on "fait marcher" des croyants et qu'on les produit.'* And in English, translated by Jean-Pierre Warnier: 'It is always in the name of something real that one can "march" the believers and produce them.' In this context, De Certeau writes about the compelling power of narratives in historiography to institute and not just document reality. He states that narrative inserts itself into the events of which it claims to be the interpreter, and all authority is based on the reality it is supposed to declare.

7 Mohan and Warnier, "Editorial: Marching the Devotional Subject," 378.

that relies on physical materials, images and actions. I distinguish the forms of these practices initially as rituals *around* digital media and rituals *for* digital media.

Digitization as a mode of representation is akin to a "social practice that intervenes in and changes the world it describes."[8] Representation "transforms what it purports to depict faithfully" by bridging or compressing "time, space and even entities."[9] Digital forms of photography and videography have become associated with ideas of progress and efficiency not only through new technological developments but also through ideas of connectivity, speed and improvement. In addition, devices, such as 'smart' phones, social networking sites, such as Instagram, and messaging applications, such as WhatsApp, may combine new technological, cognitive and affective "affordances"[10] with existing beliefs, practices and aesthetics of re-presentation to influence powerful religio-cultural imaginaries. The examples discussed in this chapter—drawn from ethnographic fieldwork conducted in 2018 in the "borderzone"[11] of Ubud, Bali—deal with usage of smart phones, social media and digital imagery. These examples position digital materiality as the transmedia physical and analytical movement between the analog and virtual, real and imaginary, and the tangible and intangible, bearing specific resonances for the study of religion.

5.2 Rituals *around* Digital Media

Beliefs in *niskala* have found their way into newer technological forms, ranging from films to, as we will see later in this section, phones and digital media.[12] The reach of communications technology is so wide that in 2016, around 70 per cent of the 55 million Indonesians who connected to the internet, did so via a mobile

---

8 Hobart, "Bali is a Battlefield," 200.

9 Edwin Jurriens and Ross Tapsell, "Challenges and Opportunities of the Digital 'Revolution' in Indonesia" in *Digital Indonesia: Connectivity and Divergence*, eds. Edwin Jurriens and Ross Tapsell (Singapore: ISEAS, 2017): 3–4.

10 See Donald Norman, *The Design of Everyday Things* (New York: Basic Books, 1988/2013), 145. Norman comes from a design perspective and defines affordance as a relationship—a combination of actual physical as well as perceived properties of an object. According to him, the interpretation of an affordance is a cultural convention.

11 Edward M. Bruner, *Culture on Tour: Ethnographies of Travel* (Chicago: University of Chicago Press, 2005), 18.

12 Adrian Vickers, "Sakti Reconsidered: Power and the Disenchantment of the World," in *Southeast Asian Perspectives on Power,* eds. Liana Chua et al. (London: Routledge, 2012), 51–66.

phone.[13] Within this framework, digital images, such as video and photography, are widely recorded, circulated and discussed. The smart phone, computer, printer and other digital (or digitally enhanced) devices are objects that through their very design and tangibility can be incorporated into religious materiality as part of annual ceremonies of purification and propitiation. For instance, the celebration of "Tumpak Landep" is the day when Balinese seek blessings for objects made out of metals, including iron *(besi)*. The term *Tumpak Landep* means "close to" and "sharp" in the ritual Javanese language, and the ceremony (always performed on a Saturday also known as *Tumpak*) is considered a means of sharpening one's thought processes. Previously, the properties of metal (strength, sharpness) would have been associated with daggers *(kris)* many of which were maintained as heirlooms and believed to carry spiritual power. Later, cars, bikes, machines and office equipment were added to the list of metal objects. Today, cash registers, telephones and any kind of business-related tool—paper punches in a binding store, for example—may also be blessed and have ceremonial offerings attached to them. Increasingly, the appliances being sanctified and propitiated have more plastic than metal[14] but when asked about the purpose of the ceremony, people continue to offer the analogy of metal's *(logam)* physical properties. As the logic of metal as a fundamental tool *(alat)* gets extended to include other materials, such as plastic, it incorporates desires for well-being and success, *Tumpak Landep* becomes a ceremony for 'digital' objects as part of a range of stuff *(barang)* vital to life and commerce.

In October 2018, I had the opportunity to observe *Tumpak Landep* ceremonies at a photo studio called "Laksamana," located on one of the many busy streets in Ubud. The morning started with a visit to the home of the owner, Wayan, who also ran a hotel and restaurant abutting the studio. In his home, Wayan showed me his collection of *kris*, performed a sanctification in his home shrine and then sprinkled a little holy water on the cameras, laptops, monitors, and keyboards that had been previously laid out on a table. Later he took me to the store, where family members had already gathered and a priest *(mangku)* was officiating (Figure 1), seated facing the auspicious direction of the sacred volcanic mountain Agung. Baskets of offerings had been piled high in front of the priest as well as being placed on the commercial-sized printers, lighting equipment, monitors and other equipment in the studio. Once the ceremony

---

13 Edwin Jurriens and Ross Tapsell, "Challenges and Opportunities of the Digital 'Revolution' in Indonesia," in *Digital Indonesia: Connectivity and Divergence,* eds. Edwin Jurriens and Ross Tapsell (Singapore: ISEAS, 2017), 4.
14 Thanks to Jessica Hughes for the observation that the quantity of metal in such objects is worth exploring further as condensation of properties such as sharpness and strength.

Figure 1: Priest performing a ceremony for *Tumpak Landep* in Laksamana photo studio. Ubud, Bali. 2018. Photo by author.

was completed in the photo shop, a small group of adults, youth and children left with suitable ritual paraphernalia to extend blessings over the rest of the property in the hotel and restaurant. For over half an hour we walked briskly along passageways, entered each hotel room, and climbed up and down numerous stairways to ensure that shrines were prayed at and holy water was sprinkled everywhere. Tiring, I noted with some gratitude the lengthier stops when the group paused and assembled to sanctify cash registers and phones in the building. Wayan also showed me his collection of vehicles, parked in the basement of the hotel and duly propitiated.

As Donald Norman[15] points out the design affordances of objects lend themselves to certain kinds of actions. While the broader surfaces of desks, printers and car hoods were suitable for flat offerings or placed in baskets, the long wires that connected computers and other devices to energy sources offered the opportunity for tying small bundles of offerings. Some of these bundles were placed near outlets and points of contact between wires and devices. Through these rituals *around* the materiality of digital technology, it seemed that both the devices and their connections were being strengthened and integrated with each other and the power of electricity, if not the universe. My conjecture about the importance of such 'magical' connectivity seemed less fanciful when a few months later, during the high tourist season of mid-late December, the increased demand for electricity in Ubud led to frequent power cuts and complaints.

Laksamana studio was one of the last photo studios in the town of Ubud, sustained by foreign tourists who needed passport images. The declining need for a photo studio in the age of smart phones raised questions in my mind about how digital technology had taken over analog media in Bali and other parts of Indonesia, and the manner in which Balinese may have perceived the introduction of cameras. Perusing Western archives for a publication on Balinese rituals and textiles[16] had previously led me to an important archive of still, black and white images (nearly 30,000) taken by Gregory Bateson, the British anthropologist, and currently stored at the Library of Congress (LoC), in Washington, D.C. Along with his then-wife, the American anthropologist Margaret Mead, Bateson conducted fieldwork in Bali (1936 – 38) and shot these photos. He developed and printed them at Sagami, a Japanese studio in Denpasar, Bali, and in atleast one instance, distributed photo prints to his research subjects, as evidenced in a black and white image[17] from 1937 depicting a healer *(balian)* carry-

---

15 Donald Norman, *The Design of Everyday Things* (New York: Basic Books, 1988/2013).
16 Urmila Mohan, *Fabricating Power with Balinese Textiles* (Chicago: BGC/University of Chicago Press, 2018).
17 Image number 06152 from a digital collection of the Bateson photographs at http://memory. loc.gov/mss/meadpp/, last accessed in 2017.

ing a photo of a young man in her bowl. This particular healer, Jero Balian Seken, was frequently shown officiating at ceremonies in the village of Bayung Gede and one wonders what she thought of the act of taking photographs. Certainly, the LoC photos depict Balinese who sometimes appear uncertain or uncomfortable, and Bateson notes that on occasion he used angular view finders when the "subject might be expected to dislike being photographed at that particular moment."[18]

In a subsequent discussion, the couple debate their use of still and ciné-cameras in Bali. Bateson's concern about the role of technology is apparent when he complains that "people are getting good at putting cameras on tripods" and that this ignored "what goes on between people."[19] Indeed, it is this anthropological emphasis on the study of relationships whether through behaviors, motions, or images that continues to find resonance in the study of digital materiality.

What is missing from these strictly empirical usages of photography is the "magic" of photography where the image is powerful as "an emanation of past reality."[20] In the image, the combination of the two subjects (healer and photo print) forces us to consider the effect of photography on the Balinese villagers. At least one Balinese woman in the 1930s asked Mead if photography would make her ill[21] and this belief finds support in practices where people avoided giving their printed photos to those they didn't trust for fear it would make them vulnerable to black magic *(ilmu hitam)*. In such rituals, the photo print was a physical object, a piece of evidence that metonymically linked ceremonial action to the human subject as the target of black magic.[22] In today's Bali, however, images of people abound on Instagram and Facebook, making it much harder to sustain such taboos. Yet, as we shall see in the following sections, core beliefs in the power and reach of the spirit world *(niskala)* persist, influencing how and when digital images are shared or not.

---

18 Gregory Bateson and Margaret Mead, *Balinese Character: A Photographic Analysis* (New York: New York Academy of Sciences, 1942), 49.
19 Margaret Mead and Gregory Bateson, "Margaret Mead and Gregory Bateson on the Use of the Camera in Anthropology," *Studies in the Anthropology of Visual Communication* 4(1977): 80.
20 Roland Barthes, *Camera Lucida. Reflections on Photography* (New York: Hill and Wang, 1981), 88–89.
21 "Majah Eeban in Poerah Tjekandik," March 30, 1937, Margaret Mead Papers, Box N12, Folder 3, Library of Congress Manuscript Division, Washington, DC.
22 There are also numerous anecdotes of how, when lovers separated or marriages fell apart, people have used 'love magic' *(guna-guna*, literally, something that is useful) on others.

5.3 Rituals *for* Digital Media

Digitization compresses time and space and this phenomenological effect is used today in online healing and divination. For example, a Balinese shaman called Putu Robinson, also known as "Balian Jaman Now" (literally, healer of the 'now' era), has become well-known in Indonesia through his YouTube (Jro Bali) and Instagram accounts (jrobalian13) where he posts videos and photos of healing sessions. The people who come to him are believed to be possessed by spirits and/or stricken with ill-health in some way. There are also those patients who make video calls on their smart phones to consult him and the comments on Robinson's Instagram site indicate that his "alternative treatment"[23] works wonders. The nickname *Balian Jaman Now* seems to underline the promise of speedy relief, facilitated by modern *(moderen)* technology. As Robinson notes in one Instagram post (Figure 2),[24] distance and time are not an obstacle for him, also stating in another instance,[25] that what he provides is a "multisystem" treatment working remotely as well as directly on the patient.

There is a strong theatrical dimension to the healing videos subsequently posted on the internet with Robinson performing various gestures—wafting incense in front of phone screens and emitting remedial sounds, ranging from softly-spoken mantras to loud screams. One of his more dramatic use of materials is the use of a single sheet of white facial tissue which he touches lightly to a patient's body as a kind of 'litmus test' of their inner state. When the patient is sick and possessed by an evil spirit the touch of a white tissue appears to cause them immense distress, leaving them screaming in pain. But when they are healed by Robinson, the same tissue elicits no reaction. Such actions cannot be performed from a distance and their presence in a video marks a moment of tension, heightened by Robinson's air of nonchalance. By explaining to the camera what he is doing and why, and often breaking his routine to chat with others, or, for instance, to show his new pair of shoes, Robinson situates these events within the everyday, and adeptly controls the emotional tone and pace of the session.

Once posted on social networking sites these videos are annotated with testimonials of cure from Balinese as well as Indonesians on other islands. In doing so, they also begin to shape perceptions of what a healing session could or should look like. Simultaneously, the very accessibility of these videos engenders

---

23 Jrobalian13. Putu Robinson healing through video call, 26.01.2018. https://www.instagram.com/p/Beb7ECwDDCg/, last accessed 5 August 2021.
24 Jrobalian13. Putu Robinson healing through video call, 26.01.2018.
25 Jrobalian13. Putu Robinson healing through video call, 30.01.2018.

Figure 2: Screen capture of Instagram post from 2018 depicting Putu Robinson waving incense as he heals a patient during a smart phone video call. 4 March 2019.

doubts as to whether Robinson's sessions could be truly effective. I shared Robinson's videos with an artist in her early thirties whom I had got to know through my interest in Balinese contemporary art. She generally visited a *balian* for her own health issues and responded that Robinson's video-call therapies could not work since a true healer would have to see the patient in person to evaluate bodily signs and prescribe medicine in highly-controlled doses. Her assessment was that Balinese healing was an ancient science and that Robinson was using technology in a "vague" rather than scientific manner. Another Balinese woman, an aide to an American expat who lived in Bali, stated that she would not go to Robinson as he was a "hypnotist." Somebody in her extended family had consulted him and had changed into a different person after the treatment. Her mother has been very ill for a while due to what she believed was black magic and for her treatment she preferred to go to a healer who was very private in his practice. At such sessions, the people gathered might shoot videos of the healer's activities but only with his permission. This woman also felt that posting such videos invaded her privacy and her desire that such knowledge be restricted to her family. This particular example marks the alignment of the healer's and patient's views on digital media and their mutual concern with privacy. Yet, it is precisely such instances that indicate potential fault lines of tension and divergence.

The actions performed by Robinson and the manner in which the rituals are affectively and performatively calibrated for social media leads one to approach them as rituals performed primarily *for* digitalization. Yet, the smart phone is also an object and through its very physicality can be incorporated into religious materiality, for instance, as part of annual ceremonies of purification and propitiation. We could consider these as rituals *around* digitalization where the 'digital' object is treated as a special, enhanced material, as we saw in the case of Wayan's celebration of *Tumpak Landep.* While making this distinction we should also note the flexibility of such boundaries, both within the categories of *around* and *for,* as well as the specific ceremony in which the digital object is embedded. For instance, when encountered in different Balinese homes, a laptop or digital camera may be re-contextualized and inserted in various ceremonies. A laptop in the home of a Balinese priest may be considered a device of knowledge and learning and thus propitiated and sanctified during the worship of the Hindu Goddess Saraswati alongside books and palm-leaf manuscripts *(lontar).* In the case of a family from the *Pande* or blacksmith caste it is highly probable that digital objects are emphasized primarily as part of *Tumpak Landep,* a ceremony when the properties of metal are celebrated.

5.4 Digital Materiality and Being 'Balinese'

5.4.1 The Issue of Digital Ease and Spiritual Unease

With tourism we have come to assume that the camera's presence is ubiquitous in Bali, but the relative (un)ease with which digital media can capture and share images is still a useful means of understanding peoples' beliefs including those in *niskala*, literally, those entities that exist outside of time. For instance, the flow of images can be curtailed depending on the demands of individual spirits. Through my fieldwork I was brought into contact with an instance of photographic "refusal"[26] on the part of a spirit. Over several months I had the opportunity to converse with a language teacher from central Bali named Ketut.[27] I would take Bahasa Indonesia language classes with Ketut and, as I tried to learn more about the culture, invariably our conversation would include events from that day or thoughts that were uppermost in her mind. As a middle-aged

---

26 Heike Behrend, *Contesting Visibility. Photographic Practices on the East African Coast* (Bielefeld: Transcript Verlag, 2013).
27 This common name in Bali is a pseudonym in this case.

woman with three sons and in-laws to care for, Ketut's life was busy with multiple responsibilities including the ever-present obligations of offerings for the ritual calendar. Ketut was worried that she constantly looked burdened and tired, resonating the Balinese emphasis on presentation of a "clear, bright face."[28] Most family responsibilities were on her shoulders and she seemed to be constantly balancing the demands of family, local community *(banjar)* and teaching work.

In early 2017 several experiences of a supernatural kind convinced Ketut that there was a spirit living behind her house. She contacted a healer *(balian)* in another part of the island for advice on how to deal with the spirit. Ketut valued the fact that this healer was "a normal person" who seemed like an ordinary Balinese housewife. She claimed the healer was well-known since she was often hired for consultations in other parts of Southeast Asia. As they were in different parts of the island, the healer asked Ketut for a photograph of the backyard in question. Ketut sent the images through WhatsApp on her smart phone. Like most Balinese Ketut relied heavily on the instant messaging application to communicate with others. (Indeed, during our conversations she would constantly receive notifications from the numerous chat groups to which she belonged.) From the photographs that Ketut sent her, the healer was able to diagnose that there was indeed a spirit who lived in the backyard and that it needed to be appeased by building a shrine. The spirit had also manifested as a snake and so a small house was built for the snake in front of the shrine.

Nearly a year and a half after the shrine was built my interactions with Ketut caused the incident of 'refusal'. Intrigued by her description of a spirit who lived in her backyard, I requested she send me photos of the shrine she had built through WhatsApp, our usual mode of communication. Ketut sent the photos to me promptly but a few months later stated that she probably should not have done so. Unusual things had been happening and she had lost money on two occasions from her house, something without precedence she claimed. The only thing she had done that varied from her normal routine was send me photos, and she concluded that the spirit had punished her for sharing images of the shrine with me. When I tried to apologize for having indirectly caused this problem with my request, Ketut seemed genuinely surprised, saying that there was no way to know and that such things were only revealed through experience. By taking her money away the spirit had communicated that she had been naughty *(nakal)*. Now that she was aware *(sadar)* she would not

---

28 Unni Wikan, *Managing Turbulent Hearts: A Balinese Formula for Living* (Chicago: University of Chicago Press, 1990), 52.

repeat the mistake. One could say that Ketut's belief in spirits and the types of punishments they could unleash on humans was a means of "searching for ways to make sense of uncertainty."[29] But what is equally relevant to our discussion is how, guided by her beliefs, Ketut was learning to use digital technology for her purposes, and in a way that would make the spirit a benevolent presence without any further disruptions.

My relationship with Ketut was certainly an example of how a non-Balinese outsider (tourist, researcher, artist, etc.) may become a participant in spirit-human interactions. But this incident also points to a process by which, aided by digitization, things that are otherwise considered secular or mundane may shift and become sacred or set apart over time. The following example helps illustrate this further. It pertains to a YouTube video (Figure 3) and discussion thread about a huge *(kolosal)* group dance of about two thousand people at Petitenget beach, Kerobokan, Bali, in late 2018 that ended with many participants going into trance *(kesurupan)*. Intended as a means to enter the Indonesian book of records (muri.org, record number 8618) the dance was part of the first ever Petitenget Festival, aimed at rebranding Kerobokan as a tourist destination.[30] The organizer explained that the trances were anticipated and that they were proof that the deity Ida Bhatara was present.[31] However, they did not deal with what motivated the deity to manifest itself through possession of dancers' bodies.

The weaving dance *(Tari Tenun)* performed by dancers was a secular, 'social realist' dance created in the 1950s by Nyoman Ridet and Wayan Likes to celebrate village labor through the actions of weaving.[32] Patronized by the then-President Sukarno and the "Old Order" government in Indonesia, the dance fell out of favor and was virtually dropped from repertoires before it was revitalized in the 1990s. In the discussion thread accompanying the video, comments in Bahasa Indonesia speculated about the dance's suitability. One viewer wondered if the dance was sacred *(sakral)*. Another clarified that in addition to the place being sacred it was a pre-requisite that the body of the trance medium be suitably purified. Some comments were critical—one questioning whether this was a form of mass hysteria. Others seemed to respond to the way the video present-

---

29 Adrian Vickers, "Sakti Reconsidered: Power and the Disenchantment of the World," in *Southeast Asian Perspectives on Power,* eds. Liana Chua et al. (London: Routledge, 2012), 65.
30 https://ubudcommunity.com/petitenget-festival-2018/, last accessed 6 August 2021.
31 Ubud Community, "Tari Tenun Kolosal Kerauhan/Petitenget Festival 2018.", YouTube, 16.09. 2018. www.youtube.com/watch?v=QuM4fnkSQNg&t=1s, last accessed 5 August 2021.
32 I Made Bandem and Fredrik deBoer, *Balinese Dance in Transition: Kaja and Kelod* (Oxford: Oxford University Press, 1995).

ed the narrative of trance and recovery through sprinkling of holy water in one continuous tracking motion of the camera.

Tari Tenun Kolosal Kerauhan / Petitenget Festival 2018

75,279 views · Sep 16, 2018

Figure 3: Screen capture of YouTube video about 2018 mass trance in Petitenget beach. The image shows staff on hand to carry away those dancers who have fallen into trance. 12 January 2019.

A comment from "tania Merah putih" asked if tourists would be frightened *(takut)* by the spectacle to which the reassuring response came from "Agus Bawa" that it was handled and that the video had sensationalized the event to get many viewers *(mendapatkan viewer banyak)*. The dramatic tone of the video was accentuated by a comment from "Komang Trima" when she asked, using the term *doohh* or an exclamation of intense emotion, what the dance was for *(mau cari apa?*, literally, what were they looking for?), adding that Bali was already well-known *(sudah tenar dimata dunia)*. Nearly three months later, "Apriyoga Kanayasa" posted a response to Komang's comment asking her not to be emotional or *ngegas*. This term implies acceleration (literally, to add fuel or gas to something) and connotes moving from calm to agitated. Apriyoga stated that the purpose was *"melestarikan budaya"* or conserving the culture and that Komang should already know this since she lived in Bali.

I shared the YouTube video link with my Balinese artist friend, Citra Sasmita, who responded to the trance phenomenon as a failure to pay attention to *desa, kala, patra,* that is, the ethic of place, time and circumstance. According to her, activities that did not follow these rules caused disharmony and destruction in contradiction to the ethic of maintaining balance and equilibrium *(keseimbangan)*. The dancers went into trance and were possessed by Ida Bhatara, a high spirit representing nature, because he was displeased that the ethic of *desa, kala, patra* was not followed. That is, since the dance was performed with the goal of setting a new world record and developing tourism, the event was not really a sacrificial offering for the deities. Here, intentionality emerges as a significant factor in the conversation about being suitably Balinese as well as relating ritual efficacy to the goal of innovation.

Between these various comments it appeared that viewers (both Balinese and non-Balinese) were trying to understand what made this performance a truly trance-inducing one as well as a distinctively Balinese practice. Although courteous in tone, there also seemed to be a need for discussion about how a dramatic mass trance event with women heaving and sobbing could be reconciled with a secular dance and tourism marketing goals. The affective tone of the video seemed intentional, designed to elicit an emotional response, but when it evoked the wrong type of response (criticism or alarm) it was firmly contained by the logic of culture as convention and what was to be expected from being, thinking and acting as a Balinese person.

5.4.2 Heritagization and Cultural Fashioning

The access to digital photography in Bali, most often through a smart phone, belies the (un)ease with which people use and perceive digital images. Images are vital for the tourism and heritage industry. So much so that, for instance, when one visits the Bali Aga village and tourist destination of Tenganan Pegeringsingan, the first place one is directed to as a visitor is a small gallery with photos of the annual ceremonies displayed prominently. The intent is that these images act as place holders for activities and even as they fail to compensate for the experience of the event, the aesthetics of these pictures (many of which are taken by renowned photographers) are powerful enough to help visitors imagine what they may have seen on another day.

The issue of heritage in Bali can be approached as "a new awareness that seeks to find novel ways to communicate with the past."[33] For instance, the "Sejarah Bali" (literally, Balinese history) website and its accounts on Instagram,

---

33 Wiendu Nuryanti, "Heritage and Postmodern Tourism," *Annals of Tourism Research* 23 (1996): 249–260.

Facebook and Twitter act as an informal archive of historic images from different regencies on the island. Announcing its mission of "loving Bali through history"[34] many of the images on these sites date from colonial times. While historic images may be connected with various endeavors, I relate it to the practice of what is known in Indonesia as "pre-wedding" *(pra-wedding)* photography.

Trends of self-fashioning as a form of consumption have been noticed in Indonesian fashion[35] and Singaporean weddings.[36] The phenomenon of pre-weddings started around 2010 in Bali, and in mid-2016, packages that included clothing rental, makeup and photography were available in the range of 3–5 million Indonesian Rupiah (IDR),[37] a more affordable rate according to one supplier. During these photo sessions engaged couples were dressed in costumes and had their photographs taken at locations that were deemed historic or *sakral* such as the royal Kerta Gosha pavilions in Semarapura, Klungkung (Figure 4), the grounds of Museum Bali, Denpasar, and the relatively newer Bajra Sandhi monument, Denpasar. In the rigid, caste-based social structure of Bali, pre-wedding photoshoots were forms of conspicuous consumption and play *(bermain)* where couples could dress in *riasan modifikasi* (modified decoration) as royalty and/or upper-castes. The mixture *(campur)* of style options made available through *modifikasi* allowed couples to create and record a fantasy. Village-style costumes and shoots were also available but the majority of pre-wedding photos emphasized the possibilities of looking like royalty or *agung*.

In her study of how people used historic images of the Philippines on Facebook, Deirdre McKay[38] describes how the past and present can be connected through the psychological need for cultural re-appropriation. In Bali, such appropriation overlaps with heritagization,[39] or the processes by which heritage

---

34 In Bahasa Indonesia, *"Cintai Bali dari Sejarahnya,"* www.sejarahbali.com, last accessed 7 August 2021.

35 Brent Luvaas, "Shooting Street Style in Indonesia: A Photo Essay," *Clothing Cultures* 1(2013): 59–81.

36 Terence Heng, "New Forms of Colonial Gazing in Singaporean Chinese Wedding Photography," in *Women and the Politics of Representation in Southeast Asia: Engendering discourse in Singapore and Malaysia*, eds. Adeline Koh and Yu-Mei Balasingamchow (London and New York: Routledge), 60–78.

37 At the time of writing in 2021 this was equivalent to $208–$347.

38 Deirdre McKay, "On the Face of Facebook: Historical Images and Personhood in Filipino Social Networking," *History and Anthropology* 21(2010): 479–498.

39 The term heritagization was first popularized in English publications by Kevin Walsh and focused on the destruction of culture by tourism. However, more recently the term has been used to refer to heritage-building processes. Kevin Walsh, *The Representation of the Past: Museums and Heritage in the Post-Modern World* (London: Routledge, 1992), 4.

Figure 4: Pre-wedding photo shoot in front of the Kerta Ghosa pavilion. Semarapura, Klung-kung, Bali. 2018. Photo by author.

is constructed, and is further complicated by the ubiquity of tourism. Tourism dovetails with religion and custom in Bali such that the island's culture has turned from "cultural tourism" to "touristic culture" *(budaya pariwisata).*[40] The performance of a calendrical cycle of rituals, as well as various traditional dances and artforms, are the basis of Bali's heritage industry with approximately 70% of the island's economy supported in 2014 by tourism-related businesses.[41]

The connection between pre-wedding photography and tourism is one that I discussed with Putu Aditya Nugraha and the creators of "Bali 1930 Rekonstruksi," a photography business and website.[42] Initiated by the photographer Gung Ama (Gusti Agung Wijaya Utama), *Rekonstruksi* features "timeless" and "konseptual" pre-wedding videos that are subsequently posted on Instagram under the name "gamaphoto1930." In general, these videos and photos feature the engaged couple and their entourage dressed in elaborate period costumes and situated in old, regal houses. *Rekonstruksi,* or reconstruction, differentiates itself from other pre-wedding shoots by paying attention to historical accuracy, down to the details of clothing worn by the participants, an aesthetic that is supported by those who deem *riasan modifikasi* to be a confused mixture *(campur).* The project produces both still images (printed as well as distributed on social media) and videos (played at wedding receptions and on social media) that are post-produced with suitable graphic effects denoting age through various digital tools such as black and white tones, film "scratches," etc. The videos also incorporate sound through traditional Balinese singing or music whose style further evokes a sense of the past as an otherworldly, ethereal space. These videos and photos thus act as nodes that mark the intersection between material and digital realms as well as the flow of visuals, ideas, and values, through image, motion, and sound, and the careful curating of *mise-en-scène* for the camera.

---

40 Michel Picard, "'Cultural Tourism' in Bali: Cultural Performances as Tourist Attraction," *Indonesia* 49 (1990): 74.

41 If tourism is represented by the tertiary sector (services sector) the contribution of tourism to the Balinese economy was 68.28% in 2014. Made Antara and Made Sri Sumarniasih, "Role of Tourism in Economy of Bali and Indonesia," *Journal of Tourism and Hospitality Management* 5 (2017): 34 – 44. Bali experiences a volume of visitors that is very high in proportion to its own population. The population of Bali in 2017 was 4,246,500. In the same year 5,682,248 visitors entered Bali through the Ngurah Rai airport in Denpasar. BPS-Statistics Indonesia, *Statistical Yearbook of Indonesia* (Jakarta: Dharmaputra, 2018), 85, 377.

42 According to the creators, the project also takes inspiration from Marlowe Bandem and Ed Herbst's Bali 1928 archival project (bali1928.net) that explores archives in the US and shares films/photos of Bali with the descendants of people depicted in them as well as the general public.

Figure 5: Screen capture of Instagram post showing a pre-wedding photo by "gama-photo1930". 22.04.2018. Text annotations describe the creator's philosophy of *kolaborasa* or affective, aesthetic collaboration in creating these images. 12 January 2019.

The creators described their intent as a mixture of commerce and preservation wherein the videos and photos helped Balinese remember *(mengingat)* their history. As one *Rekonstruksi* team member stated during a discussion in Ubud, "Nowadays...people cannot remember what it was like before. The dancing we know is the dancing used for tourism. We don't really understand how to dance, we don't really understand playing the gamelan." By stating that "smiling is conventional"[43] and posing couples with "no smile" expressions that mimicked Balinese from the 1930s Gung Ama, *Rekonstruksi's* creator, signalled that he was eschewing the aesthetic of touristic culture and its emphasis on always being cheerful and accommodating. While facial expressions (or their lack) were valued in Balinese culture, the overuse of smiles within touristic culture had clearly devalued them as gestures of genuine pleasure or references that would help others discern the wearer's (presentation of) state-of-mind.

The smile as gesture as well as reference to a person's inner states and intentionality has an analogy in *Rekonstruksi's* use of photography wherein the image (like the smile) is both an indication of feelings as well as a referent to something

---

[43] See *"Mekenyem Sube Biasa,"* literally, smiling is conventional, in https://issuu.com/gama photo1930/docs/mekenyem_sube_biasa, last accessed 3 January 2019.

else. The photograph points to something that has happened in the past and which has since been put aside—what Roland Barthes[44] describes as "irrefutably present, and yet already deferred." But, what is this deferred entity in the context of *Rekonstruksi?* The creators of *Rekonstruksi* mentioned their philosophy of *kolaborasa*, or collaboration that pays attention to sensory, perceptual affect *(rasa)* (Figure 5), in turn, drawing our attention to how digitization aids the re-enactment of certain kinds of intimacies. If, as Barthes noted, an image could truly compel or 'wound' one *(punctum)* into forgoing indifference and believing that the image's referent had existed, was there a similar compulsion or belief for *Rekonstruksi's* members that caused them to feel intensely about the past and its images?

It seemed that the serious faces of *Rekonstruksi's* pre-wedding subjects, that is, the 'no-smile' look, was both a sign of innovation as well as resonating the makers' feelings of disillusionment with contemporary life in Bali. This was especially true of those in the team who lived in and around the touristic town of Ubud and who were referred to somewhat derogatorily as 'ubudian'. Fuelled both by a sense of loss of knowledge about their history and the stress of living in contemporary Bali, the *Rekonstruksi* team felt that, like their subjects, they "could not smile" as any smile presented would be "fake." Instead, they spoke in tandem of the simpler times of their childhood as well as the period of early photography in Bali which captured "raw" Balinese culture—a time when people were not on display but simply doing things because "it is how it is." Part of this longing for quieter times, was framed as a desire for technological simplicity. By paying more attention to the concept, staging, and expression of its subjects, and using basic digital camera and equipment, the project claimed[45] to have moved away both from the relentless search for the latest tools and software and toward the more substantial goal of remembering the past and conserving Balinese history.

Through its use of digital materiality, the *Rekonstruksi* project can be considered as an example of how Balinese shape identity as well as notions of heritage albeit through a sanitized view of history.[46] With its attention to a curated 'raw-

---

44 Roland Barthes, *Camera Lucida. Reflections on Photography* (New York: Hill and Wang, 1981), 77.

45 *"Mekenyem Sube Biasa."*

46 For an analysis of how Balinese history has been sanitized of its negative aspects, ranging from slavery, feudalism and caste constraints under colonialism to the anti-communist massacre within the Indonesian republic, see James Boon, *The Anthropological Romance of Bali, 1597–1972: Dynamic Perspectives in Marriage and Caste, Politics and Religion* (Cambridge: Cambridge University Press, 1977); and Geoffrey Robinson, *The Dark Side of Paradise: Political Violence in Bali* (Ithaca: Cornell University Press, 1995/2018).

ness' and what is visible within the frame of the photograph, the images memorialize colonial Bali without criticality and, indeed, the founder Gung Ama himself is categorical that this has nothing to do with politics. However, the project does speak to a kind of contemporary Balinese self-fashioning, where in the wake of the *Ajeg Bali* movement and the pressures of a tourist economy, mimicry of colonial-era imagery (specifically, royalty) seems to express a desire for self-improvement and self-determination through "culturalization."[47] If successful, these reconstructed images operate far beyond pre-wedding shoots, become institutionalized, and help shape what is considered suitably Balinese heritage.

5.5 Conclusion: The Use of Digital Materiality to Create Images and Imaginaries

The questions I started this chapter with included whether and how the production and circulation of digital imagery influenced Balinese religious identity and values. As noted earlier, images of Bali as a tropical paradise were produced for over a century, drawing on the West's fascination with Balinese religion and arts. While this relationship continues, buoyed by tourism, each new instance of technological innovation—from print and ciné-cameras to WhatsApp and Instagram —has brought its own material and cultural distinctions to the use of imaginaries: a phenomenon that anthropology is well-suited to exploring and analysing through ethnography, archives and a large body of existing scholarship on Bali.

The subjects in this chapter used digital materiality (digital media, hardware, applications, images, objects, bodies, and associated rituals) as a means of bridging categories of the analog and virtual, tangible and intangible, and the Real and not real. Simultaneously, digital media's seeming ephemerality and ease of flow through messaging apps and social networking sites carried its own transmedia cultural specificities, promises and constraints. I had earlier invoked the ideas of De Certeau on the making of imaginaries and how the 'faithful' (in this case the Balinese) construct images via digital media to give shape to their experiences, ranging from the intervention of invisible spirits in unwanted communications to using video chats for healing rituals, as well as online dis-

---

47 See Benjamin Hegarty, "'No Nation of Experts': Kustom Tattooing and the Middle-Class Body in Post-Authoritarian Indonesia," *The Asia Pacific Journal of Anthropology* 18 (2017): 137. Following Mark Hobart's work such endeavors could be considered part of the "dissolving" effects of capitalism where every aspect of life (culture, religion, *niskala,* art etc.) is turned into a transaction. Hobart, "Bali is a Battlefield."

cussion threads on how mass trances could fulfil the multiple realities of tourism and heritage. Through rituals of digital image-making and dissemination, the Balinese subjects in these examples shaped imaginaries, and made them powerful and compelling, as well as being shaped by them. While ideas, concepts, words and symbols were certainly useful in the transformation of images and objects into something Real, what was also emphasized was the role of the subject's body, emotions, practices, and the use of material and visual culture. Digital materiality and visuality was enhanced by the subject's sensorium as we saw in the case of Robinson's use of the smartphone in distance healing sessions, Ketut's concern about the snake spirit's desires for privacy, discussants of the dramatic trance video at Petitenget beach, and Wayan's propitiation of divine forces for his businesses during *Tumpak Landep*. Objects, images and substances had to first be experienced (viewed, heard, felt, touched, smelled and grasped) by Balinese subjects, and then transformed into something Real through the state of indeterminacy of the Imaginary. Even if legitimized by discourse, digital materiality could be said to be part of the bodily and material process of the production of imaginaries towards a Real.

The role of digital materiality within Balinese religious reality as the making of devotional or spiritual 'truth' is important both for what it reinforces as well as marginalizes as unsuitable, inappropriate or false. This is not a straightforward process since seemingly different imaginaries may be working together. Indeed, ambiguities about touristic self-display, the phenomenon of trance, and Bali's status as an 'imaginary museum' on a global stage, were evident in the YouTube discussion thread about mass trance. Commenters both stated their views and monitored others for what was 'Balinese', and multiple Imaginaries were at work in this online discussion thread, attempting to turn the same event (and its dramatic imagery) into different kinds of Real for the various participants. Here, in the face of the need to assert Balinese Hindu identity in a predominantly Muslim country, beliefs in *niskala* acquired rhetorical power in a spontaneous debate. But we must not forget the affective and sensorial value of the trance video as it created unease for some, and in turn, an opportunity for others to reinforce that such seemingly uncontrolled events were integral displays of Balinese culture.

Attention to innovation in rituals helped us relate the study of Balinese religious practices and beliefs to the (in)tangibility of digital culture. Early in this chapter, I proposed an analytical point that categorized rituals depending on whether they were performed primarily *for* digitization, such as Robinson's video-chat healing sessions and his dramatic use of white tissue, or *around* digitization, for instance, when digital tools were strengthened and renewed through the traditional ceremony of *Tumpak Landep*. In the latter part of this chapter, while exploring the topic of being Balinese, these analytical modes became blurred in people's dealings with digitality, that is, a ritual *for* something could become a ritual *around* something and vice-versa. Indeed, it is hard to separate the two modes when dealing with the mass trance event and its documentation on YouTube. Nevertheless, noting the relative emphases placed on incorporating digital media and technology during the ritual performance, across these examples, was a useful starting point as it helped us focus on the role of bodies, images and objects and how power and meaning flow across media in practices.

The *Rekonstruksi* project is an example of a transmedia phenomenon that invokes both modes, *for* and *around*, creating its own hierarchy of value and negotiating between the promises of media, such as 'basic' digital cameras, and the creator's critical stance towards excessive use of technology. The subject of 'suitable' technology was related to the project's heritagization goals of determining what was worth conserving or reproducing as Balinese culture: embodied in the gesture of smiling or its lack thereof. In this case, digital materiality as rituals around as well as for the camera, helped route imaginaries into the new rituals of pre-wedding shoots. The makers of these images reclaimed a colonial visual and material aesthetic that in its seeming archaic-ness created the Real of heritage and turned away from the threat of never-ending change and technological redundancy of modern life in Bali.

Balinese culture has been called timeless, a term that crops up in *Rekonstruksi's* goals of recreating what is classic. While its creator eschews political interpretations, the project does embody a politics of identity transformation. It depicts the past as timeless—something that is literally without, or outside, time—and therefore transcendental as well as more 'real'. The past is also a product of imaginaries, and something that can be contrasted with the present. This notion of being separated from time (or atleast the present) invokes a comparison with beliefs in *niskala* or spirits who, similarly, transcend time. Beyond wordplay, however, there are relationships between these two entities, that is, stereotypical images of Bali and Balinese beliefs in the invisible world since both are sustained by digital practices of the imaginary. Focusing on the rituals of digital materiality thus helps us identify and explore those values that are important to the making of Balinese religious and cultural identity as well as the images, processes and practices by which beliefs are made real.

Acknowledgments

The research for this article was supported by a 2018–19 fellowship from the Asian Cultural Council, New York, to study textiles and religion in Bali, Indonesia. A version of this paper was presented in 2019 as part of the Ronald and Janette Gatty Lecture Series at the Kahin Center, Cornell University. I am very grateful to the attendees, especially Professor Kaja McGowan, for comments and feedback. As ever, I remain indebted to my Balinese interlocuters for their generosity and patience.

References

Allen, Pamela and Carmencita Palermo. "Ajeg Bali: Multiple Meanings, Diverse Agendas." *Indonesia and the Malay World* 33(2005): 239–255.

Antara, Made and Made Sri Sumarniasih. "Role of Tourism in Economy of Bali and Indonesia." *Journal of Tourism and Hospitality Management* 5(2017): 34–44.

Bandem, I Made and Fredrik deBoer. *Balinese Dance in Transition: Kaja and Kelod.* Oxford: Oxford University Press, 1995.

Barthes, Roland. *Camera Lucida. Reflections on Photography.* New York: Hill and Wang, 1981.

Bateson, Gregory and Margaret Mead. *Balinese Character: A Photographic Analysis.* New York: New York Academy of Sciences, 1942.

Behrend, Heike. *Contesting Visibility. Photographic Practices on the East African Coast.* Bielefeld: Transcript Verlag, 2013.

Boon, James. *The Anthropological Romance of Bali, 1597–1972: Dynamic Perspectives in Marriage and Caste, Politics and Religion.* Cambridge: Cambridge University Press, 1977.

BPS-Statistics Indonesia. 2018. *Statistical Yearbook of Indonesia 2018.* Jakarta: Dharmaputra.

Bruner, Edward M. *Culture on Tour: Ethnographies of Travel.* Chicago: University of Chicago Press, 2005.

De Certeau, Michel. *Histoire et psychoanalyse entre science et fiction.* Paris: Gallimard Press, 1987.

Fox, Richard. *Critical Reflections on Religion and Media in Contemporary Bali.* Numen Series in the History of Religions 130. Leiden: Brill, 2011.

Hegarty, Benjamin. "'No Nation of Experts': Kustom Tattooing and the Middle-Class Body in Post-Authoritarian Indonesia." *The Asia Pacific Journal of Anthropology* 18(2017): 135–148.

Heng, Terence. "New Forms of Colonial Gazing in Singaporean Chinese Wedding Photography." In *Women and the Politics of Representation in Southeast Asia: Engendering discourse in Singapore and Malaysia,* eds. Adeline Koh and Yu-Mei Balasingamchow, 60–78. London and New York: Routledge, 2015.

Hitchcock, Michael, and Lucy Norris. *Bali, the Imaginary Museum: The Photographs of Walter Spies and Beryl de Zoete.* Kuala Lumpur: Oxford University Press, 1995.

Hobart, Mark. "Bali is a Battlefield: Or the Triumph of the Imaginary over Actuality." *Jurnal Kajian Bali* 7(2017): 187–212.

Jurriens, Edwin and Ross Tapsell. "Challenges and Opportunities of the Digital 'Revolution' in Indonesia." In *Digital Indonesia: Connectivity and Divergence,* eds. Edwin Jurriens and Ross Tapsell, 1–20. Singapore: ISEAS, 2017.

Luvaas, Brent. "Shooting Street Style in Indonesia: A Photo Essay." *Clothing Cultures* 1(2013): 59–81.

Mead, Margaret and Gregory Bateson. "Margaret Mead and Gregory Bateson on the Use of the Camera in Anthropology." *Studies in the Anthropology of Visual Communication* 4 (1977): 78–80.

Mohan, Urmila. *Fabricating Power with Balinese Textiles*. Chicago: BGC/University of Chicago Press, 2018.

Mohan, Urmila. "The Indonesian Alcove at the American Museum of Natural History: Art, Culture Areas and the Mead-Bateson Bali Project." *Museum Anthropology* 44.1–2 (2021): 11–23.

Mohan, Urmila and Jean-Pierre Warnier. "Editorial: Marching the Devotional Subject: The Bodily-and-Material Cultures of Religion." *Journal of Material Culture* 22(2017): 369–384.

McKay, Deirdre. "On the Face of Facebook: Historical Images and Personhood in Filipino Social Networking." *History and Anthropology* 21(2010): 479–498.

Norman, Donald. *The Design of Everyday Things*. New York: Basic Books, 1988/2013.

Nuryanti, Wiendu. "Heritage and Postmodern Tourism." *Annals of Tourism Research* 23(1996): 249–260.

Picard, Michel. ""Cultural Tourism" in Bali: Cultural Performances as Tourist Attraction." *Indonesia* 49 (1990): 37–74.

Robinson, Geoffrey. *The Dark Side of Paradise: Political Violence in Bali*. Ithaca: Cornell University Press, 1995/2018.

Vickers, Adrian. *Bali: A Paradise Created*. Ringwood: Penguin, 1989/2009.

Vickers, Adrian. "Sakti Reconsidered: Power and the Disenchantment of the World." In *Southeast Asian Perspectives on Power*, eds. Liana Chua, Joanna Cook, Nicholas Long and Lee Wilson, 51–66. London: Routledge, 2012.

Walsh, Kevin. *The Representation of the Past: Museums and Heritage in the Post-Modern World*. London: Routledge, 1992.

Wikan, Unni. *Managing Turbulent Hearts: A Balinese Formula for Living*. Chicago: University of Chicago Press, 1990.

Part 3 **Intersections of the Digital and Material: Tools, Questions, and Processes**

Florence Pasche Guignard
Chapter 6
Material, Maternal, Embodied, and Digital: Objects and Practices in Natural Parenting

6.1 The digitalization of natural parenting: health, embodiment, media, and technology

This chapter examines selected aspects of "natural parenting" at the intersection with spirituality and religion. Its main focus is on the contrast between the use of highly mediated and digital tools and online platforms to implement and disseminate representations, discourses, and practices that, for the most part, are highly embodied and material. This particular style of parenting is also referred to as "natural mothering," "natural family living," "green mothering," "eco-parenting," or "sustainable motherhood."[1] It stands out from other styles in parenting through combining key aspects of the more well-known "attachment parenting" with environmentalist concerns, as well as elements derived from other lifestyles such as voluntary simplicity and lifestyles of health and sustainability.[2] Specialized media, marketing strategies, and scholars use these and similar labels. Some parents reclaim these designations to self-identify as such, especially on dedicated online spaces that this chapter calls attention to, whereas others resist or reject them. Practitioners and advocates of such parenting styles, as well as those who criticize them, often assign spiritual meanings to some of their typical practices, some of which this contribution will explore in more detail. Several of these practices originally developed in religious contexts or were (and often remain) strongly associated with specific religious groups, though natural parenting is not religious or spiritual in itself.

---

1 Chris Bobel, *The Paradox of Natural Mothering* (Philadelphia: Temple University Press, 2002); Chris Bobel, "Resisting, But Not Too Much: Interrogating the Paradox of Natural Mothering," in *Maternal Theory. Essential Readings*, ed. Andrea O'Reilly (Toronto: Demeter Press, 2007); and Chikako Takeshita, "Eco-Diapers: The American Discourse of Sustainable Motherhood," in *Mothering in the Age of Neoliberalism*, ed. Melinda Vandenbeld Giles (Bradford: Demeter Press, 2014).
2 Monica Emerich, *The Gospel of Sustainability: Media, Market and LOHAS* (Urbana: University of Illinois Press, 2011).

https://doi.org/10.1515/9783110608755-007

Health and embodiment, and especially women's bodies as potentially fertile, pregnant, giving birth and lactating, and the bodies of newborns and children, are at the center of many of the typical, though not exclusive, practices of natural parenting. More general topics such as education, nutrition, health, and sustainability, are recurring as well. Discourses of natural parenting tend to value whatever is culturally constructed as "natural" over what is given as technological, artificial, or chemical.[3] In addition to being regarded or marketed as (more) "natural" (than others), these lifestyles and parenting styles more generally tend to be branded as "low-tech." Such perspectives serve as the backdrop for a questioning of society's prevailing values and advocating a replacing of "the human" (rather than the economy) at the center, as well as a return to "Nature." Practitioners have a strong sense of eco-conscious consumption or "simple living" that tends to minimize—yet not completely reject—the purchase of and reliance on electronic and digital devices, placing themselves in an ambiguous relationship with technology and digital technologies of communication especially. For example, natural parents often consider breastfeeding not just as a better, healthy (and righteous) choice, but also as more "natural" option than formula feeding, even when the use of a digital breast pump and a refrigerator (to safely store pumped breast milk) are involved in maintaining or supporting the process. Furthermore, many mothers who breastfeed now seek advice and support online, or learn about it through video-sharing websites or other online platforms, rather than through in-person lactation support groups and consultants only.[4] Though they may be "low-tech," they are not "no tech."

The parents whom I read and interviewed[5] often directed their well-informed criticism not towards technology in itself, but towards "technocracy," or the attitude of systematically valuing technology. Scholars already have articulated a

---

3 For a discussion of the opposition between "natural" and "technological" in a similar context, see Pamela Klassen, *Blessed Events: Religion and Homebirth in America* (Princeton: Princeton University Press, 2001), 137–139.

4 Florence Pasche Guignard, "Discours, représentations, pratiques et modes de transmission des savoirs et des idées sur l'allaitement dans les milieux francophones du parentage naturel," in Allaiter. De l'Antiquité à nos jours / Histoire(s) et cultures d'une pratique, ed. by Francesca Arena, Véronique Dasen, Yasmina Foehr-Janssens, Irene Maffi, Daniela Solfaroli Camillocci, 2 volumes. (Turnhout: Brepols, 2022, in press).

5 This chapter features selected results from a broader study entitled "Natural Parenting in the Digital Age: At the Confluence of Mothering, Religion, Environmentalism and Technology." It was conducted between 2012 and 2017 at the Department for the Study of Religion at the University of Toronto (Canada) and at the Faculté des Lettres at the Université de Fribourg (Switzerland). I thank these institutions for hosting me during this project, and the Swiss National Science Foundation for funding my international mobility and return postdoctoral fellowships.

criticism of technocratic models of pregnancy and childbirth that can be extended to care for women's and children's health, or biomedical healthcare systems in general.[6] This chapter examines more in depth a case study that highlights some of these attitudes towards and reliance on digital technologies especially, in the management of embodiment at the confluence of the maternal (fertility and postpartum) and the material (flesh and blood), inclusive of its ritual and spiritual dimensions. Digitalization increasingly affects key moments in our human lives that once were considered intimate and, in some contexts, even sacred, in the domains of sexuality and childbirth. This contribution also outlines the new type of questions that research in the digital humanities on highly embodied, gendered, and material practices involving a variety of objects, devices or artifacts ought to ask about such processes at the intersections of the digital and the material.

In spite of the importance of digitalization, embodiment and physiology are central in analyzing the practices of natural parenting. Coats and Emerich call attention to "the ways in which spirituality [is] physiological—fermented in the vessel of the flesh through everyday practices imbued with extraordinary meanings and transformed from raw material of life into a spiritual powerhouse of health for the world, truly a healing of the self to heal the world."[7] Such focus and this terminology of "practical spirituality" informs my approach in this chapter, which also builds upon my previously published analysis of babywearing and its specifically associated objects: baby wearing wraps and carriers.[8] In fact, most of the typical practices of natural parenting fit well within such a framework of analysis: specific forms of on demand or extended breastfeeding, alternative pedagogies, conscious choices of specific diets, various reclaiming of the body or body parts, choosing washable and reusable items (such as diapers or menstrual hygiene products) over disposable ones, etc.

Such practices often combine two dimensions: the first is that of "health," sometimes at the margins or completely outside of medical practice, and the second is a spiritual dimension. The health dimension involves maintaining health

---

6 Barbara Katz Rothman, *Labor: Women and Power in the Birthplace* (New York, Norton and Company, 1982), 29–49; Robbie Davis-Floyd, *Birth as an American Rite of Passage* (Berkeley: University of California Press, 1992), 44–72; and Robbie Davis-Floyd, "The Technocratic, Humanistic, and Holistic Models of Birth," *International Journal of Gynecology & Obstetrics* 75 (2001): S5–S23.
7 Curtis J. Coats and Monica Emerich, "The Webs We Spin: Relational, Mediated, Spiritual," in *Practical Spiritualities in a Media Age*, eds. Coats and Emerich (New York: Bloomsbury, 2016), 3.
8 Florence Pasche Guignard, "Mediated Babywearing as Aesthetic Orthodoxy," in *Practical Spiritualities in a Media Age*, eds. Curtis J. Coats and Monica Emerich, 17–34 and 201–212.

or affirming the processes of the feminine or maternal body as healthy rather than as pathological and in need of medical interventions. Digital self-tracking practices, such as those of fertility awareness, also contribute to this idea of health surveillance and maintenance. Furthermore, mothers in my broader study frequently mentioned the notion of "knowing oneself" and one's body, a spiritual admonition frequently heeded to by practitioners of fertility awareness. Minimally, this spiritual dimension translates into the notion that such choices and practices have a positive effect on the self, others (such as children or future generations), and the world, and that they are "the right thing to do" and choices with moral righteousness. Additionally, the idea of letting "the natural" exist and prevail is key. This spiritual dimension is often part of a very personal or even intimate quest for well-being. In most situations, both aspects (spirituality and health) are disconnected from established religious and medical institutions, such as churches or hospitals. Home and the body are central places of focus, often with a blurring of boundaries between and subsequent redefinitions of notions such as "private" and "public," but also of "intimate."

In addition to "the natural," "home" remains another key element in natural parenting.[9] This emphasis on home (*home*birth, *home*schooling, *home*made meals, remedies, cleaning products, etc.) calls for further comments. The choice of a planned home birth, with the assistance of a professional, independent midwife, is worth discussing briefly here as an introductory example of this paradoxical mediation of intimate health choices in the domain of sexuality and motherhood. In the mostly European, francophone contexts surveyed here, the decision of a home birth may be discussed very openly and in detail with like-minded parents online, often under the cover of anonymity. In contrast, parents tend to keep their decision of a home birth selectively secret and avoid disclosing it to close relatives, friends, or regular medical practitioners.[10] In these contexts, and in others as well, homebirth generally remains an uncommon choice, one that medical professionals, mainstream media, and public opinion in general can heavily scrutinize and criticize. This especially is the case in France.[11]

---

9 Chris Bobel, in her study on natural mothering conducted in the late 1990s, before the rise of the Internet, already evidenced the significance of "home." Bobel, *The Paradox of Natural Mothering*, 111.

10 Florence Pasche Guignard, "The In/Visibility of Mothering Against the Norm in Francophone Contexts: Private and Public Discourses in the Mediation of 'Natural Parenting,'" *Canadian Journal of Communication* 40/1 (2015): 118–119.

11 Anna Fedele and Florence Pasche Guignard, "Pushing from the Margins: 'Natural Childbirth' in Holistic Spiritualities and Natural Parenting in France and Portugal," in *Sacred Inception: Re-*

Only a minority of women choose to give birth at home, but my informants commonly discussed and appreciated home birth as a valid option. In Switzerland, Belgium, and Quebec, independent, midwife-led birth centers that are not within a hospital's maternity ward are increasingly available. This is not the case in France, where both independent birth centers and home birth remain extremely marginal. For technical and sometimes financial reasons (insurances, access, etc.), very few parents could actually have the home birth that they wished for. Not all "natural moms" (*les mamans nature*) in my study were homebirthers, but, comparatively, their proportion was higher than in the general population.[12] Those who were planning or actually had had a home birth were very cautious about whom they discussed it with, or, later, shared the narrative of their generally successful home birth, even after all went well. Yet, these same mothers would give out details of their birth project, their motivations, hopes, and fears on specific online spaces where a certain degree of anonymity is possible.

During the interviews that I conducted, several mothers admitted to lying to their gynecologists or physicians in order to avoid being further questioned or subjected to moralization as "bad mothers," even after their child was born. Others complied formally with all the requirements for registering at the local hospital while knowing that, if things did go as planned, they would give birth at home. Similarly, the mothers whom I interviewed generally did not feel free to discuss some of their other choices (regarding contraception, pregnancy, birth, health, education, etc.) with most of their relatives and friends, and, even less so, with their regular medical practitioners. They were likely to receive criticism, or, at least, insistent questions about their other "less common" practices. The most controversial ones included vaccine hesitancy, long-term breastfeeding of older children and co-sleeping arrangements.[13] Mothers (and, more rarely, fathers) were likely to share about such practices done mostly at home, in intimate settings, only in partially anonymous and generally benevolent digital spaces, such as online forums dedicated to natural parenting, where they could find the advice and support that their social environment and regular healthcare practitioners could not provide them with.

---

claiming the Spirituality of Birth in the Modern World, eds. Marianne Delaporte and Morag Martin (Lanham, MD: Lexington Books, 2018), 133, 144.

12 My study focused on a qualitative, rather than quantitative, approach. Statistics on home-birth are not readily available for the contexts studied and national particularities should be taken into account. It is therefore difficult to provide data and engage in comparison. To put this into perspective, among the 30 parents I interviewed (including 4 fathers and 26 mothers), 10 mothers had had a homebirth for at least one of their babies (often the second child).

13 Pasche Guignard, "Discours, représentations, pratiques et modes de transmission."

With this context in mind, this chapter thus considers several clusters of questions. And though my focus is on the digitalization of natural parenting, several questions that I ask about this can also apply to many other aspects of our personal lives in the 21st century, as I discuss in the last section. The questions can be summed up as follows: First, how does such a practical spirituality and its material manifestations become digital? Objects tied to specific practices, such as washable diapers, baby wearing wraps, or placenta prints, make natural parenting materially visible, in addition to discourses or gestures. However, as mentioned, many of these practices are performed at home, in the private, or even intimate, domestic sphere. Thus, how important is the digitalization and, more specifically, the mediation of natural parenting online and on social media in the diffusion of these objects, practices, and worldviews or beliefs ascribed to them? If the reality of these practical embodied and material aspects of natural parenting is not always highly visible, at least not in the public space, then this reality is relayed, now more than ever before, not simply through texts or print materials, but rather through digital pictures and videos. To this end, I consider a second cluster of questions in a methodological section preceding the conclusion. These pertain to how to study such material artifacts through their digitalization, in addition to actual fieldwork and on-site interviews or participant observation, when applicable. Highlighting several of the processes and effects of the contemporary and still ongoing digitalization of natural parenting provides insights to these questions.

Before moving into the case study of digital fertility awareness as a contraceptive practice with spiritual and religious aspects, I will provide more overview and additional examples of practices typical of natural parenting. The purpose is to further illustrate how a holistic perspective on the body and the environment, including a spiritual dimension, is central in these discourses. Focusing on design, uses, and new meanings and values attributed to fertility awareness in the digital age, my analysis shows how this idea of an allegedly more "natural" treatment of a "natural" bodily function (fertility) meets with digital technology. This takes place in a context where other chemical and medicalized forms of contraception increasingly are called into question even beyond the specific milieu of natural parenting.

6.2 Natural parenting and material religion: objects, symbols, values, and identity

A perspective in religious studies that takes seriously the "material turn" should examine contemporary natural parenting along research lines that depart from those of sociology or anthropology and instead emphasize the variety of material objects significant to natural parenting. Some objects may become symbols of what has been characterized as "identity parenting" in the sense that the experiences and work of parenting shape the parents' identities and transforms them as individuals.[14] Material objects further mark them as such and are reminders of such choices on a regular basis.

In everyday practice, pragmatic compromises take place alongside a flexible continuum: for instance, natural parents stated that they used washable diapers *most of the time*, but also disposable ones sometimes, or purchased *mostly*, but not exclusively, organic food. In contrast, symbolically, certain objects or substances are pitted against each other as materializing practices that stem from or translate different lifestyles, perspectives, or philosophies of child-rearing: the breast vs. the bottle, the baby wearing wrap vs. the stroller, organic home cooked meals vs. industrial ready-made food, the side bed attached to the parents' bed vs. the crib in a separate room, the cervical mucus indicating fertility stretched between two fingers vs. the contraceptive pill, etc. Of course, books, magazines, online and print materials conveying the key ideas that the generally highly educated informants in my study were familiar with, had read, and sometimes even quoted from, still matter. In this chapter, however, my intention is to shift the focus to substances and objects, and especially to their digitalization, that make this "gospel of natural parenting" more visible than texts. In the following sections, I focus on a few examples and one in-depth case study. In all of these, objects and practices are intertwined at the intersection of the material, the maternal, the embodied and the digital. Some of these material practices are not exclusive to natural parenting, nor practiced by all natural parents, but they are not uncommon in this milieu and the topic of many discussions. These particular examples must be situated more precisely in a continuum of the material with the digital in natural parenting.

---

14 Maya-Merida Paltineau, "From Intensive Mothering to Identity Parenting" in *Intensive Mothering: The Cultural Contradictions of Modern Motherhood*, ed. Linda Rose Ennis (Bradford: Demeter Press, 2015), 131–134.

My understanding of natural parenting builds upon recent "works that emphasize the 'materiality' of religion—for example, the value attributed to bodies, things, texts, and gestures, so as to make the divine tangible in the immanent."[15] In addition to Brigit Meyer's works, Sally Promey's notions of "sensational religion" and "sensory cultures in material practices," as well as that of "dynamic materiality," are also useful in a description and analysis of sensational forms of experiences sometimes described as "sacred," or as "spiritual," though most of them were taking place outside of religious institutions or well-established traditions.[16] In contrast with such studies that looked at explicitely religious cases and contexts, in my research, the vast majority of my francophone informants did not necessarily subscribe to a notion of "the divine," even as they considered "Nature" as a key, guiding principle. The process is one of sacralization, but not of deification. Many parents identified as atheists, agnostics, non-believers, or, at least, as distant from traditional religious institutions. Yet, they saw a sacred dimension in practices and processes such as fertility, pregnancy, and, especially, childbirth. In addition, many also expressed a strong sense of "doing the right thing for myself and my children," as one mother put it, and an awareness of ethics in everyday choices in consumption, food, health, or education.

Material religion in natural parenting can be evidenced through asking two intertwined questions. First, how do the practices connect with ideas, values, or worldviews recurring in natural parenting? Second, which of these tenets of natural parenting concretely manifest through objects? A third, methodological question combines these two: How can researchers study such connections, or how can one collect and analyze data on processes that are regarded as of the domain of "the private" or "the intimate," especially those that concern women's or couples' sexual and reproductive health choices in pregnancy and childbirth? I suggest that the worldviews and values underlying natural parenting are rendered visible primarily through specific objects and embodiment, or an aggregation of both. Objects, not only discourses or gestures, make natural parenting visible to others: to those who share this style of parenting or who are interested in it, and also to those who criticize it, and to the researchers who study both the advocates and the detractors of natural parenting.

---

15 Birgit Meyer, "Aesthetics of Persuasion: Global Christianity and Pentecostalism's Sensational Forms," *South Atlantic Quarterly* 9 (2019), 743.

16 Meyer, "Aesthetics of Persuasion;" Birgit Meyer, ed., *Aesthetic formations: Media, Religion, and the Senses* (New York: Palgrave Macmillan, 2009); Sally Promey, ed. *Sensational Religion: Sensory Cultures in Material Practice* (New Haven: Yale University Press, 2014); and David Chidester, *Religion: Material Dynamics* (Berkeley: University of California Press, 2018).

Specific objects are featured more prominently than others in platforms, blogs or vlogs dedicated to natural parenting in general or to its specific key components or practices (such as co-sleeping, babywearing, breastfeeding, etc.). Most of these objects relate to the body of the parent (mostly the mother) and the child. However, classifying them into two broad categories ("parent" and "child") is often impossible since the parent and the child may use (or manipulate) these objects jointly, as in the case of the baby wearing wrap or the washable diaper. Similarly, it is difficult to apprehend such materiality only in terms of commercial value; some of them cannot be purchased or sold, and yet, to their users, become invaluable. These objects fall in four categories: homemade/handmade and highly customized artifacts, manufactured items subjected to some degree of in-home customization, mass-produced objects that retain some specificity, and high-tech devices and their connected "apps." Regardless of how an object is categorized, many of these natural parenting practices demonstrate how beliefs are materialized and, often too, participate in ritual or spiritual practices, and their consequent digitalization which disseminates objects, their practices, the discourses about them and the values that these ascribe to such objects.

The case study on digital fertility awareness methods falls in the last category, but even objects that fall in the first three categories have significance for the intersection of material religion and digital humanities. For example, what some natural parents do with placentas are great examples of the junction of embodiment, materiality, and media. Different perspectives (medical, spiritual) define placentas in contrasting ways, from "hospital waste" to "spiritual twin of the newborn." Certainly, "the label used is determinative."[17] Biomedical experts, among others, already have documented the therapeutic and clinical uses of umbilical cords and placentas, and have done so often within the institutional framework of a medical practice. Less studied are other uses, and more specifically, the discourses about these still uncommon treatments of placentas and umbilical cords after birth. Whereas tutorials on what to do with placentas are easy to find online nowadays, few studies document practices centered on placentas and umbilical cords from perspectives in the humanities and social sciences. In one of the few volumes that considers such questions, editor Nané Jordan noted that, "there are no direct analysis of faith-based protocols and scripture for handling placentas from religious traditions."[18] In some cases, mothers wishing

---

17 Valerie Borek, "A Placenta by Any Other Name," in *Placenta Wit: Mother Stories, Rituals, and Research*, ed. by Nané Jordan (Bradford: Demeter Press, 2017), 180.
18 Nané Jordan, "Introduction" in *Placenta Wit: Mother Stories, Rituals, and Research*, ed. Nané Jordan (Bradford: Demeter Press, 2017), 3.

to keep a trace of the placenta will do placenta prints. Several blogs and websites document this practice and provide tutorials on how to do it. The placenta's blood itself may be used, or additional paint may be applied. The placenta is then pressed onto a sheet of paper to leave its imprint. On blogs that detail this process and give advice on how to create a great print, the image is often compared to a tree. Mothers frequently call their print a "Tree of Life," a title that implicitly or explicitly refers to religious or spiritual symbolism. Though the fresh placenta cannot be kept forever, its image will be.

6.3 Case study: digital fertility awareness, or the secular and yet spiritual rebranding of natural family planning

Fertility awareness is a useful case study to highlight one of the paradoxes of a style in natural family living that emphasizes "the natural" while at the same time heavily relying on high-tech, digital devices for its dissemination and implementation, whether through electronic devices, apps, social media and other online spaces. Fertility awareness is an umbrella term for practices done for cognitive (gaining personal knowledge about how the body and the menstrual cycle work), procreative (achieving pregnancy), or contraceptive (avoiding pregnancy) purposes. The basic principle of fertility awareness is to identify which few days of the menstrual cycle are fertile, potentially fertile, or likely infertile through observing specific symptoms and combining them. While previous and proven less effective (in terms of contraception) methods consisted in counting or keeping track of the days of the cycle ("rhythm method" or "calendar days methods"), modern and more efficient ways of practicing fertility awareness for contraceptive purposes generally combine at least two of the following observations: basal body temperature, consistence of cervical mucus, and position and openness of the cervix. Methods based on this and practiced for the purpose of avoiding pregnancy are known as fertility awareness-based methods of contraception. Several different methods follow different rules that this chapter cannot explain in more detail. Those reputed as the most reliable ones combine observing basal body temperature at the time of waking up, as well as at least one other symptom in order to confirm that the woman is at least two days past ovulation and, thus, no longer in her fertile phase.

Personal analytics, self-tracking, and even the idea of a "quantified self" are not new, and fertility monitoring has its earlier, low-tech versions. Some religious traditions, for instance Orthodox Judaism and other highly observant forms of Judaism, demand that women track their cycle in order to obey specific rules regarding a religiously constructed idea of purity linked to menstruation and other discharges of blood. Some religious prescriptions are based on women's menstrual state, for instance those that bar menstruating or even potentially menstruating women from entering certain religious sites or buildings. For various purposes, through different media, and to different extents, women have been tracking or even recording their menstrual cycle for centuries, long before apps and current digital technologies. As I argue elsewhere, a major and still recent change in the many practices of fertility awareness is their increasing digitalization and the femtech market that this generated.[19] Dozens of fertility trackers, devices, apps, programs, support groups and communities, courses, etc., are now available, with options ranging from completely free to paying, from autonomous learning to individual coaching or group classes, in-person, and also, in most cases, online. Such access and resources have developed outside of both medical and religious institutions.[20]

In the twentieth century, one of the main communities practicing fertility awareness was that of Roman Catholic couples, which prompted an association of fertility awareness with traditional religious institutions. However, the digital turn has disentangled the practice of fertility awareness from generally more conservative forms of "natural family planning" that demand abstinence from penetrative sex during the days identified as fertile. New methods of fertility awareness, developed in more flexible and mostly secular contexts, allow or even recommend the temporary use of barrier methods, whereas earlier "natural family planning" methods did not, in those conservative spaces. Especially since its digital turn, accelerated in the mid-2010s, fertility awareness is no longer exclusively practiced and taught in institutionally religious contexts, such as Roman Catholic parishes and in prenuptial counseling, and out of obedience to the normative teachings of an institution (such as those of the encyclical of Pope Paul VI's *Humanae Vitae* of 1968).[21] Additionally, Roman Catholic and

---

19 Florence Pasche Guignard, "High-Tech Mediations, Low-Tech Lifestyles: The Paradox of Natural Parenting in the Digital Age," in *Media and Religion: The Global View*, eds. Stewart Hoover and Nabil Echchaibi (Berlin: De Gruyter, 2021), 41–62; and Florence Pasche Guignard, "Digital Tools for Fertility Awareness: Family Planning, Religion, and Feminine Embodiment," in *The Routledge Handbook of Religion, Medicine, and Health*, eds. Dorothea Lüddeckens, Philipp Hetmanczyk, Pamela E. Klassen, and Justin B. Stein (New York: Routledge, 2021), 293–307.
20 This is the case at least in the anglophone world, whereas reliable resources in other languages are still harder to find.
21 Pamela Klassen, "Contraception and the Coming of Secularism: Reconsidering Reproductive Freedom as Religious Freedom," in *Secular Bodies, Affects and Emotions: European Configura-*

other religious, mostly Christian conservative, groups and associations no longer are the primary source of information for fertility awareness, and so women and couples who are not affiliated with nor interested in the church can access secular resources on fertility awareness. In my larger study on natural parenting, women often mentioned their environmentalist concerns as one of the key reasons for going hormone-free and wanting to learn more about and try to implement fertility awareness. The turn from traditionally religious forms of natural family planning to more flexible, liberal, and secular fertility awareness-based methods of contraception was facilitated through their digitalization and the broader access to such information that it afforded, beyond specialized religious circles in which natural family planning first developed.

Several lines of analysis are relevant to this digitalization of fertility awareness. Specifically, these trends reveal how our embodied, sexual, and spiritual lives are made digital. The first is what Deborah Lupton calls the "spreading out of self-tracking cultures and practices from the purely personal into multiple social domains," which now include reproductive and recreational sexual practice, often discussed openly, though anonymously, with communities of people who share common practices and values.[22] Fertility awareness is an example of how bioinformation that once was known only to the woman (e.g. details of her menstrual cycle, date of ovulation and of sexual intercourse, etc.) is now shared not only with medical professionals, but with online communities that offer advice and support in these matters. This points out to another recurring trend: the emergence of digital communities of (self-proclaimed or peers-acclaimed) experts who benevolently offer advice or get paid for their services as coaches or fertility educators. Though their personal life stories and motivations may diverge, these online communities bring together those who emphasize "respecting the female body" and "following the natural way."

Another key point to consider at the junction of the digital, the material, and the embodied is the design of fertility trackers and, more importantly, their corresponding apps. What changed in the shift from pen and paper charts in a personal notebook or on sheets of paper to a smartphone integrated app (in most cases)? The significance of the aesthetics of (highly) feminine self-tracking cultures is part of the cluster of questions raised by the digitalization of highly embodied practices, such as fertility awareness, but also the tracking of the details

---

tions, eds Monique Scheer, Nadia Fadil and Birgitte Schepelern Johansen (New York: Bloomsbury, 2019), 17–30 and 208–209.
22 Deborah Lupton, "Self-Tracking Modes: Reflexive Self-Monitoring and Data Practices," in *Social Science Research Network*, 2014 [Online], http://dx.doi.org/10.2139/ssrn.2483549 (accessed October 3, 2014)

of pregnancy or breastfeeding. Contemporary cycle tracking apps confer fertility awareness a new digital aesthetic and a practicality that retain little in common with the stern circling of calendar days or charting on a piece of paper. The user interface of fertility tracking apps may not always reflect the seriousness of what is at stake with family planning: a pregnancy and, potentially, the new life of a child. Fancy or even playful digital designs, in line with the "gamification" of self-tracking not just in pregnancy, but also in fertility monitoring may obscure the complexity of the medical research and technological expertise needed to produce the tools (e. g. seamless Bluetooth digital thermometers, wearable trackers and sensors, etc.) and algorithms necessary for its implementation.[23] A search with the keywords "menstruation," "period," and or "ovulation," in the App Store and in Google Play yields many results: the design of the majority of apps include colors such as pink, purple, or more rarely red, and illustrations such as flowers, drops, and circles. These suggest neither bodily discipline nor the disciplining of bodies, in a Foucauldian sense, imposed on women and their partners, for a concrete and successful implementation of the practice. For instance, CycleBeads is an app based on the (old and proven less accurate) "fixed days" or "calendar days" method, different from modern and more effective 2- or 3-symptoms-based methods. The "beads" of the app, each corresponding to particular days in the cycle, are more reminiscent visually of a pill's packaging than of the prayer beads of a rosary. The designs of these apps generally do not allude to religious obligation, nor to notions that non-procreative sexual practices (albeit monogamous heterosexual ones) are "sinful," notions that are often instilled by religious teachings that are also still widely circulated, both online and offline. The "menstrual tracking aesthetics"[24] of emerging digital forms of fertility awareness challenge its traditional association with religious imperatives. Obedience to religious teachings no longer is given as a motive for choosing such methods.

The primary motives for fertility awareness methods of family planning cited by my informants were not informed by traditional religious institutions, but rather focused on a rejection of hormonal and mechanical methods of contraception for a variety of reasons. Nevertheless, a spiritual dimension is implicitly

---

23 Deborah Lupton and Gareth M. Thomas, "Playing Pregnancy: The Ludification and Gamification of Expectant Motherhood in Smartphone Apps," *M/C Journal* 18/5 (2015).
24 For an analysis of the "feminine aesthetics and often-obvious naming of apps" in relationship with gender see Sarah Fox and Daniel A. Epstein, "Monitoring Menses: Design-Based Investigations of Menstrual Tracking Applications," in *The Palgrave Handbook of Critical Menstruation Studies*, eds. Chris Bobel, Inga T. Winkler, Breanne Fahs, Katie Hasson, Elizabeth Arveda Kissling, and Tomi-Ann Roberts (Palgrave Macmillan, 2020), 739 – 740.

present through notions of following nature, respecting women's bodies and the planet, or knowing oneself better. The parents whom I interviewed and who engage in natural family living mentioned the strong links they saw between their environmentalist ethics, their interest in or practice of fertility awareness, and their contraceptive choices. As such, interfering with or against nature through chemical disruption (by taking the pill or other hormonal contraceptives) was an issue for many of them. Similarly, the hormonal residues of contraceptives found in urine and then in waters were mentioned as an environmental and moral issue. One of my informants, already a mother, put it in this way: "Why would I pollute my body and the planet with hormones? This is an issue of respect." Very few of them questioned, however, the naturalness of condoms of various materials, of using digital thermometers, or apps on their smartphones to store and even interpret such personal biodata.

Finally, another important contextual element deserves mention here. In the last fifteen to twenty years, this rapid progress of many forms of the digitalization of our daily lives, including our sexual and reproductive lives, has been taking place in a context where an increasing importance is given to discourses about the environment, or about a "return to Nature" or a "return of *the* natural." Whether or not governments or people agree with these ideas, such discourses no longer are those of a fringe, or a minority of environmental activists or green political parties. Rather, they extend to mainstream, online, and social media, public debates and the general public (e.g. discussions about climate change, new "clean" energies, etc.). Fertility management is part of such broader discussions, in relation to population overgrowth and use of resources. Pro-natalist ideas tend to be frowned upon and, certainly, natural parenting does not question contraception *per se,* but only its methods and impacts, on women's bodies, and on the environment. With an acute awareness that effective and coercive actions are not yet and probably will not be taken at the governmental level, many of the parents whom I interviewed emphasized the idea of *voluntarily* engaging in their chosen practices. Forsaking hormonal contraceptives that leave residue in the water, using washable diapers, purchasing second-hand items, or restricting their diets to local, seasonal, and preferably organic foods are examples of practices to which the parents in my research ascribed spiritual meanings and regarded as in line with their values.[25] Many stressed that they were willingly trying to "do their share" and take action at their own private, domestic level.

---

25 Florence Pasche Guignard, "Nurturing the Sustainable Family: Natural Parenting and Environmentalist Foodways in Francophone Contexts," in *Mothers and Food: Negotiating Foodways from Maternal Perspectives*, eds. Florence Pasche Guignard and Tanya Cassidy (Bradford: Demeter Press, 2016), 55–69.

This pertains mostly to the domain of personal consumption, but transmitting more sustainable habits, ideals, and environmentalist values to their children also stood out as important. More than just an informed and free choice that goes against the prevailing norms of capitalist overconsumption, natural parenting and this resurgence of and appeal to and idealized "Nature" are often regarded as resistance in the form of an individual response to a technological or even technocratic perspective. Ultimately, there remain a paradox in the fact that discourses that bridge "the natural" and "the maternal" (and sometimes also "the parental" more generally) tend to contest technocracy and technoptimism, including its digital dimensions, while at the same time they depend, now more than ever, on digital technology and media to be disseminated.

6.4 Behind my screen and in the field: methodological reflections on researching natural parenting in the digital age

The analysis of selected examples, the in-depth case study, and all aspects of natural parenting presented in this chapter derive from a broader research (see note 5). Its methodology combined cyber fieldwork and direct, on-site observation (for instance, through participating in workshops, events, or festivals on the theme of environmentalism), as well as interviews with practitioners and advocates of natural parenting. Most of them were recruited directly from the online platforms where they shared, mostly through pseudonymous names, elements of their lives as mothers, wives, daughters, workers, and many other roles. I built trust with my informants through first sharing with them some of my own questions and experiences, both online and offline, always being transparent about my own identity as a researcher. Though many of my research questions and my initial interest for this topic stem from my personal experience as a mother, I did not consider auto-ethnography as sufficient for this study. I personally had not engaged with *all* of the key practices of natural parenting to the same extent as my informants. For instance, I did practice babywearing, but I did not use washable diapers for my child. I breastfed her for more months than most women did in the Swiss national context that I was in, but this breastfeeding did not end with the "natural weaning" that many of my informants told me about and considered as ideal: my maternity leave was ending and I had to return to work in an academic environment that was neither friendly nor adapted towards nursing mothers. I certainly would not identify as an advocate of natural parenting. Yet, my informants felt confident telling me about ideas that I was already familiar with, especially after I expressed my genuine interest and (somewhat partial) practice of natural parenting. I also felt confident sharing with them some details of selected personal experiences that echoed what I had first read on the forums and that would show potential informants and actual interviewees that I could understand at least *some* of the antagonist reactions that they encountered. In their contexts and in mine, some parenting choices and practices remain quite marginal, which also explains the online building of online communities of shared values and practices. For instance, I shared with some of them how I had felt scrutinized by my local public health nurses because I insisted in continuing to breastfeed my then two-month-old baby. I was experiencing difficulties with nursing and, receiving no adequate support from these same nurses, I was being pushed towards using formula. In contexts where their choices were often marginalized, scrutinized, or openly criticized, these mothers were reluctant to voice out their personal journey into natural parenting to friends, relatives, and their regular healthcare practitioners.[26] Instead, they shared some of their ideas or challenges online and then to me, during the interviews, with some confidence that even if I did not identify strongly with nor promoted these choices, I could, at least, have some understanding of what they were talking about, including in terms of personal and embodied experience. This prompted an important methodological question for me as a researcher. How can scholars bridge the gap between what is discussed and shared online, in digital spaces, and the real, raw, everyday practices of mothers? More specifically, how do the objects featured digitally in online spaces reflect actual practices and inevitably variable discourses ascribed to them?

For example, I recruited Fabienne, a French mother in her early thirties who self-identified as "agnostic," for an interview through writing to her directly in a forum dedicated to natural parenting. When I asked her if she had done "anything special" around the birth of her first child, she replied that they had not organized anything. Yet, later in the same interview, Fabienne gave me many details about the family event organized for her daughter's first birthday; with other relatives, the family buried the placenta in the backyard of their newly built eco-home. This ritual is known as a "placenterre," the burial of the placenta in the ground, or as the French term suggests, giving it a place in the earth. She had "saved" (*récupéré*) her placenta after her home birth, and kept in the freezer

---

26 Anna Fedele, "When Homebirth 'Goes Wrong': Holistic Mothers Who End Up Giving Birth in a Portuguese Hospital," Etnográfica 22/3 (2018), 152, n26; Pasche Guignard, "The In/Visibility of Mothering Against the Norm in Francophone Contexts;" and Fedele and Pasche Guignard, "Pushing from the Margins," 133 and 140.

for a whole year. On top of this placenta, the family planted a tree salvaged from Fabienne's own grandparents' property, located elsewhere in France. In this case, the planted tree stands as a visible reminder, growing like the child, but the buried placenta will decompose in the ground, no longer materially here to be seen or displayed. In all cases that I encountered, even when no tree was planted, families selected a specific and meaningful location for burying the placenta, with the idea of "giving it back to the earth" also mentioned. The timing of this ritual also is important: the freezer, a modern technology, allows to keep the placenta for longer periods of time.

In addition to such discourses collected through semi-structured interviews, I also considered a variety of publicly accessible platforms that did not require any identification and that anyone can search for and read them online. Other platforms require some form of identification. On these free and public internet platforms, parents share stories, some of them very intimate and personal, as in the case of home birth and fertility awareness. While the case study presented here did not pull from stories shared on such social media groups or forums, my awareness about them and the role of specific practices and objects in the natural parenting community informed my understanding of some situations brought up in the interviews, such as the logistical difficulty for women in France to access the proper midwifery care necessary for a safe home birth, or in-person support groups or secular educators in fertility awareness (in contrast with an easier access to online resources). Methodologically, I went back and forth between the online, purely digital and often anonymous expressions, and the in-person and very personal stories of the informants talking to me in their kitchens, in public parks and cafés, or through Skype. It should also be noted that the scope of my research did not allow me to include large-scale data mining or the use of bots for the purpose of systematically scraping the public data of users of online platforms dedicated to natural parenting. Moreover, this would also have raised new questions in research ethics that were only emerging in the (francophone) digital humanities at the time I started this study. We can question whether new research ethics protocols already have or will be put in place regarding such issues, depending on the awareness of various boards responsible for authorizing research with human beings.

Another advantage afforded by online spaces is that they transcend temporality, which also allows researchers to see how certain practices evolve over time, or become more accepted and less marginal in any given national context over the years (for instance, babywearing or breastfeeding in the context of France). Moreover, digital expressions and intimate accounts of mothering may (or may not) remain accessible as archives for a long time. For instance, a mother facing a specific problem with breastfeeding or interpreting a fertility chart could consult an online forum or social media group to find what another mother with the same issue wrote earlier, as well as the comments or responses by other active contributors. In most cases, it would not matter to the mother presently seeking information if the post was three years, three months, three days or three hours old; what she needs to read is available at all times in a click, whereas her lactation consultant or her regular healthcare practitioner may not answer her calls at 3:32 am.

Besides collecting data for the specific purpose of research, the epistemological relevance of analyzing publicly accessible online discourses is justified in the case of an interdisciplinary perspective that combines the digital humanities with other, more common approaches in the social sciences (anthropology and sociology). In order to understand natural parenting and its spiritually ascribed meanings in the digital age, it is necessary to reach out to potential informants where they are. Beyond babywearing workshops, lactation clinics, or environmentalist festivals, many of these parents are also active on a diversity of online spaces. Because many of their practices are considered as alternative to the mainstream ones, or are even regarded as suspicious, such online spaces may play an even more important role for these parents.[27] For some practices, their religious origins and religiously conservative association, may also play a role in their marginalization, especially in highly secularized contexts, such as that of France.

As a stranger or even as a friend, receiving a personal invitation to attend a ritual celebration centered on the mother during pregnancy, such as a mother raising or blessing way, let alone just to a regular baby shower or another traditional ritual taking place during pregnancy is a rare event. Being invited to attend a homebirth *as a researcher*––and not as a supportive friend––would be an even more rare occasion. Though there is a trend in inviting professional birth photographers, with their technology (the camera), for the purpose of recording image (and sometimes videos, too) of birth, especially in the case of a planned home birth, researchers allowed to take fieldwork notes and document the whole process would often be out of place. Behind the screen and in person, during some of the interviews, I had the occasion to witness breastfeeding sessions of various lengths with children of various ages. Mothers showed me specific objects, such as baby carriers, washable diapers, or eco-certified wooden toys. As a researcher, my chances are very slim to be invited to attend a home birth, to witness a "placenterre" ritualization or the making of a placenta

---

27 Pasche Guignard, "The In/Visibility of Mothering Against the Norm in Francophone Contexts;" and Fedele and Pasche Guignard, "Pushing from the Margins."

print, or to see a woman take her basal body temperature upon waking up, from this same anthropological perspective. Yet, through the many digital expressions found online, I gained access to such uncommon practices and, through interviewing parents at a convenient time for them, through online communication, I could document more precisely some of these objects, practices, and discourses.

6.5 Concluding remarks

This chapter considered representations, discourses, and practices of "natural parenting" at their intersection with material religion and digital technology. There is a continuous trend in associating natural parenting with religion, spirituality, or ritualization, even if not all practices of natural parenting had been initially associated with specific religious movements at their origins. Some typical practices actually do have religious roots, historically at least, or are also commonly performed within specific religious groups: fertility awareness practiced as a conservative form of natural family planning (without barrier methods) is an example of this. In addition, some practitioners insist on a vocabulary of morality, of "doing the right thing" for themselves, their family, future generations, and the planet, engage in new ritualizations that often borrow from traditional ones, or ascribe new spiritual meanings to what they do. Objects, such as placentas, babywearing wraps, washable diapers or digital thermometers, often carry such meanings and display the tenets of what these parents believe and enact in everyday choices beyond embodiment, but in a continuum with the body, especially the maternal body and the body of the baby. These objects reflect how choices in lifestyle and, more specifically, in consumption, values, practices and the environment intertwine.

To some of the questions asked in the previous section, about how to bridge the gap between online, digital representations, and the everyday, embodied, material and maternal practices and objects, as well as the various discourses ascribed to them, several answers emerged. First, without fully engaging in a methodology of autoethnography, acquiring in-person experiences of the said practices and objects, even to a limited extent, can usefully inform our scholarship. Then, the movement of reading general online discourses against the backdrop of what informants say about *their own* practice, and vice-versa, is also relevant. Finally, I suggest that such methodological reflection may also be relevant beyond the academic study of religions, for instance, in thinking about the ways in which topics such as food, sports, or sexuality are apprehended through such a reflexive perspective in the digital humanities and not just in anthropology or religious studies. Around these topics (and many others, too) the discrepancy between the mediated practices and the embodied, material reality can also be enormous. Let's think, for instance, of the gap between homecooking and the now many cooking shows on television or Netflix.[28] Another striking example worth mentioning here is the distance –and sometimes the causal the relationship of how the digital representations influence the physical, actually embodied and highly gendered practices– between mainstream pornography and sexuality as lived and reflected in anonymous online counselling columns by various experts, including religiously affiliated ones.

In the early twenty-first century, the academic study of religions has experienced two critical disciplinary advances in embracing the "material turn" and the "digital turn," almost coincidentally, in a movement seeking innovative methodological paths and taking an adequate and reflexive distance from purely "textocentric" approaches in the discipline. This chapter has demonstrated how the recent and still increasing digitalization of daily lives further leads to certain practices and objects carrying values and meanings. Like placentas, these objects can be exceptional and extraordinary for most people, uncommonly seen and touched directly, but now more commonly visible through their digital images and materialization under many forms, such as placenta prints, or trees planted as markers of a placenterre ritual. These objects can also be part of the everyday, intimate lives of parents who show and discuss them in the framework of their highly curated, digital lives. The contrast found in the use of highly mediated and digital tools and online platforms to implement and disseminate ideas and practices that, for the most part, relate to embodiment and materiality is particularly significant in the case of natural parenting. In the process of this seemingly paradoxical practice, these parents create a unique space for their community. Of course, parenting is not the only domain that digital technologies have transformed in the past decades, but the insistence on "the natural" and an awareness of and respect of "the body" is now relayed mostly through digital media rather than through official medical institutions (e. g. at the family doctor's office) or older forms of activism and self-awareness groups (e. g. as in feminist groups in earlier decades).

The discussion of selected aspects of natural parenting presented in this chapter, has emphasized new questions and new sites of analysis that arise from paying attention to the digital side of being human and embodied, or, in

---

28 An exception to this may be shows that highlight, precisely, this distance between professional chefs and what ordinary, untrained people actually are capable of doing in the kitchen. Such examples include *Nailed It!*, airing on Netflix since 2018, where the cakes made by the participants generally are far from resembling the model that they have to bake from scratch.

other words, to the digitalization of our daily lives with a particular focus on women's health and bodies. More than ever, these stand at the junction of the embodied, the material, the maternal, the spiritual, and, now, the digital as well.

References

Bobel, Chris. *The Paradox of Natural Mothering*. Philadelphia: Temple University Press, 2002.

Bobel, Chris. "Resisting, But Not Too Much: Interrogating the Paradox of Natural Mothering," in *Maternal Theory. Essential Readings*, ed. Andrea O'Reilly. Toronto: Demeter Press, 2007.

Borek, Valerie. "A Placenta by Any Other Name," in *Placenta Wit: Mother Stories, Rituals, and Research*, ed. by Nané Jordan. Bradford: Demeter Press, 2017.

Chidester, David. *Religion: Material Dynamics*. Berkeley: University of California Press, 2018.

Coats, Curtis J. and Monica Emerich, "The Webs We Spin: Relational, Mediated, Spiritual," in *Practical Spiritualities in a Media Age*, eds. Coats and Emerich. New York: Bloomsbury, 2016.

Davis-Floyd, Robbie. *Birth as an American Rite of Passage*. Berkeley: University of California Press, 1992.

Davis-Floyd, Robbie. "The Technocratic, Humanistic, and Holistic Models of Birth," *International Journal of Gynecology & Obstetrics* 75 (2001): S5–S23.

Emerich, Monica. *The Gospel of Sustainability: Media, Market and LOHAS*. Urbana: University of Illinois Press, 2011.

Fedele, Anna. "When Homebirth 'Goes Wrong': Holistic Mothers Who End Up Giving Birth in a Portuguese Hospital," *Etnográfica* 22/3 (2018): 691–714.

Fedele, Anna and Florence Pasche Guignard, "Pushing from the Margins: 'Natural Childbirth' in Holistic Spiritualities and Natural Parenting in France and Portugal," in *Sacred Inception: Reclaiming the Spirituality of Birth in the Modern World,* eds. Marianne Delaporte and Morag Martin. Lanham, MD: Lexington Books, 2018.

Fox, Sarah and Daniel A. Epstein, "Monitoring Menses: Design-Based Investigations of Menstrual Tracking Applications," in *The Palgrave Handbook of Critical Menstruation Studies,* eds. Chris Bobel, Inga T. Winkler, Breanne Fahs, Katie Hasson, Elizabeth Arveda Kissling, and Tomi-Ann Roberts. Palgrave Macmillan, 2020.

Jordan, Nané. "Introduction" in ed., *Placenta Wit: Mother Stories, Rituals, and Research*, ed. Nané Jordan. Bradford: Demeter Press, 2017.

Klassen, Pamela. *Blessed Events: Religion and Homebirth in America*. Princeton: Princeton University Press, 2001.

Klassen, Pamela. "Contraception and the Coming of Secularism: Reconsidering Reproductive Freedom as Religious Freedom," in *Secular Bodies, Affects and Emotions: European Configurations,* eds Monique Scheer, Nadia Fadil and Birgitte Schepelern Johansen. New York: Bloomsbury, 2019.

Lupton, Deborah. "Self-Tracking Modes: Reflexive Self-Monitoring and Data Practices," in *Social Science Research Network*, 2014 [Online], http://dx.doi.org/10.2139/ssrn.2483549. Accessed October 3, 2014.

Lupton, Deborah and Gareth M. Thomas, "Playing Pregnancy: The Ludification and Gamification of Expectant Motherhood in Smartphone Apps," *M/C Journal* 18/5 (2015), https://doi.org/10.5204/mcj.1012

Meyer, Birgit, ed., *Aesthetic formations: Media, Religion, and the Senses*. New York: Palgrave Macmillan, 2009.

Meyer, Birgit. "Aesthetics of Persuasion: Global Christianity and Pentecostalism's Sensational Forms," *South Atlantic Quarterly* 9 (2019): 741–763.

Paltineau, Maya-Merida. "From Intensive Mothering to Identity Parenting" in *Intensive Mothering: The Cultural Contradictions of Modern Motherhood*, ed. Linda Rose Ennis. Bradford: Demeter Press, 2015.

Pasche Guignard, Florence. "Digital Tools for Fertility Awareness: Family Planning, Religion, and Feminine Embodiment," in *The Routledge Handbook of Religion, Medicine, and Health*, eds. Dorothea Lüddeckens, Philipp Hetmanczyk, Pamela E. Klassen, and Justin B. Stein (New York: Routledge, 2021), 293–307.

Pasche Guignard, Florence. "Discours, représentations, pratiques et modes de transmission des savoirs et des idées sur l'allaitement dans les milieux francophones du parentage naturel," in Allaiter. De l'Antiquité à nos jours / Histoire(s) et cultures d'une pratique, ed. by Yasmina Foehr-Janssens and Daniela Solfaroli Camillocci, 2 volumes. (Turnhout: Brepols, 2022, in press).

Pasche Guignard, Florence. "High-Tech Mediations, Low Tech Lifestyles: The Paradox of Natural Parenting in the Digital Age," in *Media and Religion: The Global View*, eds. Stewart Hoover and Nabil Echchaibi. Berlin: De Gruyter, 2021.

Pasche Guignard, Florence. "Mediated Babywearing as Aesthetic Orthodoxy," in *Practical Spiritualities in a Media Age*, eds. Curtis J. Coats and Monica Emerich. New York: Bloomsbury, 2016.

Pasche Guignard, Florence. "Nurturing the Sustainable Family: Natural Parenting and Environmentalist Foodways in Francophone Contexts," in *Mothers and Food: Negotiating Foodways from Maternal Perspectives*, eds. Florence Pasche Guignard and Tanya Cassidy. Bradford: Demeter Press, 2016.

Pasche Guignard, Florence. "The In/Visibility of Mothering Against the Norm in Francophone Contexts: Private and Public Discourses in the Mediation of 'Natural Parenting,'" *Canadian Journal of Communication* 40/1 (2015): 105–124.

Promey, Sally, ed. *Sensational Religion: Sensory Cultures in Material Practice*. New Haven: Yale University Press, 2014.

Rothman, Barbara Katz. *Labor: Women and Power in the Birthplace*. New York, Norton and Company, 1982.

Takeshita, Chikako. "Eco-Diapers: The American Discourse of Sustainable Motherhood," in *Mothering in the Age of Neoliberalism*, ed. Melinda Vandenbeld Giles. Bradford: Demeter Press, 2014.

James Edmonds
Chapter 7
(Re)Enchanting the Digital: Technological Manifestations of Baraka

Figure 1: Habib Syech on his phone in the middle of a performance being recorded by someone else on stage. Photo by the author.

7.1 Introduction

Tens of thousands of people descend upon the fields, town squares, and stadiums to watch, listen, feel, and participate in the performances of *selawat* (devotional songs about the virtue of prophet Muhammad) led by Habib Syech bin Abdul Qadir Assegaf. These events take place between fifteen and twenty-five times a month, and they have been taking place since 1998. A cacophony of sensory information fills the space between the bodies participating in this gathering of devotional piety. The fields are lit by mesmerizing stage lights accompanied by thousands of small LED lights from participants' smart phones. Some

https://doi.org/10.1515/9783110608755-008

of the thousands of video recordings find their way onto YouTube, Facebook, and other social media, but most do not. Many participants travel to multiple events in a month, making new recordings at every new location. The amount of new recordings every year is in the millions, but the number of recordings that can be found online does not match the number of recordings that are being made. Thus, a question arises: how are participants using these recordings and for what purpose? As I will argue throughout, these recordings become a part of the *selawat* milieu in which individuals who attend these events are seeking *baraka*. *Baraka* is often translated as blessings, holiness[1], charisma[2], or "nearness that allows for prosperity."[3] I define *baraka* as "the infinite possible manifestation of gifts, not dependent on reciprocation, from God, the one and only source of *baraka*, in both the visible and invisible world impacting the spiritual, economic, and social lives of people."[4] However, here, I will be focusing on how technology as a medium operates as a spiritual materiality and material spirituality lived, operated, and constantly exchanged through the digital. The use of digital technology in and beyond these events creates a possibility for imagining the (re)enchantment of the material.

My first introduction, like many Indonesians, to Habib Syech was digital. My first fieldwork in Indonesia brought me to the events of Syekh[5] Abah who was a Naqshbundiyya Syekh in rural Central Java. The Naqshbundiyya Sufi Order has a long and significant history in Indonesia as a foundational component and motivating factor in the spread of Islam across the archipelago.[6] After he suffered a stroke, Syekh Abah encouraged me to meet with Habib Syech because of his mass appeal in Indonesia. In the summer of 2012, I searched social media sites for a schedule and information on where he was to perform. I found the

---

1 Edward Westermarck, *The Moorish Conception of Holiness (baraka).* (Helsingfors: Akademiska Bokhandeln, 1916). Clifford Geertz. *Islam Observed: Religious Development in Morocco and Indonesia.* (New Haven: Yale University Press, 1968).
2 Pnina Werbner and Helene Basu, *Embodying charisma: Modernity, Locality, and Performance of Emotion in Sufi Cults,* 1st ed. (New York, London: Routledge, 1998).
3 Dietrich von Denffer, "Baraka as basic concept of Muslim Popular Belief," *Islamic Studies* 15 (3), 1976: 167–186.
4 James Edmonds, "Smelling *Baraka:* Everyday Islam and Islamic Normativity" in "(Mis)Representations of Islam: Politics, Community, and Advocacy," ed. Timothy P. Daniels and Meryem F. Zaman, special issue *American Journal of Islamic Social Science* 36, no. 3 (Summer 2019): 21–48.
5 The term Syekh here refers to Abah's position as the head of the local Naqshbandiyya order. This differs from the use of Syech in Habib Syech's name that does not indicate a position but rather indicates that "my father was a teacher."
6 See Martin van Bruinessen, *Tarekat Naqsyabandiyah di Indonesia: survei historis, geografis, dan sosiologis* (Bandung: Mizan, 1992).

official Facebook page for Habib Syech's fan club, Syekhermania,[7] "Syekherma-nia Pusat."[8] As of January 2019, 628,810 people had "liked" Habib Syech's Fan-club page, Syekhermania Pusat (Central Syekhermania). I have followed Sye-khermania Pusat for seven years, and the number of followers has increased by the thousands every month. Habib Syech's Twitter account (established in June 2013), syaikhassegaf, has over one million followers. Hundreds of Facebook pages dedicated to local Syekhermania groups or competing sites to Syekherma-nia Pusat have tens of thousands of members as well. Over the last ten years, the social media presence of Habib Syech and his Fanclub have flooded the media-scape of Indonesia forming transnational communities. However, the use of technology goes well beyond Facebook groups and social media posts.

Indicating the contexts in which these *selawat* events form is essential to un-derstand the relationship between digital technologies and these massive per-formances that bring millions together across Asia each year. Both digital tech-nology and the prominence of these events combine in the historical genealogy of Syekhermania to create a fan club that provides a sense of online community while Syekhermania and Habib Syech indicate a deep distrust of these cyber-Is-lamic environments. Participants make recordings and seek out new recordings in order to capture *baraka*, if only for a moment. The desire to capture *baraka* indicates a different milieu in which these videos, pictures, and audio recordings circulate.

As Manuel Castells has argued, "the protocols of communication are not based on the sharing of culture but on the culture of sharing."[9] The internet and social media sites have enabled exponential access to communication that is multifaceted, digital, and open to more individuals. This global form of communication, however, has also changed the nature of communication. The web and social media are built on a culture of sharing that has made people less dependent upon centralized media. In Indonesia, an example of an Islamic figure whose popularity is built on marketing and branding through traditional forms of media and social media is Kyai Haji Abdullah Gymnastiar.[10] Eventually his popularity would wane due to taking a second wife, but his popularity was built on an engagement with the culture of sharing propelled by his extensive marketing that brought Islam, Western pop-psychology, and technology together

---

7 This is sometimes spelled Syechermania as well.
8 "Syekhermania Pusat," *Facebook*. https://www.facebook.com/SYEKHERMANIA.PUSAT/. Ac-cessed January 2019.
9 Manuel Castells, *Communication Power* (Oxford : Oxford University Press, 2009), 167.
10 James Hoesterey, *Rebranding Islam: Piety, Prosperity, and A Self-Help Guru* (Stanford: Stan-ford University Press, 2015), 11.

in the media that appealed to Islamic piety across Indonesia.[11] The recordings of Habib Syech appeal to many of these same Muslims across Indonesia, but his disavowal of technology and individuals' uses of the recordings are not being harnessed to indicate a participant's presence at the event by sharing the recording online. These events and their recordings are not defined by a culture of sharing.

This use of technology also emerges as a challenge to a reading of digital technology and social media as carriers of the project of modernity. Multiple modernities,[12] liquid modernity,[13] varieties of modernity,[14] and reflexive Modernization[15] have all been used to fight against the universalizing narrative of modernity. However, science and technology are still assumed to be the "two most salient forces" of modernity.[16] That is to say that digital technologies are a part of "a general economy of power which has the form [of], or which is at any rate dominated by, the technology of security."[17] Facebook, Instagram, and other online environments have become spaces dominated by governmental apparatuses of security through surveillance under the guises of freedom and privately owned entities operating outside of the constraints of public trust.

Many of the recordings do not make their way into social media and are, therefore, not as easily surveilled by the state. Although I am not certain of how, if at all, individual recordings are surveilled, the lack of social media presence has led to the presence of state officials and anthropologists sponsored by foreign governments at these events. Habib Syech was always quick to not only disavow technology but also any political stance. He did, however, agree to work with the Indonesian government to eradicate drug and alcohol use. He has always promoted a drug and alcohol-free lifestyle, and for a period of time, he gave more sermons that encouraged participants to stay away from drugs and alcohol. Surveillance must often take place at the ground level, rather than

---

11 Hoestery, *Rebranding Islam*, 10 – 11
12 S. N. Eisendtadt, *Comparative Civilizations and Multiple Modernities* (Leiden, Boston: Brill, 2003).
13 Zygmunt Bauman, *Liquid Modernity* (Cambridge, Malden, MA: Polity; Blackwell, 2000).
14 Volker Schmidt, "Multiple Modernities or Varieties of Modernity?" *Current Sociology.* 2006; 54(1): 77– 97.
15 Ulrich Beck, Anthony Giddens, and Scott Lash, *Reflexive Modernization: Politics, Tradition and Aesthetics in the Modern Social Order* (Cambridge, UK: Polity, 1994).
16 Sheila Jasanoff, "Future Imperfect: Science, Technology, and the Imagination of Modernity," in *Dreamscapes of Modernity: Sociotechnical Imaginaries and the Fabrication of Power*, Sheila Jasanoff and Sang-Hyun Kim, eds. (Chicago: The University of Chicago Press, 2015), 8.
17 Michael Foucault, *Security, Territory, Population: Lectures at the College de France, 1977– 1978*, Graham Burchell trans. Michel Senellart ed. (London: Palgrave Macmillan, 2004), 25.

through social media or digital technology. These recordings, therefore, are often saved to individual smartphones and occasionally shared through social media or apps such as WhatsApp. This is also partially due to the way that media has been surveilled through Indonesian history, as I will indicate in the first section of the chapter. In May 2019, the Indonesian government blocked WhatsApp, Facebook, and Instagram across Indonesia due to violence around the election.[18] Even with state surveillance at the events, the fact that these recordings are kept by participants and not shared as readily indicate a tactic by which Indonesian Muslims are subverting technologies of security, even if incompletely.

Another feature of technology and its relationship with the project of modernity is an assumption that they are disenchanted. Smartphones and digital recordings are part of the systemization and rationalizing process pointed out by figures such as Max Weber.[19] Smartphones are a material technology that are assumed to be engaged with the 'real' world and devoid of any supernatural or magical elements. The recordings of *selawat* performed by Habib Syech are captured within the phone using digital technology. The smartphones themselves are a material, physical object that participants can hold in their hands. Following this logic, smartphones and their recordings should partially engage with and be defined by the culture of sharing that inundates digital technology. However, this material technology is not only a participant in the history of mass media in Indonesia, the culture of sharing, and the rise of Islamic preachers. Indonesian Muslims' use of these material technologies reveal how technology and the ineffable come together. Participants recording *selawat* are seeking the material and spiritual prosperity given by Allah through *baraka*, transmitted through smartphones. *Baraka* is never guaranteed, and not every individual recording these events is doing so for the same reason. However, for many, these material technologies allow Allah's gifts to be experienced throughout their day, even if they can never be captured.

7.2 Mass Media in Indonesia

Previous restrictions of technology under both Sukarno (1945–1967) and Suharto (1967–1998) as well as community based and decentralized technological organization loom large in the Indonesian context. In the same way that Bubandt re-

---

18 Fanny Potkin, "Indonesia curbs social media, blaming hoaxes for inflaming unrest," *Reuters*, May 22, 2016.
19 Max Weber, *The Sociology of Religion* (Boston: Beacon, 1963), 209.

minds us that authoritarianism and the "political ghost of Suharto" still haunt contemporary Indonesian democracy,[20] technology as a mode of both authoritarian control and subversion of that control are intricately mixed in the formation of the contemporary mediascapes of Indonesia. I am using mediascapes in the manner in which Arjun Appadurai uses the term referring to both the means of production and dissemination of the media as well as the "images of the world created by these images." [21] It is in both the modes of production and the representational images that these productions indicate that the "collectively held, institutionally stabilized, and publicly performed visions of desirable futures, animated by shared understandings of forms of social life and social order attainable through, and supportive of, advances in science and technology."[22] Although Jasanoff allows for the possibility of multiple sociotechnical imaginaries, the prime mover in these imaginaries is science and technology. This is an important corrective to the assumption that technology is primarily a feature of and mover of modernity, but in focusing on the advances in science and technology as the object of investigation for understanding social life that animates "institutionally stable" visions of the future, fixes science and technology as the defining feature of social life in the assemblages of mediascapes informing the performances of Habib Syech. Rather, I see technoscientific imaginaries as one attempt to deal with the complexity of the digital, but in privileging science and technology as a corrective to other formulations of the imaginary is insufficient in understanding the discursive field of the performances that is used by, changed, and navigated by participants leading to new forms of piety. Science and technology are one ambiguous part of the context into which Syekhermania and their use of digital technology are born.

The explosion of possibilities for media following the downfall of Suharto, as well as the genealogies that inform technological innovation, picked up steam before his downfall, and in the space opened up by a loosing of regulations, Indonesia's most prominent tele-dai (television preacher), AA Gym rises and falls as one of the most significant figures in contemporary Indonesian Islam. Hoesterey describes him as "as a combination of prosperity gospel televangelist Joel Osteen and TV psychologist Dr. Phil (Einstein 2008), with Oprah

---

20 Nils Bubdant, *Democracy, Corruption and the Politics of Spirits in Contemporary Indonesia* (New York: Routledge, 2014), 133.

21 Arjun Appadurai, *Modernity at Large: Cultural Dimensions of Globalization*, Public Worlds; v. 1. (Minneapolis: University of Minnesota Press, 1996), 35.

22 Sheila Jasanoff, "Future Imperfect: Science, Technology, and the Imagination of Modernity," *Dreamscapes of Modernity: Sociotechnical Imaginaries and the Fabrication of Power*, Sheila Jasanoff and Sang-Hyun Kim, eds. (Chicago: The University of Chicago Press, 2015), 4.

Winfrey's power of personal brand (Lofton 2011)."[23] The task at hand is to place Syeckhermania, Habib Syech, and the performances themselves within milieu of Indonesia in reference to not only the prominence of figures like Aa Gym but also the rise in figures like him on the international Islamic stage. In doing this, it will become clear how Habib Syech is not a tele-dai and actively reject attempts to place him in that category.

Indonesia's first vice president and revolutionary against colonialism, Muhammad Hatta, was essential in introducing "cooperates operated not just as pragmatic systems of production but as technologies of social justice."[24] Hatta envisioned the Indonesian future as progressing with individual communities creating a technological and economic future run by multiple individuals. It was a bottom-up vision for Indonesian democracy that took power out of the elites of society. This, however, was not the vision that Sukarno or Suharto had for Indonesia.

Sukarno worked to build industrial complexes run by elite members of society. Hatta retired from the vice presidency in 1956 as a critique to Sukarno's "politicization of cooperatives," among other things.[25] Hatta's critique of Sukarno's 'Guided Democracy' as authoritarianism in democratic clothing landed Hatta in prison. Suharto's New Order worked to further consolidate economic and political power by consolidating military power over political life, reorganizing institutions in order to control these organizations at the furthest level possible, and justified authoritarian rule.[26] From independence in 1945 until the fall of Suharto in 1998, Hatta's ideas of economic cooperates at the base of society dramatically impacted the landscape under which Onno Purbo emerges, "the father of the Indonesian internet."[27]

For members of the general public, authoritarianism that seeks to control every aspect of economic and political life enforced by the military becomes the standard power relationship under which Indonesians had to operate. This

---

23 Hoesterey, *Rebranding Islam*, 11.
24 Suzanne Moon, "Building from the Outside In: Sociotechnical Imaginaries and Civil Society in New Order Indonesia," in *Dreamscapes of Modernity: Sociotechnical Imaginaries and the Fabrication of Power*, Sheila Jasanoff and Sang-Hyun Kim, eds. (Chicago: The University of Chicago Press, 2015), 179.
25 Moon, "Building from the Outside," 181
26 Edward Aspinall, *Opposing Suharto: Compromise, Resistance, and Regime Change in Indonesia* (Stanford, CA: Stanford University Press, 2005), 22–23.
27 Joshua Barker, "Guerilla Engineers: The Internet and the Politics of Freedom in Indonesia," in *Dreamscapes of Modernity: Sociotechnical Imaginaries and the Fabrication of Power*, Sheila Jasanoff and Sang-Hyun Kim, eds. (Chicago: The University of Chicago Press, 2015), 200.

is clearly indicated by Suharto's launching of the Palapas satellite in 1976 that sought to unify Indonesia by shaping and controlling the Indonesian conscious-ness.[28] Bottom-up enterprises that were not endorsed by the New Order had little chance of success, and yet, Purbo begins building the foundations for Indonesia's internet through " 'guerilla' (*gerilya*) tactics in their 'struggle' (*perjuangan*) to bring a 'free net' to Indonesia."[29] The formation of the internet was very much a part of the tactical struggle against the strategic power of the New Order. This is significantly different from the way in which, for example, the internet develops in the United States as an extension of the state.[30] It is in the vein of struggle and freedom that the internet develops.

Purbo began developing the first interconnected computer network in the 1990s between the Institute of Technology in Bandung and other campuses.[31] Although Suharto introduced his Palapas satellite in 1976, the internet as free net was under constant negotiation at the Institute of Technology in Bandung. [32] The development of the activist internet run by those subverting power became even more significant as Purbo wanted to create a wire infrastructure that was independently controlled. However in 2007, he writes, "money, technology and government help are not the keys. The dedication of many Indonesian volunteers to community education processes is the most important factor in developing this infrastructure."[33] Rather than laying cables through the Bandung campus and Indonesia as a whole, he now sees the wireless internet as the future of com-munity-based infrastructure. This sense of the internet as a place in which au-thoritarian regimes attempt to consolidate power and the internet as a place of community-based, bottom-up tactics for improving Indonesia. For Onno, the internet was a "self-organized public" that "should provide participants with a form of sociality that is characterized by a set of shared technical practices, heightened reciprocity, less hierarchy, more speed, greater immediacy, and great-er intimacy."[34] It is in this environment that the Islamic tele-dai emerges.

---

28 Joshua Barker, "Engineers and Political Dreams: Indonesia in the Satellite Age," *Current Anthropology* 46, no. 5 (December 2005), 708.

29 Barker, "Guerilla Engineers," 200.

30 Byung-Keun Kim, *Internationalizing the Internet: The Co-evolution of Influence and Technology*, New Horizons in the Economics of Innovation (Cheltenham, UK; Northampton, MA: E. Elgar, 2005).

31 Barker, "Guerilla Engineers," 200.

32 Barker, "Guerilla Engineers," 205.

33 Onno Purbo, "Getting Connected." *Inside Indonesia*. July 29, 2007. Accessed February 8, 2009. https://www.insideindonesia.org/getting-connected.

34 Barker, "Guerilla Engineers," 214.

7.3 The Rise of the Tele-dai and Digital Islamic Authority

Increased access to the internet and the rapid development of technologies such as television and cassettes have dramatically changed the dynamics of Islamic authority, authenticity, and the "self-conscious Islamic identity and practices (prayer, religious lessons, meetings, and anti-Christian rhetoric) and paraphernalia (clothing, mosques, books, and cassettes) that enact, embody, and inculcate it."[35] The increased use of and dispersal of digital technology has created distinctly digital forms of Islam, such as the initiation into the Naqshbandi Sufi Order through taking digital *bay'a*, oath of allegiance.[36] The increase in "cyber-Islamic environments" as spaces that "represent varied Muslim worldviews within the House of Islam, all of which present a reference point of identity with a conceptualization of Islam," provide a diverse frontier for new forms of purely digital Islam as well as new reference points for everyday engagement with Islamic identities, practices, and beliefs.[37] This can be seen with Charles Hirschkind's work on cassette sermons which significantly reconfigures not only the political, religious, and communal configurations in the Middle East, but also the "affects, sensibilities, and perceptual habits" of contemporary Muslims.[38]

In the Indonesia context, the developments of digital technology must be seen as coupled with the *da'wa* movements of the twentieth century. I follow Michael Feener who identifies the "*da'wa* paradigm" of the twentieth century as characterized as bringing "together mutually-reinforcing currents of Islamic reform, Indonesian nationalism, and economic developmentalism."[39] The goal of these *da'wa* movement of the New Order under Sukarno were in line with the larger movement in global Islamic revival that sought the "Islamization of the modern experience."[40] The form and direction of this Islamization is diverse,

---

35 Lila Abu-Lughoud, *Dramas of Nationhood: The Politics of Nationhood in Egypt* (Chicago: The University of Chicago Press, 2004), 135–136.
36 "Bay'a," *Sufi Live*, Accessed, January 16, 2019. https://sufilive.com/baya/.
37 Gary R. Bunt, *iMuslim: Rewiring the House of Islam* (Chapel Hill, NC: The University of North Carolina Press, 2009), 1.
38 Charles Hirschkind, *The Ethical Soundscape: Cassette Sermons and Islamic Counterpublics* (New York: Columbia University Press, 2006), 1.
39 Michael Feener, *Shari'a and Social Engineering: The Implementation of Islamic Law in Contemporary Aceh, Indonesia* (Oxford: Oxford University Press, 2014), 4.
40 Voll Haddad, John Obert, and John L. Esposito, *The Contemporary Islamic Revival : A Critical Survey and Bibliography* (New York: Greenwood, 1991), 24.

but the drive of these multiple interrelated revivals often connects pre-modern concepts with contemporary conditions. This is clearly demonstrated in AA Gym's rise to prominence in Indonesia in the late twentieth century. He developed a brand around his *da'wa* which took global popular psychology, especially from New Age America, and found an Islamic base that both critiqued and built on the popular psychology. He, furthermore, used his brand and platform developed through the expansion of this brand to "shame the state."[41] Aa Gym demonstrated a type of political Islam beyond the creation of an Islamic State that was able to discipline the state through a blend of Islamic and psychological concepts established in his brand.

Development of media such as television, cassettes, and smartphones have dramatically changed who gets to stand as an Islamic authority and the methods by which Islamic teachings are dispersed. However, unlike television, the cassette sermons of Hirschkind's work, or the Islamic blogosphere of Gary Blunt's work,[42] the recordings of the events of Habib Syech are not shared in the same way. Habib Syech does not make a habit out of giving sermons or commands. He performances of *selawat* as his personal *da'wa* (invitation to follow Islam as the prophet Muhammad commanded) are changing Islamic sensibilities, but simply listening to the content of his songs is not sufficient in determining how these are changing. This is additionally complicated by the history of the internet in Indonesia which acts as a place for both attempted authoritarianism and active resistance through community-based infrastructure. Habib Seych's performances of *selawat* and their digital presence within this history of the internet in Indonesia and the rise of the tele-dai manifest most clearly in the formation of his Fanclub on Facebook.

7.4 Habib Syech's Playful Disavowal of Technology

The use of social media as a platform for dispersing information is not intended to solidify Habib Syech's control over the crowd of people who identify as a part of his fan club, Syekhermania. However, as already indicated, social media sites such as Facebook, Instagram, and YouTube have millions of members who identify as members of Syekhermania through these sights. Habib Syech's statement

---

41 James Bourke Hoesterey, *Rebranding Islam: Piety, Prosperity, and A Self-Help Guru* (Stanford: Stanford University Press, 2015), 149.
42 See Chapter 4 of Bunt, *iMuslims: Rewiring the House of Islam*.

during Ramadan in 2014 reveal his own contentious relationship with social media:

> "Do not trust what you see on the media. Do not believe what you see on Facebook. I do not have a Facebook. I do not have a Twitter. I have an Instagram to share the activities of my events. However, I do not communicate on Instagram. There are many who claim to be me on Instagram, but they pretending to be me to use my name to sell things. There are many Islamic preachers on television, but do not believe them because they are only selling Islam."

Habib Syech and other members of Syekhermania have a deep distrust of technology and social media. Habib Syech frequently publicly performs his disavowal of technology while simultaneously encouraging people to use the lights on their cellphones to sway back and forth to his music. He posts on Instagram, but this is primarily to "share the activities of his events," while others are using it to sell Islam. The one-time Habib Syech has used his Instagram to post a direct message that took place very recently in reference to the upcoming election. In September of 2018, videos surfaced comparing the interaction between Habib Syech and Jokowi as well as a separate interaction between Habib Syech and Jokowi's challenger, Prabowo Subianto.

The first video shows Habib Syech embracing Jokowi in Habib Syech's building in Solo, Indonesia. The second video shows an awkward interaction between Habib Syech. Habib Syech sits at a round table with others preparing for events, and Prabowo suddenly appears immediately extending his arms for a hug. He wraps his arms around the shoulders of Habib Syech as Habib Syech ducks his head and says, "please sit, sit." Prabowo doubles down on the hug and tries to reach even further around Habib Syech. This elicits laughter from Habib Syech who leans further away from the hug and urges him to sit. These two instances are then taken as an indication of his choice for president. Habib Syech releases a statement on Instagram. He writes:

> "I am not an ulama. I am nobody. I only want to urge society to love the Prophet through *selawat*. I will surely perform *selawat* whenever and wherever, whoever wants to come, *Ahlan wa sahlan, silahkan*. I do not know political affairs. All citizens of the nation are free to determine their political choices including choosing a president. However, if there is already someone chosen, that means God's decision must be respected by everyone. As citizens of the nation which are good, all of us must support and direct that which is true, because the president will work for what is important for us as a nation."[43]

---

43 Syaikhassegaf, *Instagram*, Accessed September 14, 2018. https://www.instagram.com/p/Bnv C8xZhnko/.

This is the only post made by Habib Syech on social media that contains an official written statement. The above statement highlights that he is actively trying to stay out of politics even when others continually drag him into the ongoing political debates. However, more importantly, he indicates where he sees himself in reference to other types of religious officials. He is not an ulama (Muslim scholar). He only wants others to love the Prophet through *selawat*. *Selawat* is his *da'wa*, and he is not interested in being identified as anything more than someone who performs *selawat*. His evasion of the question of where he stands as a religious official both in this form as well in my fieldwork again places him both within the rise in digital or cyber-Islamic authority and yet not a tele-dai or religious figure who simply provides concise descriptions of what it means to be a 'good' and 'pious' Muslim. It is only through his *selawat* that the intention and repercussions of these performances reveal themselves.

7.5 Syekhermania

Syekhermania Pusat's (Central Syekermania) Facebook site has over 600,000 followers. In the about section, the group describes itself in the following way. The tone indicates excitement and reads like someone speaking through a megaphone to hype up a large crowd:

> 'Syekhermania" is the vessel for the Community of Lovers and Practitioners of 'Selawat of Prophet Muhammad SAW' who are full of sincerity in praying because of the encouragement from 'The Selawat Motivator' Habib Syekh bin Abdul Qadir Assegaf as the Caregiver of the Majeli s Ta'lim and Selawat of 'AHBAABUL MUSTHOFA' from Solo in Central Java. He always galvanizes young souls who are lulled by the glittering of life in the world to remember *selawat* for the Prophet Muhammad. Through the method of dah'wa 'Habib Syech *selawat*' also on the basis of 'Community' which he always emphasizes, invites, and guides us to.[44]

The original web post announcing the events of Habib Syech and Ahbaabul Musthofa presence was through the creation of a blog by "the initiator" titled Ahbaabul Musthofa.' Around the same time, another blog, "Central Ahbaabul Musthofa,' arose.[45] It is unclear when exactly the sites were first created. Habib Syech began performing in 1997, and by 2009, most of the focus was on the Facebook

---

[44] Syekhermania PUSAT Facebook page, https://www.facebook.com/Syekhermania.PUSAT/. Accessed January 19, 2022.

[45] The precise dating of these websites is difficult to ascertain. What I seek to indicate here is the collective momentum of this virtual presence.

site Syekhermania Pusat. The name changed from Ahbaabul Musthofa because to Syekhermania because there were so many new groups popping up with the name Ahbaabul Musthofa. Local manifestations of individual communities following the group were creating their own sites and for the initiator and others this created the perception that there was competition.

After 2009, 'lovers of Habib Syech' were consolidated into the group Syechermania. Habib Syech has an Indonesian textile factory that makes jackets, flags, and other apparel. He also makes non-Syekhermania gear such as sarongs and the white shirts characteristic of the *santri* (Islamic boarding school attendee). Recently, he made a deal with the water brand Clavio for the creation of Syekher Water. Although the water is not officially presented as containing *baraka*. Instagram posts, perception by the members of Syekhermania, and in informal conversation with sellers indicate that the water potential contains *baraka*. *Baraka* is commercialized in the form of Syekher Water. This water is, furthermore, distributed by members of Syekhermania. Rather than through traditional forms of commercial exchange. Motorbikes, vans, and trucks owned by members of Syekhermania transport the water from Solo to other parts of Indonesia. Stores dedicated singularly to selling the water have also arisen.

This community of lovers of Habib Syech create complex systems of economic and spiritual exchange over Indonesia, but also to other countries. Syekhermania Taiwan and Malaysia, also, has its own official Facebook page. The Burmese man who attended Habib Syech's events also bought large amounts of merchandise to take back to Burma. These exchanges are always framed in the attempt to create community, peace, and friendship. There is no particular ritual or rite that makes someone a part of Syekhermania besides perhaps listening to and participating in the performances by Habib Syech. Purchasing and wearing the merchandise is a way to display allegiance. However, as compared to initiation into a Sufi order or participating in a self-help seminar led by Islamic elite, the group is rather open to anyone and the identity is simple, followers of Habib Syech. Many members of Syekhermania have furthermore never been to an event. They simply follow the events of Habib Syech through YouTube and Facebook, and the videos that are recorded are shared from one person to another. They are often sent through WhatsApp rather than posted publicly. However, this still does not account for the vast number of recordings that take place, and this does not explain what seems to bring Syekhermania together. The Facebook site mostly posts about when and where the events will take place. Why and what then are the lights in the below picture recording?

Figure 2: Smartphones begin to emerge in preparation for Habib Syecha' arrival and participants attempts to capture the performance of *selawat.* Photo by the author.

7.6 Technological *Baraka*

I sat on a busy corner in Yogyakarta, Indonesia, with two shop owners while three young children played next to a busy street corner. It was dusk, and the street was alive with the lights and the insistent sound of car and motorbike horns. As we sat on the cool tile floor, we talked about their lives and my experience in Indonesia. They repaired broken bags and shoes for a living and often slept on the floor where they worked. I asked if one of them had ever heard of *selawat.* They laughed and said, "well of course." I then asked if they had ever heard of Habib Syech bin Abdul Qadir Assegaf, and they again said, "yes, of course; he is the leader of sholawat." However, they had never been to any of his events. It was not unusual to find someone who knew of Habib Syech only through his presence in social media sites. Habib Syech's presence in social media sites increases rapidly as thousands of new pictures and videos are uploaded every day. In some ways, this mimics what you would expect from a popular musician. However, the conversation then moved to *baraka.*

I said, "many people say they go to these events for *baraka,* what do you think of that?"

One of the shop owners energetically motioned to his phone and said, "yes, when you watch it [Habib Syech's performance] on your cell phone, and you focus on understanding and take it very seriously. You may start to cry. You can feel it." He motioned as if tears were running down his cheeks to his feet. I asked, "you feel what?" He responded, "*baraka.*" This was the first moment of my fieldwork where I realized that something different was going on with these recordings. This individual was watching the recording of Habib Syech's performance on YouTube; so, the recording was a part of the culture of sharing. The drive to watch the recordings was driven by an attempt to experience, feel, emote *baraka*.

This shop owner was not the only one to indicate that in watching a recorded version of one of Habib Syech's events one could feel *baraka*. My realization that these recordings were not circulating in the same way that cassetts, CDs, or sermons arose from my fifth trip into the field. The first night that I arrived in Indonesia, I went and spent time with Habib Syech in his private home. One of the Indonesians who assist Habib Syech snapped a picture with me, and I thought nothing of it. The next day, I woke up to 100s of messages on WhatsApp, Facebook, and other messaging services of individuals who now knew that I had arrived and that I was looking "fatter than last year." The photograph had circulated in private channels. In a similar way, the recordings of *selawat* are present on YouTube, Facebook, and Music streaming services, but their primary circulation is between individuals, much like the initial ideas behind the 'guerilla' Indonesian internet. The circulation of these recordings was between individuals in messaging applications, and the veracity of their circulation was driven by a desire to experience *baraka*. Experiencing *baraka* does not require the participant to be physically present at the event; it extends through the videos and photos posted on social media platforms. This is a new form of experience of *baraka* that slips into everyday life in a way that it previously did not, but the further from the source of the recording an observe get, the less efficacy the recording has due to its entanglement with *baraka*.

The transference of *baraka* has typically required touch or presence at the place through which it moves. For example, Habib Syech tells the story of the prophet Muhammad going to the house of a poor family. There was only one portion of rice for 14 people. However, after Prophet Muhammad, a vessel through which *baraka* is said to move, touched the rice with his hand, there was not only enough food for everyone, but there was excess food. Bottles of water are, additionally, regularly brought to religious figures like Habib Syech to bless by reciting Qur'anic verses and blowing or touching the water. Those seeking *baraka* would have to travel to the religious figures *pesantren* (Islamic school) or wait to get close to the figure. Furthermore, although the Qur'an is a source through which *baraka* moves, reading Arabic or learning to recite the Qur'an is often restricted to these Islamic schools making physical presence at the mosque or Islamic boarding schools necessary to experience Quranic recitation. Recordings that are shared either from peer-to-peer or on social media platform make the potential of experience *baraka* accessible with the push of the play button on

YouTube. However, the closer to the recording that an individual can get makes the efficacy of "really feeling" *baraka* more possible due to the perceived nature of *baraka* requiring physical presence.

Baraka is unhinged from the present moment and resonates beyond the events through smartphones. The smartphone is transformed into a medium for experiencing blessings, an increase in usefulness, or the spiritual power emitted from Allah said to be present at these events. This inexplainable feeling of *baraka* can manifest at any moment even in-between fixing shoes.

7.7 Conclusion: (Re)Enchanting the Digital

Smartphone recordings are not reaching the typical mechanisms of dispersal, and although the context of Indonesia opens up the conditions of possibility for the emergence of Syekhermania and the recording of *selawat*, digitally, the use by everyday Muslims evades the intention and use behind many of these digital technologies. Habib Syech and these events furthermore do not fit within the rise of media and cyber-Islamic authority. They rather open up a space for the infinite possible manifestation of gifts from God that cannot be rationally understood but can be felt and experienced by concentrating on the screen projecting the event of *selawat*. The effects of this can range from "calming the heart," "making better Muslims," or "making business ventures succeed." However, they do not operate according to rationalist logic. Watching and listening to *selawat* might result in *baraka*, but it might not result in *baraka*, and the moment one assumes that *baraka* can be captured in this medium or any other material medium the spiritual nature of the force dissipates as if you were trying to grasp smoke. Technology is a medium for the intangible force that blends spiritual and material prosperity and gifts in the everyday life of Indonesian Muslims forcing us to reconsider the way technology is used and reflected upon by modern Indonesian subjects.

References

Abu-Lughoud, Lila. *Dramas of Nationhood: The Politics of Nationhood in Egypt*. Chicago: The University of Chicago Press, 2004.

Appadurai, Arjun. *Modernity at Large : Cultural Dimensions of Globalization*. Public Worlds; v. 1. Minneapolis: University of Minnesota Press, 1996.

Aspinall, Edward. *Opposing Suharto: Compromise, Resistance, and Regime Change in Indonesia*. Stanford, CA: Stanford University Press, 2005.

Barker, Joshua. "Guerilla Engineers: The Internet and the Politics of Freedom in Indonesia," *Dreamscapes of Modernity: Sociotechnical Imaginaries and the Fabrication of Power.* Sheila Jasanoff and Sang-Hyun Kim ed. Chicago: The University of Chicago Press, 2015.

Barker, Joshua. "Engineers and Political Dreams: Indonesia in the Satellite Age," *Current Anthropology* 46, no. 5 (December 2005).

Bauman, Zygmunt. *Liquid Modernity.* Cambridge: Malden, MA: Polity; Blackwell, 2000.

Beck, Giddens, Lash, Giddens, Anthony, and Lash, Scott. *Reflexive Modernization: Politics, Tradition and Aesthetics in the Modern Social Order.* Cambridge, UK: Polity, 1994.

Bubdant. Nils. *Democracy, Corruption and the Politics of Spirits in Contemporary Indonesia.* New York: Routledge, 2014.

Bunt, Gary. *iMuslims: Rewiring the House of Islam. iMuslims.* Chapel Hill: The University of North Carolina Press, 2009.

Bruinessen, Martin van. *Tarekat Naqsyabandiyah di Indonesia: survei historis, geografis, dan sosiologis.* Bandung: Mizan, 1992.

Denffer, Dietrich von. "Baraka as basic concept of Muslim Popular Belief. Islamic Studies 15 (3), 1976: 167–186.

Duggan, Maeve. "Photo and Video Sharing Grow Online," *Pew Research Center.* October 28, 2013. http://www.pewinternet.org/wp-content/uploads/sites/9/media/Files/Reports/2013/PIP_Photos-and-videos-online_102813.pdf

Edmonds, James. "Smelling Baraka: Everyday Islam and Islamic Normativity" in "(Mis) Representations of Islam: Politics, Community, and Advocacy," ed. Timothy P. Daniels and Meryem F. Zaman, special issue. American Journal of Islamic Social Thought 36, no. 3 (Summer 2019).

Eisenstadt, S. N. *Comparative Civilizations and Multiple Modernities.* Leiden; Boston: Brill, 2003.

Feener, Michael. *Shari'a and Social Engineering: The Implementation of Islamic Law in Contemporary Aceh, Indonesia.* Oxford: Oxford University Press, 2014.

Geertz, Clifford. *Islam Observed: Religious Development in Morocco and Indonesia.* New Haven: Yale University Press, 1968.

Haddad, Voll, John Obert, and John L. Esposito. *The Contemporary Islamic Revival: A Critical Survey and Bibliography.* New York: Greenwood, 1991.

Hoesterey, James Bourke. *Rebranding Islam: Piety, Prosperity, and a Self-help Guru.* Stanford: Stanford University Press, 2016.

Hirschkind, Charles. *The Ethical Soundscape: Cassette Sermons and Islamic Counterpublics.* New York: Columbia University Press, 2006.

"Indonesia, fourth highest number of Facebook users in the world." *The Jakarta Post.* March 4, 2018. https://www.thejakartapost.com/life/2018/03/04/indonesia-fourth-highest-number-of-facebook-users-in-the-world.html

"Jadwal Habib Syech," *Syekhermania.* (Archived here: https://web.archive.org/web/20170313132230/http://syekhermania.or.id/jadwal-habib-syekh-update-bulan-februari-2017). Accessed January 19, 2022.

Kim, Byung-Keun. *Internationalizing the Internet: The Co-evolution of Influence and Technology.* New Horizons in the Economics of Innovation. Cheltenham, UK ; Northampton, MA: E. Elgar, 2005.

Moon, Suzanne. "Building from the Outside In: Sociotechnical Imaginaries and Civil Society in New Order Indonesia." *Dreamscapes of Modernity: Sociotechnical Imaginaries and the Fabrication of Power*. Sheila Jasanoff and Sang-Hyun Kim ed. Chicago: The University of Chicago Press, 2015.

Purbo, Onno. "Getting Connected." *Inside Indonesia*. July 29, 2007. Accessed February 8, 2009. https://www.insideindonesia.org/getting-connected.

Schmidt, Volker. "Multiple Modernities or Varieties of Modernity?" *Revista De Sociologia E Politica* 28 (2007): 147–160.

Syaikhassegaf. *Instagram*. Accessed September 14, 2018. <https://www.instagram.com/p/BnvC8xZhnko/>

"Syekhermania Pusat." *Facebook*. https://www.facebook.com/SYEKHERMANIA.PUSAT/

Weber, Max. *The Sociology of Religion*. Boston: Beacon, 1963.

Werbner, Pnina and Helene Basu. *Embodying charisma: Modernity, Locality, and Performance of Emotion in Sufi Cults*. 1st ed. New York, London: Routledge, 1998.

Westermarck, Edward. *The Moorish Conception of Holiness (baraka)*. Helsingfors: Akademiska Bokhandeln, 1916.

Barbara E. Mundy and Dana Leibsohn

Chapter 8
Beyond Recognition? Orphan Objects, Decolonization, and Religious Histories of the Spanish Americas

8.1 Introduction

It was the bitter end of July in 1646 when Constanza de Escobar dictated her testament to a notary in Santiago, Chile. As was the case with many Indigenous
women living in cities in the Spanish Americas, Escobar embraced Catholic beliefs and social practices.[1] Her will commits funds to purchase masses for her
soul. It also describes her desires to gift (rather than sell) some of the religious
images she owned, "these two images, one new without frame, of Our Lady of
the Rosary and another of the Guardian Angel. I order that these two be given
to the stewards of the cofradía of Our Lady of Guadalupe to be placed on her
altar."[2] In making such donations, Escobar did nothing unusual. By the mid-seventeenth century, tens of thousands of Indigenous people were living in urban
centers; nearly all of these people relied upon objects to forge relationships
with the world of the saints and with other faithful Catholics, both in life and
in death. Other genres of prose like sermons and catechisms complement testaments in the archival record, some written in Indigenous languages rather than
Spanish. Read alongside each other, these works reveal the centrality of writing
and printing in the Spanish Americas. They also remind us how few Indigenous
people were writers, how rarely their own words from the seventeenth, or even
the nineteenth century, have been preserved.[3] From the early 1500s through

---

1 The first Iberian and Catholic claims to territories that would become the Americas were made
in the late fifteenth century. Spanish rule lasted into the early nineteenth century for most places, although Cuba, Puerto Rico and the Philippines were held by Spain through the nineteenth
century.

2 Archivo Nacional, Chile, Escribanos de Santiago, vol. 200 A, fol. 48. The original Spanish, with
an English translation and a short history of publication, can be found in Dana Leibsohn and
Barbara E. Mundy, *Vistas: Visual Culture in Spanish America, 1520–1820* [https://vistas.ace.
fordham.edu/lib/17th/amerindian/].

3 For recent scholarship in English on Indigenous writing and literacies, see for instance, Alcira
Dueñas, *Indians and Mestizos in the "Lettered City": Reshaping Justice, Social Hierarchy and Political Culture in Colonial Peru* (Boulder: University Press of Colorado, 2010), Alan Durston, "Na-

https://doi.org/10.1515/9783110608755-009

the early 1800s, other religions took root in the Americas, but in the Spanish Americas, Catholicism held sway. And Indigenous and Afro-Indigenous people were among its most numerous adherents. The recognition of material traces of their religious experiences and the questions those traces raise for modern historians of religion, form the central themes of this essay—and here, we go back to the roots of "recognize" taking it to mean "to know again," to acknowledge that historical knowledge is partial and changes over time. Surviving colonial objects have often been known to their custodians, be they local communities or museum curators. Historians' identification of objects as colonial and Indigenous is not a discovery but a recognition, a re-knowing, of what others may have already (if not always) known.

As in many places and at other times, Escobar and her compatriots experienced "Catholic religion" as a continually unfolding set of practices—rigidly proscribed rituals of the Mass, spontaneous toasts at the feast of a patron saint, deathbed utterances. Her religious life was distinctive in having been shaped by urban customs and gendered expectations, and also by policies and permissions related to her Indigenous ancestry.[4] In the Spanish Americas, Indigenous peoples were assigned membership in a corporate community, a *pueblo de indios*, whose political status and historic roots in the pre-Hispanic past shaped legal rights and obligations, and the religious practices and beliefs of its members. In the cities of Spanish America, the boundaries between Indigenous lives and those of others often blurred; in the mid-seventeenth century, however, urban Indigenous women often worshipped together, sharing their devotional labor, prayers, and material objects. Escobar was one such woman. While not required to testate upon her deathbed (indeed, many Indigenous people could not

---

tive Language Literacy in Colonial Peru: The Question of Mundane Quechua Revisited," *Hispanic American Historical Review* 88, 1 (2008): 41–70, Justyna Olko, John Sullivan, and Jan Szeminski, eds. *Dialogue with Europe, Dialogue with the Past: Colonial Nahua and Quechua Elites in their Own Words* (Louisville: University Press of Colorado, 2018), Joanne Rappaport and Tom Cummins, *Beyond the Lettered City: Indigenous Literacies of the Andes* (Durham, N.C: Duke University Press, 2012), Camilla Townsend, *Annals of Native America: How the Nahuas of Colonial Mexico Kept Their History Alive* (Oxford: Oxford University Press, 2016), Peter Villella, *Indigenous Elites and Creole Identity, 1500–1800* (Cambridge: Cambridge University Press, 2016).

4 In her will Escobar identifies her parents as caciques. She also lists a number of Indigenous-style garments, at least one of which she wishes to be sold for an outfit for the Virgin of Guadalupe. The scholarship on Indigenous wills is now substantial; in writing this essay, we found particularly useful both Karen Graubart, "Catalina de Agüero: A Mediating Life," in *Native Wills from the Colonial Americas*, ed. M. Christensen and J. Truitt (Salt Lake: University of Utah Press, 2016), 19–39 and Frank Salomon, "Indian Women of Early Colonial Quite as Seen Through Their Testaments," *The Americas* 44, 3 (1988): 325–341.

afford the notarial fees or paper), in choosing to do so, she registered for posterity something still too often overlooked: images and objects, not only words, served as crucial mediators between the social and sacred. Religious objects were not likely the most expensive things Escobar owned, but they bound her into networks that she trusted—some of which extended across generations, some across the city streets of Santiago, and some into heaven.

The works Escobar gifted to the Virgin of Guadalupe's altar are no longer known. Indeed, tragically few of the religious prints, paintings and sculptures that circulated through Indigenous hands in the past survive today. This is one outcome of settler colonialism in the Americas, which as part of the denial of territorial, cultural, and legal autonomy to Indigenous peoples, has privileged English, French, Portuguese, Spanish and creole histories and the works associated with them. Thirty years ago this observation could have been surprising to many. Today, the fate of objects like those Escobar once owned may not be news, but reckoning with the effects of that fate remains intellectually and politically challenging.

Decolonization, that is, unwinding the violent effects of settler colonialism, has no set recipe. Nor is the work of decolonization the same everywhere: Africa is not Australia, nor is it Latin America. Writing in the North American context, Eve Tuck and K. Wayne Yang have argued that decolonization involves uncomfortable, unsettling change; as an elsewhere, rather than end, decolonization is a project of ontological incommensurability, not reconciliation.[5] Other scholars and activists engaged in decolonization, who focus more explicitly on epistemologies, are challenging the fundamental assumptions of disciplines like anthropology and history about culture, subjectivity and narrative. In the context of museums, especially in western, Euro-American settings, decolonization includes not only the reworking of catalog information and display labels but also physical and digital repatriation of objects in museum custody (see discussion below).[6]

---

5 Eve Tuck and K. Wayne Yang, "Decolonization is Not a Metaphor." *Decolonization: Indigeneity, Education & Society* 1, 1 (2012): 1–40.

6 Decolonization has been differentially defined in recent years. Historically, the fight for political and cultural independence from colonial powers grounded writing about decolonization; in this regard, the work of Frantz Fanon has been especially influential; see, for instance, *The Wretched of the Earth* (New York, Grove Press, 1963). Other important writers, who have emphasized the cultural work of decolonization include Edward Said, *Orientalism* (New York: Pantheon, 1978), Ngũgĩ wa Thiong'o, *Decolonising the Mind: the Politics of Language in African Literature* (London: J. Currey, 1986), and Linda Tuhiwai Smith, *Decolonizing Methodologies: Research and Indigenous Peoples* (London: Zed Books, 1999). See also Raymond F. Betts, "Decolonization: A Brief History of the Word," in *Beyond Empire and Nation: The Decolonization*

Decolonization, as a transformative project in the academy gaining force in the 1980s, coincided with the worldwide web's early promise to democratize knowledge. Given that a colonialist world ordering dominated traditional structures of knowledge, the flexible, malleable web seemed to offer an alternative, allowing other modes of knowing to become more accessible and responsive to diverse public interests, including often marginalized Indigenous communities. So did other forms of mass media: Indigenous communities began to run radio stations that broadcast in Indigenous languages and disseminate their own films.[7] For objects from the colonial past, though, the web's promise was less clear. For instance, it is true that Constanza de Escobar's will and the colonial objects that *do* survive from Indigenous networks open onto religious histories that are not possible to know from written texts alone. And today, some of these objects are held in Indigenous communities, among families and in churches, while others are kept by private collectors far from their sites of origin. Could making their images widely available online be a productive initial line of redress? Presumably, visual accessibility *could* counter the invisibility of Indigenous objects in conventional published histories and museum galleries. Setting such images into an online space, rather than the colonialist world-ordering schema of art and anthropology collections, *could* challenge decontextualization and the fragmentation of Indigenous knowledge. Or...perhaps not.

As non-Indigenous scholars, we have long been interested in the possibilities of the web to both decolonize knowledge and grant greater recognition to religious practices of the Spanish Americas. But as art historians, we also know that the connections among "visual accessibility," decolonization, and recognition are rooted in theories of vision in the West, specifically the assumed relationship between vision and knowledge. Since vision is a historically situated practice, any decolonizing project that relies upon recognition through new technologies as a first step in addressing the historical fragmentation of Indigenous knowledge must also contend with the fact that "visual accessibility" carries its own epistemological burdens. This essay is one such contention. In what fol-

---

of African and Asian Societies, 1930s–1970s, ed. E. Bogaerts and R. Raben, 23–38. Leiden, Nederlands Instituut voor Oorlogsdocumentatie, 2012.

7 Analyses of the growth of "Indigenous media," and now "Indigenous new media," while peripheral to this essay, can be found in Valerie Alia, *The New Media Nation: Indigenous Peoples and Global Communication* (New York: Berghahn Books, 2010), Jennifer Wemigwans, *A Digital Bundle: Protecting and Promoting Indigenous Knowledge Online* (Regina: University of Regina Press, 2018), and Jennifer Gómez Menjívar and Gloria Elizabeth Chacón, eds, *Indigenous Interfaces: Spaces, Technology, and Social Networks in Mexico and Central America* (Tucson: University of Arizona Press, 2019).

lows, then, we do not seek to reconstitute the realm of Catholic practice forged by Escobar and other Indigenous people (indeed, we are not sure such a thing is even possible); rather we wish to reckon with questions posed by modern desires to recognize, see, and know Indigenous objects from the Spanish Americas.

The online presentation of a silver gilt chalice now in the collection of the Los Angeles County Museum reveals some of these complexities (Figure 1). The chalice was created in Mexico City between 1575–1578 and therefore may be one of the earliest surviving liturgical objects from colonial Mexico. Not currently on view in the Los Angeles museum, it is searchable and viewable on the museum's website.[8]

On first glance, this chalice, with its late Renaissance design, might seem to be a close copy of a work made in Spain, but the text points out that it "fus[es] Spanish silverwork and indigenous artistic traditions." And scrolling through the 20 photographs of the work, many offering close detail, one can see traces of an Indigenous contribution in the carved figural plaques whose colored backgrounds were formed by the thin application of the feathers of tropical birds, likely hummingbirds. No one expects any website to "say everything" and museums have distinctive policies about the range of topics that can be discussed (and the tone that can be used). Thus, while the website does make the image accessible, its emphasis on Indigenous religious practice is limited. It does not say, for instance, that feathers, because of their iridescence and their seeming ability to generate light out of nothing, were long associated by Nahuas (a majority Indigenous group of Central Mexico) with the unseen (and therein spiritual) energies of the cosmos. Nor does it connect the presence of these feathers on this Catholic liturgical object to histories of conversion (including extirpation) in the Spanish Americas. While the museum provides viewers like us with the valued opportunity to see physical evidence of specialized Indigenous knowledge and skill, and of modes of creativity that were (and still are) valued highly, it does little to identify them as such online.[9]

More explicit recognition would begin to offer redress, but such gestures are not simple: recognition is never just a project of saying more or adding text. Moreover, visual accessibility is not a value-neutral move. For the museum website does another kind of work which has implications for the critical scholarship of religion. It changes this work—which was once a ritual object, seen and

---

8 At the time of this writing, the URL: https://collections.lacma.org/node/228992. Clicking on this page will display a range of close up views and details of the chalice.

9 For a serious, very recent scholarly study, see Ilona Katzew and Rachel Kaplan, "Like the Flame of Fire" A New Look at the "Hearst" Chalice," *Latin American and Latinx Visual Culture*, 3, 1 (2021): 4–29.

Figure 1: "Chalice (Cáliz)," Los Angeles County Museum of Art. Website in the public domain: https://collections.lacma.org/node/228992. Last accessed September 29, 2021.

used by privileged viewers—into a work of art open for public inspection.[10] Anyone with an internet connection and the correct URL can zoom in, pan across the chalice's surfaces, and click through different views, some of which show the chalice disassembled. As if to compensate for the absence of the ability to touch (a highly restricted activity, now and in the past), web viewers are offered promiscuous visual access.

So while the museum's website implicitly remedies the invisibility of Indigenous craftsmanship, now shown in the detailed photographs of the featherwork, its remedy comes in the form of a new visual experience that shares little

---

10 This is common in museum websites that display ritual objects from the past. See discussion below on the implications of restricted viewing access.

with the historical uses of this object. For one, photographs show nothing of the iridescent qualities of the feathers, which would have been a most important feature—beyond the gilt and the iconography—to an Indigenous (if not also European) viewer. In addition, the website minimizes the experiences created through scale, high and low relief, and weight. The online display also flattens the hierarchies of visibility that were conditioned by inequality in the historical past. Because not just anyone could hold this chalice or visually appreciate its expensive materials, accessibility was enmeshed with power relations. Given contemporary digital fluencies and expectations, these points may seem so obvious they are barely worth making. Yet when it comes to Indigenous histories, in privileging "modern sight," which takes for granted visible accessibility online, over "historical sight," digital technologies can eclipse the mutually buttressing relationships between vision and settler colonialism.

What are we to make of this eclipse? Are the relations it obscures inevitable or do they carry some decolonizing promise? In what follows, these questions guide our thinking. While our focus on the Spanish Americas is regional, we have cast this essay to resonate with other settings marked (if not also made) by settler colonialism. We first sought to address some issues, particularly the recognition of colonial objects as Indigenous, in the course of developing our online project, *Vistas: Visual Culture in Spanish America*.[11] Other matters we grapple with grow out of the decolonizing projects of Indigenous activists, scholars, students, and curators who are actively repatriating their histories; while today, repatriation is taken to mean a return of stolen or illicitly taken objects, we use it somewhat differently to indicate practices that return Indigenous knowledges to their homelands—their *patria*. Of particular import to our argument are projects that seek to develop digital technologies to respond to and register Indigenous epistemologies and traditional knowledge. But this repatriation paradigm, albeit important, does not extend everywhere. Outside its ken are objects that have no present-day Indigenous claimants, often because they lack specific markers or features that explicitly connect them to an existent (and active) Indigenous community. At the end of the essay, then, we home in on these "orphan" objects which offer an aporia to progressive digital technologies, thereby pointing to a future challenge, and perhaps direction, in digital scholarship.

---

11 Today the project is hosted by Fordham University [https://www.fordham.edu/vistas] and runs in WordPress and Omeka. Since its initial inception, *Vistas* has passed through multiple incarnations, including short Spanish and English interpretations of object with low-resolution images (which can still be seen at: https://www.smith.edu/vistas), and a peer-reviewed DVD published by the University of Texas Press in 2010 that linked to a Luna database.

8.2 Appearances

We begin with a simple observation: recognizing objects from the past that were fashioned by, or circulated through the hands of, Indigenous people remains a persistent challenge. Take, for instance, the prints that Constanza de Escobar left in her will, which were likely mass produced works on paper, made in a metropolitan center, perhaps Lima, or even Antwerp. Essential to the networks that bound the Indigenous faithful together, such prints usually bore no marker or tag that identified them as having once been owned by an Indigenous person. And even if the fragile, ephemeral objects that mattered enough to Constanza de Escobar that she willed them to her church *had* survived, such things have historically been of little interest to preserving institutions. They were not precious or unique enough for the art museum, nor "Indigenous" enough for the anthropology collection. In contrast, the chalices, lamps, pyxes and book stands used during the celebration of the Catholic Mass are common in public collections today. Often wrought of costly and stunning materials and safeguarded for decades, if not centuries, in church collections, such objects have been transformed from precious church goods to valuable museum objects. For instance, the LACMA chalice, discussed above, was almost certainly preserved across the colonial period for the value of its gold and silver rather than its feathers. So histories of the Spanish Americas that take seriously Indigenous religious practice and seek to distinguish those works that were, in fact, used by native communities, converts, and worshippers from the (often, better-preserved) works that were not, are confronted with an archive of absence.

Nearly twenty years ago, we were more optimistic about the work that digital technologies could do in bringing recognition to Indigenous objects, making visible what *did* exist in the fragmentary public archive. With funding from the National Endowment for the Humanities and our home institutions, we created *Vistas: Visual Culture in Spanish America, 1520–1820*. This online, curated collection was designed to be widely accessible and, through the often overlooked or unstudied works that it featured, open onto histories of the colonial past, especially those that cast light onto the roles of Indigenous actors. This period of Latin American history was chosen for two reasons. On one hand, it was between roughly 1500 and 1800, that people of European, Indigenous, African and Asian descent were forced to reckon with, and engage each other in ways that were previously unknown. On the other, this same period was often neglected by constructions of Latin American nationalism which emphasized a modernity produced by independence movements that brought the colonial period to an end, or, particularly in Mexico, favored a tale of national origins rooted in the pre-Hispanic period. These might not have been the issues most central to scholars elsewhere, but these were the early modern and modern histories we wanted to engage, and, no less importantly, begin to revise.

Today, it is easy to call out the naïveté of embracing a project that hinged primarily on recovery and accessibility, but 1999, when we wrote our first grant proposal, was an early day in digital scholarship, especially in art history. And both recovery and accessibility seemed to be crucial decolonizing projects at that moment. Drawing upon art history's disciplinary habits, we researched public museum collections, queried curators, and scoured storerooms to find works that captured, in a wide variety of ways, the dynamic world of colonial religious practice.[12] Of particular interest were objects that shone light on Indigenous practices that involved public forms of expression—be those the practices of Nahuatl or Aymara speakers—because too many histories of colonial Latin America had long presumed their invisibility. To be sure, our focus on museum collections betrays the biases of our field, which has hardly been immune to colonialism's racialized thinking and habits of knowledge-formation. But we wanted to feature works that were no longer in use for worship and that had effectively been removed from market circulation. Focusing on public institutions, *Vistas* included works that were usually kept in storerooms rather than exhibition galleries yet could no longer be sold or subjected to the whims of private collectors.[13]

A festival hat from Bolivia, home of the silver-rich mine of Potosí, the famed Cerro Rico, and now in the collection of the Brooklyn Museum, was one such work (Figure 2). On a velvet substrate, the maker sewed flat silver pieces worked to render miniature images of Cerro Rico and its surrounding landscape. The hat, laden with heavy ornament, was almost certainly worn in public performances as part of a dance costume. It is no longer possible to know who first crafted or wore this hat, nor is it possible to know how the hat was valued by either person. As explained in *Vistas*, "It is easy to imagine the silver of the hat gleaming in the sun when its owner marched through town—perhaps to celebrate a Church feast day, a historic moment in the city's past or a change in political leadership

---

12 We turned to public institutions and collections since their missions tend to embrace both stewardship and education. Yet in those early days more than one metropolitan museum refused us permission to make photographs from their collection publicly visible online.

13 Of course, art and anthropology museums are bound up with histories of settler colonialism and the violence wrought by salvage-paradigm collecting. While these histories surfaced in annotations for selected objects in *Vistas*, and our approach would be different were we to be designing the project today, when we started it seemed the most important revisionism could come from calling attention to works that were largely unknown and un-studied rather than the dark history of collecting.

Figure 2: Creator(s) name(s) is/are not currently known, possibly Aymara. Festival Hat, 18th century. Repoussé silver plaques on velvet, glass beads, wire, 4 15/16 c 13 ¼ x 13 ¼ in. (12.5 x 33.7 x 33.7 cm). Brooklyn Museum, Museum Expedition 1941, Frank L. Babbott Fund, 41.1275.274c.

in the Viceroyalty of Perú."[14] What we did not emphasize then, but would now, is the weight of the silver—not only for those who danced the hat but also for those who chose neither to pawn nor melt the metal to buy or create other things.

Within the context of *Vistas*, we also asked this hat to perform anew. Enlisted in intellectual work, the hat indexed the ephemeral practices that gave form and substance to religious belief and it pointed to the participation of Indigenous actors within an increasingly global Catholicism. Reading for form and history (and not only performance), *Vistas* also called out the hat's silver plaque in the shape of the Cerro Rico, tracing in this image of a mountain, long held sacred to native Andeans, the pre-Hispanic bedrock of Indigenous religious practice. The online image was not, however, allowed (or expected) to convey all this on its own. We wrote annotations, originally in English and Spanish, that addressed materials

---

14 Dana Leibsohn and Barbara E. Mundy, *Vistas: Visual Culture in Spanish America, 1520–1820.* [https://vistasgallery.ace.fordham.edu/items/show/1723], 2015.

and collecting histories, iconography and facture. With regard to religious history, we stressed how the physical interactions of people with objects constituted religion-as-practice. As the dancer transformed by costume (including the hat) traveled in procession through the streets of a city or town to mark a festival like Corpus Christi, that sight—before the gathered crowd—presented and reinforced shared beliefs among communities of the faithful.

Central to the presentation of objects in *Vistas* was high resolution imagery, with zoom functions. By allowing (if not encouraging) viewers to see objects in detail, we sought to open an evocative space onto religious experiences of the past. We also sought to present objects in conversation with each other, and so developed a suite of themes that, when searched, would sort objects into related groups (e.g., Otherworldly Visions, Political Force of Images, Mestizaje). We remain convinced that this kind of curatorial work is still compelling, for students in particular, and also for others unfamiliar with the Spanish American material. Yet how revisionist was this? Even at the level of metadata—the terms we accepted from museums to explain date, culture, title—these objects were reigned in and assigned to Western art categories.[15]

But perhaps more troubling is that while imagery featured online brings recognition to Indigenous objects, *Vistas* and most other museum-sourced databases offer the beauty shot. That is, they show the object as it has been conserved (and sometimes restored) and presented under careful photographic lighting. Viewers have few clues about professional interventions made to or upon the object, nor is there a way of showing that its current condition may not be the one in which Indigenous people in the past used the work most extensively. The hat in the art museum may not be unique in this, but we raise the point because beautiful digital images travel so quickly, and reiteration creates evidentiary authority. When passed from tweet to tweet, museum website to Instagram, and from Twitter to tee-shirt, images obscure—not only index— aspects of Indigenous history that matter but are too rarely acknowledged.

The festival hat, for example, sits not on its original base, but upon a later, probably nineteenth-century replacement. We cannot say for sure, but perhaps heavy use wore out the first one. After the work of the original maker was finished, the tiny spray of glass flowers at the top seems to have been added, as if the

---

15 In recent years, the colonialist origins of metadata in museums and archives has become a topic of considerable debate (and, amongst those who work with indigenous materials and communities, a source of no small anxiety) .See, for instance, Kimberly Christen "Opening Archives: Respectful Repatriation," *The American Archivist* 74 (2011): 185–216 and the essays in Christina Gish Hill and Medeia Csoba De Hass, eds., "Digital Representation of Indigenous Peoples through Sharing, Collaboration, and Negotiation," *Museum Anthropology Review* 12, 2 (2018).

landscape rendered on the hat led one of its custodians to analogize the hat's crown with the generative earth. These renovations, however, are ignored by most online presentations (including those in *Vistas*). While the path of many colonial objects from Indigenous hands into metropolitan museums is often difficult to trace, it is along this path that some of the most poignant and traumatic Indigenous history lies. In this case we know the festival hat was collected in 1941 by Herbert Spinden, a longtime curator at the Brooklyn Museum who saw in "folk" objects from Latin America the potential to stimulate design in the mid-century industrial age of Brooklyn, New York.[16] Works that would speak to this "lesson" were those that caught his eye. What we don't know are the conditions under which people (or a community) released, were forced to release, or unwittingly released this object to the market. Nor do we know how much the hat was changed by its penultimate owner to attract the interest of a buyer like Spinden. Once the hat entered the museum, it may have been cleaned but it was no longer re-made (or danced). The hat we now know—and that can be seen at multiple websites—is the hat that existed when it was sold for the last time.[17] By making widely available archival- or museum-style sanctioned photography that tends to frame objects, and certainly religious objects, at the point that they became commodities, what kinds of religious histories are digital technologies promoting?

8.3 Super-vision

The ways in which digital technologies invite—and normalize—dehistoricized modes of viewing are not incidental. They impinge upon any decolonizing project. Accessibility and the commodification of religious objects from the past are but two aspects of this. No less important are modern expectations that close-looking produces viable knowledge. Among the objects created in the Spanish Americas that have consistently caught scholars' eyes are images

---

16 Diana Fane, "From Pre-columbian to Modern: Latin American Art at The Brooklyn Museum, 1930 – 50," *Converging Cultures: Art and Identity in Spanish America* (Brooklyn: Brooklyn Museum of Art, 1996), 14 – 27. In Spinden's benefit was a general lack of export protection that national governments afforded colonial-period objects at the time, as opposed to pre-Columbian ones.
17 In contrast to art museums, which tend to privilege both visually exquisite objects and stunning photography, anthropology and natural history museums often own objects that were not reworked for the modern art market and these museums tend to sell scholars photographs of their objects from storage facilities. It is not surprising, then, that fewer of these "unbeautiful" objects and images circulate online on social media.

made from feathers, often as part of liturgical objects.[18] The silver gilt chalice in the LACMA collection with its feather inlays is one example, and others have survived in which featherwork takes pride of place. We do not know how many, but dozens upon dozens of Indigenous craftsmen in New Spain worked with local and imported materials—tropical feathers of parrots and quetzals, silver and gold wire, amatl paper and cotton—to create vestments, banners, and portable shrines. When Catholic objects were first made of feather-mosaic in the sixteenth century, this was an art of ongoing innovation. Well before Europeans arrived in the Americas, extensive trade networks for feathers existed. The Mexica of Tenochtitlan, for instance, collected tribute in feathers from certain regions of the empire, sometimes requiring these precious materials to be fashioned into outfits or shields for military display and sometimes demanding that unprocessed feathers be sent to the imperial capital in bulk. When Hernán Cortés overthrew Mocteuzuma, local environments were ravaged and daily life in central Mexico was disrupted. However, neither the trade networks nor the specialized knowledge required to fashion spectacular objects from feathers disappeared: both were tapped by the new regime. As Catholicism took root in the Spanish Americas, Indigenous craftsmen worked feathers under the watchful eye of European-born friars, drawing inspiration from imported prints. Christ as Salvator Mundi (Figure 3) represents one such example. The names of those who created this feathered Christ—with fingers raised in blessing and left hand supporting an orb—have not survived and the banner's original visual effects are muted. Now tattered in places, the featherwork has lost some of its iridescence. When new and when marched in procession in bright sunlight, this image of the Christ and his orb would have changed colors as it moved, appearing to have had the ability to generate light, the mark of animacy among the Mexica.

In the early modern past, the flickering sheen of feather mosaics was considered both beautiful and dazzling. Crafted by Indigenous hands, feathered religious objects were frequently sent to Europe and Asia as gifts from friars and missionaries. At least one object known from the sixteenth century was commissioned by an Indigenous ruler, but usually patrons for such works were members of the Church. Feathered mosaics therefore circulated as exquisite forms of evi-

---

18 Feather-work objects created in New Spain have long been known, and were mentioned in the sixteenth-century inventories of objects Hernán Cortés sent to the Spanish court. For a range of approaches to featherwork in, and from the Spanish Americas, see Alessandra Russo, Gerhard Wolf and Diana Fane, eds., *Images Take Flight: Feather Art in Mexico and Europe, 1400–1700* (Munich: Hirmer Verlag, 2015). On early modern perceptions of iridescence, see, for instance, Brendan McMahon, "Contingent Images: Looking Obliquely at Colonial Mexican Featherwork in Early Europe," *Art Bulletin* 103, 2 (2021), 24–49.

Figure 3: Creator(s) name(s) is/are not currently known, possibly Nahua. Christ as Salvator Mundi, ca. 1550–1600. Museo Nacional del Virreinato, Tepozotlán. Reproduction authorized by the Instituto Nacional de Antropología e Historia, Mexico.

dence, demonstrating to court and religious officials the successes of conversion efforts. For these same viewers, feathered religious objects also made manifest— in material forms that could be touched and worn and therefore embodied—how sophisticated Indigenous handwork and visual innovation could be. Indigenous experiences, whether of the craftspeople (almost certainly men) who specialized in feather-working or those who saw their iridescence, are more difficult to describe. Among the phrases used by the Mexica for precious featherwork was "Shadows of the Sacred Ones," which historian Inga Clendinnen describes as "marvelous projections into this dimmed world of light."[19]

Much easier to apprehend is the assembly of these objects: the weave of cotton substrates and the fibrous bark paper that lent support, the bending and inlay of wires of precious metals; the technique of laying longer feathers over shorter ones to add dimension and increase color density (Figure 4). This kind of knowledge of the craft specialist would have been largely inaccessible to most people in the past, including those who counted upon feathered objects to mediate their encounters with the sacred. Narratives of facture, miraculous and otherwise, circulated widely in the early modern Catholic world, in writing and oral tradition, yet it was rare for those who were not artisans to view, directly, processes of facture. And so, worshippers in sixteenth-century New Spain certainly admired the luster of feathers painstakingly arrayed in this exquisite work, but very few of those people ever observed the detailed traces of labor required to fashion the Salvator Mundi, or, in fact, most religious objects.

For modern viewers, however, digital technologies that bring detailed views to the screen and allow scopic exploration through panning and zooming are wholly expected. Millions of times a day, people navigate the world by pinching and flexing their fingers, shifting the scale of screen images on demand. For many in the twenty-first century (but certainly not all) this practice and its associated modes of vision are so common they tend to catch attention only when something goes awry. Digital technologies encourage us to notice their effects, not their habits of working. And they imply that zooming in to read a city map is fundamentally akin to zooming in to see the fibers that support the feathers of a religious object from the past. In certain ways, this is true. It is nevertheless clear that digitally-enabled and enhanced close-looking of sacred objects is not precisely comparable to viewing an image (like a Google map) designed for the zoom. How, then, does close-looking foster the work of historians of religion? We do not pose this question flippantly, for no good historian would zoom to details of a high-resolution image and expect to see religious practice revealed. Nonetheless, the ways in which digital technologies expose certain physical features of the object, especially intimate details of facture usually visible only to

---

19 The phrase, "sombra de los dioses" in Spanish, comes from friar Diego Durán, *Historia de las Indias de Nueva España e Islas de la Tierra Firma*, Ángel María Garibay K., ed. 2ⁿᵈ ed. (Mexico City: Editorial Porrua, 1984), vol. 2, ch. 25, p. 206, translated and cited in Inga Clendinnen, *Aztecs: An Interpretation* (Cambridge: Cambridge University Press, 1995 [1991], 308).

Figure 4: Detail of Figure 3.

the object's maker, and occlude others invisible to sight (touch, weight, smell) are important to the kinds of knowledge created through objects, particularly religious objects. Because certainly, debates about where the sacred conjoins the physical world and how material objects incarnate the divine presence have long shaped the history of Catholicism, fueling more than a few wars, and in their wake, reform of the Roman Church and its teachings. The question we are asking about what knowledge close-looking produces, then, concerns the ontology of the object under examination—and for Catholics in the early modern period, this might well have been the central question. This question, mutatis mutandis, relates to other parts of the world, but we find the colonial context particularly charged.

Since we are interested in histories of Indigenous creations, we focus here upon facture—the skills, labors, and materials involved in assembling religious objects—rather than iconography, which has been well served by new technologies. Impressive digital efforts have been directed at church interiors in Latin America, with zoom technology illuminating the iconography of large mural campaigns and revealing the physical (and presumably theological) relationships among works of art set on walls and over altars.[20] Facture is a different matter. A detail of the featherwork Salvator Mundi seen in figure 4 provides a standard example. It reveals something of the object's creation by exposing the materials and their relationships. This renders the work less mysterious, and, perhaps, less wondrous. Whether knowledge of material use was once held secret or guarded in the ways medieval guilds protected certain craft practices, we cannot say. Certainly, such knowledge was highly specialized. Panning across and zooming into a high-resolution photograph, it is possible to see layered feathers and their veins, how different colored feathers were arranged to create warm highlights in Christ's hair and the illusion of fabric folds. A similar kind of visual experience is constructed by the LACMA website: online photographs of the chalice include zoom-able details that reveal tiny boxwood sculptures and the silversmith's stamps; the site also displays photographs of the disassembled object, revealing imagery that would have been known to some, but not all, of the chalice's makers. It is the work of conservators, photographers, web-designers, and internet providers that constitutes modernity's rituals of viewing.[21] There is wonder in what they do, but it is hardly the wonder of the sixteenth century.

---

20 See, for instance, the essay by Emily Floyd and Meg Bernstein, in this volume.
21 For a range of examples of this kind of work on objects from the Spanish Americas, see, for instance, Joanna Ostapkowicz, et al. "Integration the Old World into the New: An 'Idol from the

It is easy to forget, but eyes are culturally habituated, and sight is historically constituted. Women like Constanza de Escobar, who lived and died in the city of Santiago in the 1600s, would have had far more experience viewing holy images illuminated by candlelight than most people today, far less experience with aerial perspectives. And no technology that currently exists can replicate her mode of perception. In part this is because her vision was mediated and shaped by early modern Catholicism as it took root in the Americas. For the faithful in different times and places, holy images, particularly icons, themselves were capable of sight. Close-looking cannot, in and of itself, bring historians of religion closer to the experiences of the sacred that people of the past valued. Given that vision was both a physical and a metaphysical capacity of the viewer, and at times, of the image itself, modern habits of close-looking tend to level the hierarchies so central to Catholicism that structured sight. Zoom technologies and their photographic supports therefore do little to close the temporal and cultural chasms between those who saw the Salvator Mundi marched in a parade and those who see it now on screen or even in the museum. In many respects, zoom technologies pry open and widen those gaps.[22]

When understood as critical practice, rather than transparent or normative, digital looking can ask historians to reckon with the shifting status of facture. It can also—and we suggest, crucially—invite new thinking about how different the viewing of sacred objects was in the past, not only because of the conditions of visibility, but also because of the historically and culturally constituted act of sight. Approaching digital zoom technologies from an oblique angle, we observe that they expose a theme little discussed outside specialist circles, but which carries significant political weight: conservation. Through their autopsy-like functions, contemporary digital technologies make it possible to better understand facture and thus how to keep works like the Salvator Mundi clean and safe, how to minimize further decay. One consequence of this is that new technologies for conservation have emerged (and still are emerging) that offer longer lives for works from the past. Indigenous creations from the Spanish Americas, however, are not just any creation. In addition to being more rare and often more fragile because of their materials, many embody connections to descendent communi-

---

West Indies,'" *Antiquity* 19, 359 (2017): 1314–1329, Stefan Hanß, "Material Encounters: Knotting Cultures in Early Modern Peru and Spain." *The Historical Journal*. Published online 1 January 2019: 1–33; and Barbara E. Mundy, ed., "Dialogues: Contours of Practice in Colonial Artworks," *Latin American and Latinx Visual Culture*, 1, 2 (2019): 94–130.

22 From our perspective, the chasms opened by digital zoom technologies differ from those created in other viewing contexts because of the elasticity of scale that digital zoom viewing enlists and depends upon.

ties. Who can (and should) look closely at these things? Who can (and should) intervene in their longevity? These are some of the most difficult decisions pressured by the spread of digital technologies that seek to both expand visibility and enhance sight.

8.4 Orphans

To write religious histories that turn upon objects from the Spanish Americas is to write about works that, more often than not, are claimed by nation states. It is not unusual to see a work created by Indigenous hands in the sixteenth or seventeenth century displayed today in a Latin American museum with the label "Mexican" or "Colombian."[23] In the global north, museums often follow suit, but one also sees Maya or Mapuche, the names of Indigenous groups rather than national monikers. Regarding works created in the Spanish Americas that now lie within the national borders of the United States—primarily California, the southwestern states, and parts of the southeast—Indigenous histories tend to be more explicitly marked. For instance, while the vessel depicted in figure 5 may have been made in the Spanish Americas in the seventeenth century, it is a decidedly Zuni creation, the result of the cultural connections that have been made between certain works created in the Spanish Americas—not always, but often quite directly—and with descendant communities, some of which hold sovereign lands. In North America (e.g., the U.S. and Canada) Indigenous sovereignty is defined by laws that have few parallels in Latin America; this is one reason the pot is Zuni, the Salvator Mundi is Mexican (rather than Mexica).

When we began *Vistas*, we could see that a shift in the Anglophone historiography of religious practice in the Americas was underway, and it was driven by Indigenous communities—especially in the United States, Canada and Australia—as they sought to reclaim not only ancestral objects, but also languages, spaces and narratives from and about their past. Our work with Indigenous communities was highly mediated and organized via the permissions process. When we asked the School for Advanced Research (SAR)[24] for permission to include the Zuni pot—an object held in the SAR collection—our request and interpretive texts were vetted by an advisory board that included Indigenous members. Zuni tribal members had long been active in seeking the physical return of their objects, so

---

23 There are of course exceptions, Guaraní represents one, as does the region of Bolivia where Indigenous people lived on Jesuit missions, Mojos.

24 At that time, and until 2007, the institution was named the School of American Research.

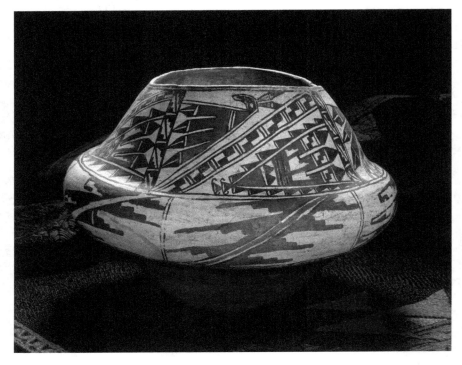

Figure 5: Creator(s) name(s) is/are not currently known. Zuni Vessel, ca. 1680–1700. Courtesy School for Advanced Research, cat. no. IAF.1.

this did not surprise us. Yet working with the SAR in this way (even in the early 2000s!) represented a new model of scholarship for us. It was also a model quite different from that invited by objects we sought to include and interpret from Bolivia, Peru and Ecuador, objects for which no descendent communities have yet been identified or for which national institutions have historically been accepted by residents of Latin America—Indigenous and otherwise—as the primary custodians.

Across the last two decades, as Indigenous communities in the Americas have established new agendas and working paradigms, conversations and decolonizing projects have moved well beyond the return of physical objects.[25] In

---

25 Several of the projects that have been published were developed (or are being developed) by Indigenous stakeholders in collaboration with non-Indigenous allies. For Latin American materials, this often involves partnerships with North American institutions. Examples include the

the United States, the Native American Graves Protection and Repatriation Act (NAGPRA, passed in 1989) has been influential, even though its effects have been both uneven and fraught. As D. Rae Gould reminds us, NAGPRA is a compromise and it applies primarily to ancestors and sacred belongings.[26] Other emergent models of decolonizing practices include consultation among Indigenous community members and archivists, the virtual return of objects and documents through digital means, and the enlistment of open source platforms designed to meet Indigenous rather than outsider objectives.[27] This kind of repatriation is important, if difficult work. And much still transpires as experiment. When it succeeds, though, knowledge of Indigenous languages and histories has the potential to become largely (if not exclusively) Indigenous once again. For outsiders, one of the unsettling effects of this mode of digital repatriation—as such work is sometimes called—is that information, including visual imagery, no longer circulates freely. Instead, those who have the appropriate rights, privileges, and preparation share information selectively. For example, the Sípnuuk Digital Library, which preserves material related to the Karuk Tribe (in present-day California) states on the "About" section of its website

> Any materials containing Karuk traditional knowledge are the intellectual and cultural property of the Karuk People, and we will therefore make these materials available according to our Karuk cultural protocols regardless of their current copyright assignment. In any

---

Hijuelas Project, the Nahuatl Digitization Project, and the Ticha Project. Notably, all of these endeavors focus on documentary records and language, not objects. We thank Hannah Alpert-Abrams for sharing information on these three examples.

26 See her important essay, "NAGPRA, CUI and Institutional Will," in *The Routledge Companion to Cultural Property*, ed. Jane Anderson and Haidy Geismar, 134–151 (Abingdon and New York: Routledge, 2017). The NAGPRA literature is extensive. For a range of perspectives, see, for instance, for instance, Sagita Chari and Jaime M.N. Lavallee, eds. *Accomplishing NAGPRA: Perspectives on the Intent, Impact, and Future of the Native American Graves and Repatriation Act* (Corvalis: Oregon State University Press, 2013). For comparative perspective, see Catherine Bell and Robert Paterson, eds., *Protection of First Nations Cultural Heritage: Laws, Policy and Reform* (Vancouver: University of British Columbia Press, 2008) which offers parallel accounts of US and Canadian laws.

27 The open source platform MUKURTU, is best known in this regard. For its use in a recent California context, see Karuk Tribe, Lisa Hillman, Leaf Hillman, Adrienne Harling, Bari Tally and Angela McLaughlin, "Building Sípunuuk: A Digital Library, Archives and Museum for Indigenous Peoples," *Collection Management* 43, 3–4 (2017): 294–316. For examples of digital projects and models that do not involve territories or people once part of the Spanish Americas, see Aaron Glass, "Indigenous Ontologies, Digital Futures: Plural Provenances and the Kwakwaka'wakw collection in Berlin and Beyond," in *Museum as Process: Translating Local and Global Knowledges*, ed. Raymond Silverman (London: Routledge, 2015), 19–44 and Amiria Salmond, "Uncommon Things," *Anthropologica* 59 (2017): 251–266.

case, the Karuk Tribe asserts primary ownership of all cultural knowledge specific to our Tribe. Parties who have questions or who wish to contest the use of specific works may contact: Karuk Historic Preservation Officer.[28]

Among the custodians of Karuk histories, images, and documents, decisions about access to material online is for Karuk to make. Open (or indiscriminate) access aligns with the violences wrought by settler colonialism and its handmaiden, the salvage paradigm, and as such runs against current practices of Karuk sovereignty. It is too soon to know how such digital turns will re-shape the field of religious history, but we sense significant promise, and in its wake, fundamental change.

Far less clear is how objects and architectural sites that have not been claimed by any Indigenous group will—or should fare—in this shifting landscape. Many works were made by communities that have no current corporate identity, others, like the (no-longer extant) printed images of Constanza de Escobar, bear few recognizable markers of Indigenous presence. Settler colonialism scarred the Americas differently, but one implication for the history of religions is that some colonial objects and spaces have homes, others became orphans. Our concept of "orphan" is resonant with the "culturally unidentifiable" (CUI) designation in the United States, which has emerged in response to NAGPRA; however, we see the orphan as a historiographic problem (rather than a legal category) existing across the Americas, not just in the United States.

The problem of the orphan for the historian prompts different responses in the global north than it does in Latin America; it also relates differently to architecture and mobile objects.[29] For instance, in what is today the southwestern United States, Pueblo communities have long built kivas. In Kewa Pueblo and Nanbé Owingeh (both in New Mexico) kivas stand in public plazas. In the colonial past, many kivas were sunken into the ground, covered with flat roofs; such spaces are also found archaeologically in pre-contact period sites across the southwest. An example of one colonial-era kiva has been preserved at San Gregorio, Abó (today in New Mexico) (figure 6). This kiva, built as it is, within the walls of a colonial church compound, represents an unusual practice and has been taken to mean that the custodial priests at San Gregorio grasped the impor-

---

28 See https://sipnuuk.karuk.us/about {last accessed 26 September 2021}. The site contains more information about the site and its dedication to tribal sovereignty and the revitalization of Karuk culture.

29 On the challenges of working through the "CUI" (culturally unidentifiable) designation in the United States and for discussion of how institutional "retentive philosophies" confound tribal claims, see Gould, "NAGPRA, CUI and Institutional Will."

tance of kivas and, at least for a while, tolerated their use within the compound. This enmeshed history is one reason we included the image in *Vistas*. Also of interest were the ways this structure challenged traditional thinking about who could enter or use kivas (e. g., they were not traditionally designed as Catholic spaces). Because the kiva and church—indeed, the entire site of San Gregorio —had been abandoned centuries ago—and is now "governed" by the U.S. federal government and open to visitors, the architecture seemed to us appropriate for public display. But this is not true for all colonial-era kivas. At Awatovi, which sits on Hopi lands, kivas have been abandoned for centuries but access to the entire site is forbidden. Some readers might argue that Hopi practices are the better guide for outsiders' relationships to kivas—if not Indigenous architecture and objects from the Spanish Americas—more broadly. Following this line of reasoning, we have overstepped in displaying San Gregorio's architecture (both online, in *Vistas,* and again, here). This point has resonance for us. We also know that objects and sites from the colonial past that are orphans today may be claimed by tribal members in the future. Yet it gives us pause to observe the power of modern geographies and claims to political sovereignty in all this. Because of the custodial reach of the nation state, orphans are—and remain—more widespread in Mexico and Colombia than in California or Texas.

Figure 6: Creator(s) name(s) is/are not currently known, San Gregorio, Abó, with Kiva, ca. 1623–1670, Abó, New Mexico. Photograph courtesy of Carolyn Dean.

When it comes to granting permission—that is, who allows whom to see, touch, photograph, know—appropriate stakeholders should be making the decisions.[30] This is fundamental to any serious decolonizing project. And as the Sípnuuk website suggests, this is something digital technologies can, increasingly, facilitate. These technologies, however, cannot resolve the dilemma posed by works that, as yet, have no descendent community to claim them. A great many such works were made, and used, in regions of the Spanish Americas that, today fall south of the Rio Grande, where laws and constructions of Indigeneity follow different paths than do those to the north. While it would be possible to interpret Indigenous works from sovereign nations through similar gestures, whose sovereignty should take the lead? As scholars and authors, we are in no position to adjudicate whether Indigenous people in Guatemala or Ecuador should take their cues from those living elsewhere. What we can be sure of is that works, objects and spaces as yet unconnected to descendant communities, abound in Latin America, and this did not happen by accident.

It is tempting to say, straight out, the cause is settler colonialism. This would not be wrong; yet, for the Americas, it would also be far too simple. In part, this is because historical constructions of "the Indigenous" are still embedded in national legal frameworks. For histories of the Spanish Americas—which are our primary interest—the differences among the United States, Canada, and the nations of Latin America are significant. In the United States, sovereignty (and resultant legal agency) of federally-recognized tribes—itself a contested designation—is defined by federal law (an irony not lost on Indigenous governments and communities). This situation finds parallels with Canada's First Nations. In North America, then, both the arrival of settlers and the creation of the nation, which are themselves linked projects, form inviolate horizons against which Indigenous histories are constructed—the very idea of "First" nations, or "Native" Americans is contingent on the existence of a "second" nation (Canada) or non-natives who are also Americans. Across Latin America, Indigenous people have not been designated as sovereign in exactly the same way. Moreover, interest in colonial works was traditionally eclipsed by creations of greater antiquity, specifically sites and objects that predate the arrival of Europeans, often by centuries. In some countries, these interpretive traditions predate any decolonizing project, as in the nationalist narratives in Mexico that privilege descent from a noble Mexica or Maya past. Across the twentieth century, however, national in-

---

30 The category "appropriate stakeholder" is itself a theme of considerable debate and, increasingly, a site of decolonized thinking and action. This is true for settings across the Americas but also in Australia, New Zealand, Africa and Southeast Asia.

stitutions in Latin America (if not also state institutions) have required non-nationals to work with the national government, and at times, to also work collaboratively with local residents. Some archeologists now partner with local communities to ensure their participation, therein strengthening communities' ties to the archeological past.[31] In some instances, these local communities are Indigenous but not always. Further complicating this landscape is the fact that many Latin American communities now devalue their local image-saturated Catholic environments—many of them rich with colonial-era paintings and objects—as they embrace Protestant religious practices.

When claimed by no descendent community, colonial objects in Latin America slip through the net. Consider again the Salvator Mundi featherwork (Figures 3, 4). Based on its similarity to another featherwork of known provenance, this one was likely made in an Indigenous community in Mexico City. The Nahuatl-speaking Mexica who lived the city were a corporate community until the 1800s, but their lands and legal status were dismantled as part of the mid-19th century liberal reforms. No sovereign Indigenous group exists to claim the Salvator Mundi (or for that matter, the spectacular pre-Hispanic featherwork known as "Moteuczoma's headdress" now in Vienna). And the nation has stepped in—the Salvator Mundi is held by a national museum dedicated to colonial arts, and it is the Mexican nation that is advocating for the return of "its" feather headdress from Vienna as national patrimony. While we know that Indigenous peoples across the Americas made works and spaces to express and contain religious practices, those spaces and things are not necessarily coded as "Indigenous" any longer, nor do the colonial works fit seamlessly into local communities' own ongoing constructions of their pasts.

So we close this section with a dilemma. Many decolonizing projects are arising from and within Indigenous communities. Consequently—and rightfully—what constitutes a valid narrative about one's ancestors or the appropriate conditions of visibility are changing, especially in the digital realm. But what then of the "orphaned" Indigenous colonial object or space, the ones that have no Indigenous descendants to claim them? Surely, further research can (and will) shift the status of some of these works. Yet current paradigms of interpretation for these materials, including those of repatriation (broadly conceived) and Indigenous intellectual property, are not sufficient. Whether resolution is possible, we cannot say, but orphan objects from the colonial past should concern us because they are among those that circulate most freely online.

---

31 Patricia A. McAnany, *Maya Cultural Heritage: How Archaeologists and Indigenous Communities Engage the Past* (Lanham, MD: Rowman & Littlefield, 2016).

8.5 Conclusion: Beyond Recognition

In this essay, we have discussed themes that bear upon and color historians' understanding of Indigenous religious practice in the Spanish Americas as more and more related material is launched online. Within the framework of recognition, greater access has been—and indeed remains—one of the key promises of digital imagery. When coupled with data transfer technologies, digital media expand opportunities: people can see a greater number of objects made by Indigenous people, in greater detail. When first developed in the early 2000s, *Vistas* built upon this now mundane fact. Our project sought to introduce scholars and students to works from the Spanish Americas that were too often sequestered in dusty store rooms, too rarely granted exhibition space. Yet our goal was not simply visibility. Rather, we curated the *Vistas* collection to counter outdated narratives about colonial visual culture which centered on the objects and spaces of settler colonists. By broadening knowledge of the objects and object types that organized lived experiences in the colonial past, we sought to pressure the canon of early modern art, in which European objects consistently occupied center stage. In seeking to emphasize Indigenous objects and spaces, we attempted to decolonize knowledge (although these were not the terms we were using in the moment).

As it turns out, digital access is not as uncomplicated as anyone once supposed. And while no one ever imagined that simply presenting more images online would (or could) fundamentally change colonialist histories, the fact remains that more images are now there. It is also clear that objects from the past that circulate via digital media have vibrant public lives; in many cases, the same images tend to appear time and again. We therefore observe with a grain of irony that a new canon is being created, one that may embrace objects of Indigenous facture, but again foregrounds objects in collections of the global north, where there are deeper veins of finance to build, present, and maintain online collections.[32] Moreover, the digital display of objects (and this is a point not reserved to colonial Latin America) promotes kinds of visual access never available in the past as a means of knowing.

One effect of digital accessibility is that, if untethered from a critical practice of viewing, it normalizes digital technologies, so that the ubiquitous zoom and the close-up are rarely understood as antithetical to modes of viewing in the past. For instance, visual accessibility (or lack thereof) was actively enlisted in

---

32 Two important exceptions are the websites of the Museo de Arte de Lima (Peru) and the Museo Nacional del Virreinato (Mexico).

settler colonial societies to produce inequalities; visual access to objects such as the chalice with featherwork was not merely a product of hierarchies forged abroad through Catholic ritual and its social practices. To lose track of this fact, and ignore it in new digital projects, would both reinscribe and reinforce colonialist practices in the present. And finally, embracing the paradigm of repatriation—in its sense of welcoming objects back to their epistemic homelands—may have the unintended consequence of turning those objects whose actual and symbolic patria have been eradicated into the most widely known and eloquent objects in histories of Indigenous religion written by (non-Indigenous) outsiders. Whether this represents an unfortunate side-effect or a progressive aspect of decolonization (that is a bug or a feature), remains for now, an open and vexed question.

Acknowledgements

We would like to thank Hannah Alpert-Abrams for her perceptive comments and careful reading of an earlier draft of this essay, as well as the volume editors, Emily Suzanne Clark and Rachel McBride Lindsey, for both the invitation to participate and their feedback. Ongoing conversations with Emily Floyd have enriched our thinking about the relationship of the colonial to the digital. Any errors, of course, are ours.

Bibliography

Alia, Valerie. *The New Media Nation: Indigenous Peoples and Global Communication*. New York: Berghahn Books, 2010.
Bell, Catherine and Robert Paterson, eds. *Protection of First Nations Cultural Heritage: Laws, Policy and Reform*. Vancouver: University of British Columbia Press, 2008.
Betts, Raymond F. "Decolonization: A Brief History of the Word." In *Beyond Empire and Nation: The Decolonization of African and Asian Societies, 1930s–1970s*, ed. E. Bogaerts and R. Raben, 23–38. Leiden: Nederlands Instituut voor Oorlogsdocumentatie, 2012.
Chari, Sagita and Jaime M.N. Lavallee, eds. *Accomplishing NAGPRA: Perspectives on the Intent, Impact, and Future of the Native American Graves and Repatriation Act*. Corvalis: Oregon State University Press, 2013.
Christen, Kimberly. "Opening Archives: Respectful Repatriation." *The American Archivist* 74 (2011): 185–216.
Clendinnen, Inga. *Aztecs: An Interpretation*. Cambridge: Cambridge University Press, 1995 [1991].

Dueñas, Alcira. *Indians and Mestizos in the "Lettered City": Reshaping Justice, Social Hierarchy and Political Culture in Colonial Peru*. Boulder, Co: University Press of Colorado, 2010.

Durán, Diego. *Historia de las Indias de Nueva España e Islas de la Tierra Firma*, Ángel María Garibay, K., ed. 2nd ed. Mexico City: Editorial Porrua, 1984.

Durston, Alan. "Native Language Literacy in Colonial Peru: The Question of Mundane Quechua Revisited." *Hispanic American Historical Review* 88, 1 (2008): 41–70.

Fane, Diana. "From Precolumbian to Modern: Latin American Art at The Brooklyn Museum, 1930–50." *Converging Cultures: Art and Identity in Spanish America*. Brooklyn: Brooklyn Museum of Art, 1996, 14–27.

Fanon, Frantz. *The Wretched of the Earth*. New York: Grove Press, 1963.

Gish, Christina Hill and Medeia Csoba DeHass, eds. "Digital Representation of Indigenous Peoples through Sharing, Collaboration, and Negotiation." *Museum Anthropology Review* 12, 2 (2018).

Glass, Aaron. "Indigenous Ontologies, Digital Futures: Plural Provenances and the Kwakwaka'wakw collection in Berlin and Beyond." In *Museum as Process: Translating Local and Global Knowledges*, ed. R. Silverman, 19–44. London: Routledge, 2015.

Gómez Menjívar, Jennifer, and Gloria Elizabeth Chacón, eds. *Indigenous Interfaces: Spaces, Technology, and Social Networks in Mexico and Central America*. Tucson: University of Arizona Press, 2019.

Gould, D. Rae. "NAGPRA, CUI and Institutional Will." In *The Routledge Companion to Cultural Property*, ed. Jane Anderson and Haidy Geismar, 134–151. Abingdon and New York: Routledge, 2017.

Graubart, Karen. "Catalina de Agüero: A Mediating Life." In *Native Wills from the Colonial Americas*, ed. M. Christensen and J. Truitt, 19–39. Salt Lake: University of Utah Press, 2016.

Hanß, Stefan. "Material Encounters: Knotting Cultures in Early Modern Peru and Spain." *The Historical Journal*. Published online 1 January 2019: 1–33.

Karuk Tribe, Lisa Hillman, Leaf Hillman, Adrienne Harling, Bari Tally and Angela McLaughlin. "Building Sípnuuk: A Digital Library, Archives and Museum for Indigenous Peoples." *Collection Management* 43, 3–4 (2017): 294–316.

Katzew, Ilona and Rachel Kaplan, "Like the Flame of Fire" A New Look at the "Hearst" Chalice," *Latin American and Latinx Visual Culture*, 3, 1 (2021): 4–29.

Leibsohn, Dana and Barbara E. Mundy. *Vistas: Visual Culture in Spanish America, 1520–1820*. [https://www.fordham.edu/vistas], 2015.

McAnany, Patricia A. *Maya Cultural Heritage: How Archaeologists and Indigenous Communities Engage the Past*. Lanham, MD: Rowman & Littlefield, 2016.

McMahon, Brendan. "Contingent Images: Looking Obliquely at Colonial Mexican Featherwork in Early Europe." *Art Bulletin* 103, 2 (2021), 24–49.

Mundy, Barbara E. ed. "Dialogues: Contours of Practice in Colonial Artworks," with contributions by Ellen J. Pearlstein, "Bishop's Miter and Infulae, a Feathered Masterpiece from Museo degli Argenti in Florence"; Davide Domenici, "Codex Mendoza and the Material Agency of Indigenous Artists in Early Colonial New Spain"; Dorothy Mahon, Silvia A. Centeno and Louisa Smieska, "Cristobal de Villalpando's Adoration of the Magi: A Discussion of Artist Technique"; and Joseph Fronek, Observations on Miguel Cabrera after the Conservation of One of His Casta Paintings." *Latin American and Latinx Visual Culture*, Vol. 1, Number 2, pp. 94–130.

Ngũgĩ wa Thiong'o. *Decolonising the Mind: The Politics of Language in African Literature*. London: J. Currey, 1986.

Olko, Justyna, John Sullivan, and Jan Szeminski, eds. *Dialogue with Europe, Dialogue with the Past: Colonial Nahua and Quechua Elites in their Own Words*. Boulder, Co., University Press of Colorado, 2018.

Ostapkowicz, Joanna, Fiona Brock, Alex C. Wiedenhoeft, Rick Schulting and Donatella Saviola, "Integrating the Old World into the New: An 'Idol from the West Indies.'" *Antiquity* 91, 359 (2017): 1314–1329.

Rappaport, Joanne and Tom Cummins. *Beyond the Lettered City: Indigenous Literacies of the Andes*. Durham, N.C: Duke University Press, 2012.

Russo, Alessandra, Gerhard Wolf and Diana Fane, eds. *Images Take Flight: Feather Art in Mexico and Europe, 1400–1700*. Munich: Hirmer Verlag, 2015.

Said, Edward. *Orientalism*. New York: Pantheon Books, 1978.

Salmond, Amiria. "Uncommon Things." *Anthropologica* 59 (2017): 251–266.

Salomon, Frank. "Indian Women of Early Colonial Quite as Seen Through Their Testaments." *The Americas* 44, 3 (1988): 325–341.

Smith, Linda Tuhiwai. *Decolonizing Methodologies: Research and Indigenous Peoples*. London: Zed Books, 1999.

Townsend, Camilla. *Annals of Native America: How the Nahuas of Colonial Mexico Kept Their History Alive*. Oxford: Oxford University Press, 2016.

Tuck, Eve and K. Wayne Yang. "Decolonization is Not a Metaphor." *Decolonization: Indigeneity, Education & Society* 1, 1 (2012): 1–40.

Villella, Peter. *Indigenous Elites and Creole Identity, 1500–1800*. Cambridge: Cambridge University Press, 2016.

Wemigwans, Jennifer. *A Digital Bundle: Protecting and Promoting Indigenous Knowledge Online*. Regina: University of Regina Press, 2018.

Emily Suzanne Clark and Rachel McBride Lindsey

Conclusion
Challenges and Possibilities in Digital
Humanities and Material Religion

As the chapters in this volume suggest, there are opportunities and challenges at the intersection of digital humanities and material religion. Rather than defining the bounds of a new field of inquiry, the essays in this volume make a compelling case, collectively and on their own, for the interpretive creativity required of the humanities in the digital age. In this way, "digital material" is an intentional paradox, a kind of riddle that makes us pause and see anew what has long been before our eyes. We are not naive enough to believe that material worlds can be translated to digital media and platforms without fundamentally transforming the object of study. The question that remains is to what extent scholars seek to access embodied, material worlds through digital translations and, in turn, to build their interpretive castles.

That constructed, and too often unnamed, association between the "material" and the "digital" has been on display in this volume's chapters as authors have interrogated the role of sacred space, questions about embodiment, the importance of decolonization, and processes of creating religious networks, among other key points of inquiry. These are of course familiar interpretive threads within the study of religion writ large. What these chapters raise, and what we are now pressed to consider, is how—and to what lengths—digital worlds enrich the discipline and to what lengths digital technologies command new epistemologies, new methods, and the definition of new objects of study.

Among the various questions that this volume has prompted, perhaps the most urgent is to ask whether digital tools have generated new questions in the study of material religion or, instead, whether they allow us to ask our existing questions in new ways? A diplomatic answer would be to acknowledge the possibility of both: that is, both new approaches to and new perspectives on the study of religion. But while there is certainly a mood if not demonstrable proof that digital tools and worlds have changed the field, the chapters in this volume have presented an opportunity to test those assumptions. The utilization of digital tools to complete tasks or support institutions that grew out of previous techno-cultural regimes is hardly revolutionary. (No more than, say, utilizing social media to bolster attendance at a local school board meeting necessarily addresses the systemic racism behind the boundaries of the school district).

https://doi.org/10.1515/9783110608755-010

Studies of material religion have long prompted reflections on how people engage with a variety of religious technologies. And furthermore, from printing in the sixteenth century to photography and telegraph in the nineteenth century to television, radio, and the internet in the twentieth century, the warp and woof of religion has always been caught up in emerging technologies of communication, commerce, and empire. Does digital technology expand the field in new directions? Is this technological moment of a different order than those that have come before? Further projects and publications will reveal the expanses and limits of digital material religion, as will the ways in which technology and everyday life changes. If nothing else, we hope that this volume prompts further scrutiny of the production of the field and its coconstitution with intersecting fields of power, from race and gender to the arrayed technologies of empire.

As this volume was being written, the coronavirus pandemic that began in the early months of 2020 (and that as of late 2021 has yet to abate) prompted additional questions for scholars of material religion and the digital. For example, Jewish Passover and Christian Easter season fell early in the U.S. pandemic and they further revealed the challenges and opportunities for religious communities when moving religious practice into virtual spaces. In St. Louis, a Catholic priest filled the pews with photographs of parishioners when he live-streamed mass.[1] Seder tables via Zoom conference calls and live-streamed Stations of the Cross allowed for connection to material religious practice in a pandemic. And yet, traumatic as it was for communities across the globe, this intersection of the material and digital was not new. Hindu temples in the US and beyond began this conversation over a decade ago with live-stream feeds of deities, in the form of statues, enabling a digital version of darshan. The blessing of seeing and being seen by the deity *seemed to* translate through the internet.

As careful as we have been to capture the diversity of this emerging terrain of scholarly inquiry, there are many roads not traveled in this volume. For instance, one digital tool that this volume did not address is virtual and augmented reality. VR and AR have become as ordinary in our current historical moment as cameras were at the turn of the twentieth century—far more accessible to middle and upper classes than a generation earlier and on a rapid clip of improving user experience. To stretch back even farther, before the language of "virtual reality" had been coined, from the 1860s into the early 1900s stereoscopes created opportunities to explore "sense horizons" untethered to physical space. As is almost always the case, our current media innovations are grounded in historical

---

1 Erin Heffernan, "Priest fills St. Louis County church with photos of congregation to unite, despite pandemic," *St. Louis Post-Dispatch*, 12 April 2020.

precedents and, often enough, present new variations of longstanding paradigms of human experience. Still, modern religious communities have taken advantage of virtual and augmented reality in a variety of ways. Shortly after the
release of Second Life in 2003, religious communities turned to this online virtual world program to develop virtual versions of themselves. Perhaps more
striking, however, was the creation of new religious communities. For example,
some LGTBQ+ Christians found new communities of support and affirmation de-
nied to them in their immediate social and physical environments. Additionally,
with digital avatars, transgendered worshippers were able to create digital versions of themselves that felt more authentic than their physical bodies.[2] Virtual
reality also provides unique opportunities for scholars of destroyed landscapes
to engage the intersection of material religion and digital humanities. Lithodo-
mos VR is an Australian-based company run by trained archeologists to enable
virtual archeology for scholars and tourists. Their work invites the viewer to experience cities, like Pompeii and Jerusalem, as they are now and as they were
centuries ago by layering the virtual recreation of the city on top of the physical
city where the viewer stands. Vivid paint colors, decorative statues, religious temples, and more appear where ruins now remain. The viewer, just by raising and
lowering their smart phone from their eyes, can toggle between the virtual, old
world and the material, contemporary world. With virtual reconstructions of ancient cities, virtual reality, like the 360º photography discussed by Emily C. Floyd
and Meg Bernstein in this volume, might prompt a new kind of pilgrimage practice. In July 2020, we saw a simple version of this when the Sanctuaire de
Lourdes in France live-streamed the day-long celebration of masses, sayings of
the rosary, processions, and more to allow for virtual pilgrimage on the feast
day of Our Lady of Lourdes as the coronavirus pandemic raged unchecked.[3]
While there were no reported Marian apparitions that day, people across the
world could experience the divine through digitally mediated devotional practice. We look forward to more scholarship that interrogates VR, AR, and other
emerging technologies as well as the assumptions we have made in outlining
the digital material as a framework of analysis in the study of religion.

A final thought to conclude this volume. When scholars attempt to define
digital humanities, a common point of emphasis is that the field uses digital
tools and technology to ask new questions of our subject material. What do
we do with the realization that our tools and technologies are also those of

---

2 "Born Digital and Born Again Digital: Religion in Virtual Gaming Worlds," Religion and Popular Culture Group, American Academy of Religion Annual Meeting, 2007, San Diego, California.
3 "Catholic holy site Lourdes holds first online pilgrimage," AP News, 16 July 2020, https://ap
news.com/534720ff747c815727345457aed7c1f4

the people we study? During the pandemic, for instance, religious studies scholars at work on ethnographic projects found their previous methods of research difficult. Once processes and expectations had been adjusted, some of their interlocutors asked for assistance on how to use Zoom and other video technology in their religious practice. In this way, digital platforms created spaces where worlds collided. Scholars relied on video conferencing to do their work and religious people used digital tools to sustain their communities and maintain their religious practice. Unlike other places of contact, virtual meeting spaces collapsed—or perhaps expanded?—notions of the sacred into researchers' own homes and offices. While common utilization of video conferencing platforms might not make interlocutors into digital humanities scholars, it makes them akin to digital humanities practitioners. Perhaps reckoning with this realization will be part of the next shift in the study of material religion and digital humanities: what new questions and challenges are our subjects facing in light of the new, (post?) Covid-19 world we now inhabit? What tools and methods will scholars need to study and analyze these new religious practices and communities? While answers to these questions will likely reveal themselves only in hindsight, we hope this volume has initiated a conversation of consequence to the study of religion.

Index

https://doi.org/10.1515/9783110608755-011